THE TWO POETS OF *Paradise Lost*

The Two Poets of *Paradise Lost*

Robert McMahon

Louisiana State University Press
Baton Rouge and London

Manufactured in the United States of America
First printing
07 06 05 04 03 02 01 00 99 98 5 4 3 2 1

Designer: Amanda McDonald Key
Typeface: Galliard by Carter & Cone
Typesetter: Impressions Book and Journal Services, Inc.
Printer and binder: Thomson-Shore, Inc.

Library of Congress Cataloging-in-Publication Data

McMahon, Robert, 1950 Oct. 28–
The two poets of Paradise lost / Robert McMahon.
p. cm.
Includes bibliographical references (p.) and index.
ISBN 0-8071-2188-6 (cloth : alk. paper)
1. Milton, John, 1608–1674. Paradise lost. 2. Christian poetry, English—History and criticism. 3. Epic poetry, English—History and criticism. 4. Milton, John, 1608–1674—Characters—Poets. 5. Bards and bardism in literature. 6. Blind in literature. 7. Poets in literature. 8. Persona (Literature) I. Title.
PR3562.M36 1998
821′.4—dc21 97-24426
CIP

The paper in this book meets the guidelines for permanence and durability of the Committee on Production for Book Longevity of the Council on Library Resources. ♾

For my parents,

first and best teachers,

and for my wife,

tanto gentile

Contents

Acknowledgments

I first studied *Paradise Lost* in a graduate seminar taught by Thomas Vogler and H. Marshall Leicester, Jr., at the University of California at Santa Cruz, almost twenty years ago. They sent their students to read Harry Berger, Jr.'s essays on John Milton, and Don Ryall compelled me to read and discuss them with him. While at Santa Cruz, I also had conversations about Milton with Berger and with George Amis. All of these good people helped me come to grips with Milton's poetry. I am responsible for defects in my grasp.

I wish also to express my gratitude to other teachers. Gary Miles led me through Vergil's poetry; Mary-Kay Gamel taught me to read Ovid. Ronald L. Martinez showed me how subtly an allusion can ramify through a work. Robert M. Durling taught me how to think about several works while reading one. Thanks to his tutelage and example, the best questions I learned to ask about Milton came from Dante, Vergil, and Ovid.

My colleagues at Louisiana State University have helped in many ways. Larry Sasek and Anna Nardo provided bibliographic advice, and Anna's thoughtful comments on my prose have enabled me to clarify many obscurities. Gale Carrithers and Jim Hardy gave me their book, *Milton and the Hermeneutic Journey,* while still in manuscript, and it taught me things I could not have found elsewhere. Christine Cowan meticulously reviewed the entire manuscript, suggesting many improvements in clarity and grace. I prize the learning and friendship of them all.

Work on this book was materially aided by two grants from Louisiana State University: a Manship Faculty Summer Fellowship and a Council on Research Summer Stipend. I am also grateful to my former chairman, John Fischer, who arranged a leave from teaching that enabled me to complete this book.

The Two Poets of *Paradise Lost*

INTRODUCTION

The Two Poets of *Paradise Lost*

There are two poets of *Paradise Lost:* John Milton, its author, the poet behind the poem; and his narrator, the Bard, the poet within the poem. John Milton was a person in history, the author of many works, a writer who composed his epic in whatever sequence of operations he found suitable. The Bard is a literary figure who exists in the present. He is the speaker of *Paradise Lost,* composing it "now" in the order of its self-presentation, "singing" it in the ongoing present of our reading: "Half yet remains unsung" (VII, 21); "I now must change / Those notes to Tragic" (IX, 5–6).[1] Subsequently, the Bard composes *Paradise Regained,* not because John Milton published it later than *Paradise Lost,* but because its opening lines tell us so: "I who erewhile the happy Garden sung, / By one man's disobedience lost, now sing / Recover'd Paradise" (*PR,* I, 1–3). There are two poets of *Paradise Lost,* but they have not always been distinguished. Both of them have most often been called "Milton."

Anne Ferry first distinguished Milton from his Bard in *Milton's Epic Voice: The Narrator in "Paradise Lost,"* which appeared in 1963. Although her book has been widely admired, Miltonists have generally not followed her in making this central distinction. She argues that "the blind bard," like "the bird," symbolizes the poetic Speaker on

1. All quotations from Milton in this book are taken from John Milton, *Complete Poems and Major Prose,* ed. Merritt Y. Hughes (New York, 1957).

his quest for vision, and she cautions against the habit in criticism of taking this imagery as autobiographical for the historical Milton. She grants that Milton's blindness "must have partly determined his choice of metaphors, and our knowledge of that fact gives added poignancy" to the image. But she insists that the voice of the poem was invented by Milton to achieve certain ends and that it "can never be equated with his total personality."[2] Ferry's subtle position has not persuaded most Miltonists, for a long critical tradition has explored and enjoyed the presence of the historical Milton in his poem. Although Ferry does not, in fact, sunder Milton from his Bard, most Miltonists seem to feel that she does.

Yet Ferry's distinction corrects the ambiguity in scholars' use of "Milton." Allan H. Gilbert complained of this lack of clarity in 1947, in his book *On the Composition of "Paradise Lost": A Study of the Ordering and Insertion of Material.* The nature of his topic led him to explore Milton's "saltatory composition," that is, how the author stitched together the various parts of the poem, composed and revised over many years. Gilbert pointed out that critics had generally failed to take this into account. "It has been conventional to say that the first book of *Paradise Lost* is the work of John Milton fresh at his task and Book XII his product when he was worn down by much writing."[3] This conclusion holds only if Milton composed the work in the sequence of its self-presentation, and all the evidence tells against that assumption. We do not have to accept Gilbert's reconstruction of Milton's saltatory composition to see his point.

If Gilbert felt keenly the ambiguity in critics' use of "Milton," he did little to clarify it. He, too, thought of the poet as John Milton, a single figure, an author, and so he did not see clearly how the poem itself points to its being composed in the sequence of our reading. The ambiguity of "Milton" ensnared him even as he inveighed against its effects.

For "Milton" points indiscriminately to the historical author of the poem as a whole and to the narratorial voice of the poem at every point. If the poem were a treatise, this ambiguity would present little difficulty. It would be no different from speaking of Immanuel Kant

2. Anne Ferry, *Milton's Epic Voice: The Narrator in "Paradise Lost"* (Chicago, 1983), 27–28, 49.

3. Allan H. Gilbert, *On the Composition of "Paradise Lost": A Study of the Ordering and Insertion of Material* (Chapel Hill, 1947), 4.

in relation to the various stages of his argument in the *Critique of Pure Reason* as well as to the whole. But *Paradise Lost* is not a treatise but an epic poem, narrating a story in a variety of styles as it moves from beginning to end. What the poem says at its various points and what its historical author thought or believed are not necessarily the same. Moreover, if we want to understand Kant's thought in the *Critique,* we must give pride of place to his conclusions and understand the stages of his argument in relation to them. Similarly, if we wish to use *Paradise Lost* as evidence for the views of the historical Milton, we should consider the epic as a whole and give pride of place to the final two books. We should "remember the ending," since plots are constructed to emphasize endings. As Anne Ferry insisted, however, the critics' use of "Milton" blurs all distinction between what the voice of the poem asserts at its many points and what the historical Milton thought. We may distinguish the historical Milton from his Bard and still argue that they hold the same view on an issue, but the ambiguity of "Milton" prejudges their unanimity, with the inevitable loss of critical clarity.

This ambiguity deserves a brief historical analysis: to see how it arose may help to free us of its enchantment. It arose, of course, from critical tradition on the epic. From ancient times, Homer has been understood to be both a historical person and the poetic voice of the *Iliad* and the *Odyssey.* We cannot distinguish between what the historical Homer thought and what this poetic voice says, for we know Homer only through these poems. The critical situation for Vergil, however, proves more complex.[4] The "gods of Homer," for example, means indiscriminately "the gods whom Homer believed to exist" and "the gods whose acts his poems narrate." We have no way of telling these apart. But "the gods of Vergil" refers solely to those deities represented in his poems, since we have some evidence of his religious skepticism, typical of his era. Knowledge about the historical Vergil has enabled readers for centuries to distinguish his view, at many points, from what his poems assert. Nevertheless, until recently, critical convention has called both the historical person and the voice of the *Aeneid* by the same name. This ambiguity blurs the

4. Modern scholarship has established that "Vergilius" is the correct spelling of Vergil's name, and classicists have increasingly preferred "Vergil" to "Virgil" as the proper spelling in English.

distinction between a person's thought and what he wrote in his fictions. It enabled Augustine in Book I, chapter 13, of the *Confessions,* for example, to criticize Vergil for offering in his poem, as though they were true, what he knew to be falsehoods. Even John Dryden felt obligated to defend Vergil for the anachronism of Aeneas' meeting Dido, as though a poet ought to be a historian.[5]

Only in recent decades have critics distinguished the author of a poem from its speaker. The New Critics won this battle on the field of the lyric, once considered an author's most personal utterance. Subsequently, the distinction was adapted to prose fiction, and students of the novel began to treat "narrators" and "implied authors." Yet scholars of epic have generally resisted this practice. Doubtless, the nature of their work attaches them to traditions critical as well as literary (the bibliography on epic spans centuries, not decades), but perhaps more telling are the requirements of epic itself. As Dryden observed, "A heroic poem, truly such, is undoubtedly the greatest work which the soul of man is capable to perform."[6] It makes the utmost demands on a poet's powers of invention, disposition, learning, and skill. Whereas a novelist may write many works in the course of a career, a poet labors a lifetime to shape his powers for a single epic. Hence, scholars have felt that an epic represents the poet's views on all the matters of moment he takes up.

The ambiguity of "Milton," which arose from this tradition and continues to be sustained by it, also has other sources. Samuel Johnson observed of the proems that "perhaps no passages are more frequently or more attentively read than those extrinsic paragraphs," and they attract readers by their felt relation to Milton himself.[7] Romanticism and historicism have further nourished our desire to see the historical Milton in his poem, and the achievements of scholarship in this vein speak for themselves. Hence, Ferry's distinction between

5. Augustine, *Le Confessioni,* ed. M. Skutella, rev. Michele Pellegrino (Rome, 1982), Vol. I of *Opere di Sant' Agostino,* 34 vols. projected; John Dryden, "Dedication of the *Aeneis,*" in *Virgil's Aeneid,* trans. John Dryden (New York, 1909), 33–36. The translations from the Latin text of Augustine are mine, unless otherwise noted.

6. Dryden, "Dedication of the *Aeneis,*" 5.

7. Samuel Johnson, "Life of Milton," *Selected Poetry and Prose,* ed. Frank Brady and W. K. Wimsatt (Berkeley, 1977), 434.

Milton and his Bard has made little headway because it labors against currents of criticism old and deep, strong and various.

Yet its value has increasingly come to be recognized. Margarita Stocker, for example, writes of Milton's narrator, and James A. Freeman treats the Speaker of *Paradise Lost.* The ambiguity in critics' use of "Milton" is slowly giving way to the clarity provided by the distinction between author and narrator. But the consequences of this distinction have not yet been fully explored. Harry Berger, Jr., began that task over twenty-five years ago in his essay "*Paradise Lost* Evolving," but his insights have not been noticed by Miltonists.[8] The present work takes them up to examine the Bard's experience in singing his epic.

We do not know in what sequence of operations John Milton composed *Paradise Lost,* but we do know the sequence of the Bard's composing, for he sings the poem in the sequence of its self-presentation. John Milton was a historical person, and I write of him only in the past tense. As an author, he enjoyed the possibilities open to any writer of any work. He composed the various parts of his epic in whatever sequence of operations he found suitable, working now on one part, now on another, drafting here, revising there, over many years. The Bard does not enjoy these possibilities, for as a "singer" in the literary present, he has no access to them. *Paradise Lost* explicitly presents itself as being composed in the ongoing present of our reading. According to this self-presentation, our reading witnesses the original composition of the poem. The Bard, as a speaker, exists in a literary present: when we read the poem, we are hearing him compose it. Hence, the poem presents itself as an unrevised performance—unrevised because unrevisable, for it is taking place "originally" in an ongoing present recreated in our reading. The Bard can

8. Margarita Stocker, *Paradise Lost* (London, 1988), 67–85; James A. Freeman, "Milton and Heroic Literature," in *The Cambridge Companion to Milton,* ed. Dennis Danielson (Cambridge, Eng., 1989), 59; Harry Berger, Jr., "*Paradise Lost* Evolving: Books I–VI. Toward a New View of the Poem as the Speaker's Experience," *Centennial Review,* XI (1967), 483–531. See also Berger's remarks on the poem in "Archaism, Vision, and Revision: Studies in Virgil, Plato, and Milton," *Centennial Review,* XI (1967), 24–52.

thus alter an utterance only by saying something further. He can qualify, modify, or undermine something he has said, but he cannot properly revise it.

This distinction between Milton and the Bard simply insists on the self-presentation of *Paradise Lost,* on its artistic integrity. Granted, these aspects of its self-presentation are implied in the epic convention of oral composition. An oral poet necessarily composes in the present, and though he may stumble and correct himself, he cannot revise what he has uttered because he cannot call back what has left his teeth's barrier. Although Miltonists have often noted this convention, they have also dismissed it as merely conventional. They have assumed as axiomatic that the historical Milton was speaking in propria persona throughout the epic. But this axiom I deny. Rather, I contend, Milton exploited in an original way the poetic resources in the epic convention of an oral Bard. The Bard should be understood, not as a convention for "Milton," but as one of Milton's characters in *Paradise Lost.*[9]

Here, I depart from Ferry and so must clarify our differences. We agree that the Bard should be understood as the narrator of all of *Paradise Lost* and not of the proems only, as is sometimes understood.[10] Raphael and Michael, for example, are the Bard's secondary narrators. The third proem makes clear that the Bard has been in "the Heav'n of Heav'ns" (VII, 13) in vision, singing Raphael's story of the war. All of *Paradise Lost* presents itself as the Bard's composition.

Ferry and I differ on the nature of that composition and the character of its singer. Although she calls the Bard a narrator, she treats him as a consistent authorial consciousness. In her view, he has already made up his mind about everything in his poem, and he does not change his mind as he narrates it. In this regard, Ferry's narrator proves much like Milton the author, except that the Bard does not represent Milton's "total personality," for that cannot be done.

In my view, the Bard changes in the course of narrating his poem. He changes the way he portrays some of his characters, most fa-

9. Roger B. Rollin argues that the Bard is one of Milton's characters in "*Paradise Lost:* 'Tragical-Comical-Historical-Pastoral,' " *Milton Studies,* V (1973), 29–33. See also Jason P. Rosenblatt, "The Mosaic Voice in *Paradise Lost,*" *Milton Studies,* VII (1975), 207–32.

10. For this view, see Barbara Kiefer Lewalski, *"Paradise Lost" and the Rhetoric of Literary Forms* (Princeton, 1985), 25–27.

mously, Satan. He changes the stylistic register of his poem radically between Books I and II and XI and XII, as many have complained. He comments retrospectively on his own work, worrying about the audacity of his war in Heaven ("Standing on Earth, not rapt above the Pole, / More safe I sing" VII, 23–24) and criticizing the glorification of war in Book XI (683–99). The twelve books of *Paradise Lost* encompass substantial changes, and these have long been grist for scholarship, but because Miltonists have been writing about "Milton," they have not seen these as evidence for change in the narrator of the poem. Berger, however, argues that Milton's epic evolves as the changing experience of its Speaker, and Roger B. Rollin and Jason P. Rosenblatt have seen that the proems dramatize changes in Milton's narrator. With these scholars, I argue that substantial changes in the poem suggest significant change in the poet and that Milton designed the movement of his epic to reveal his Bard's growth. In other words, the Bard does not simply tell the story of the poem; his narrating the poem tells a story about him. The Bard is not simply a poetic voice for Milton but one of his characters. The present work aims to argue this thesis by telling the Bard's story.

The rest of this introduction treats the general view of *Paradise Lost* implied in the distinction between poet and narrator. Examining some representative scholarly works in its light should clarify the consequences of this view. In *Before and After the Fall,* Kathleen Swaim contrasts Raphael and Michael as secondary narrators in *Paradise Lost.* She terms Raphael's discourse "prelapsarian": it treats the order of Nature before the Fall as an established unity, a ladder of analogies from earth to heaven. Michael's teaching is postlapsarian: it treats the typological order of salvation history and instructs Adam in right moral choices. Where Raphael's ladder of Nature is constructed on the analogy of space, Michael's discourse treats time as the medium of salvation in the history of the race and in the person. The order of salvation history, unlike the order of unfallen Nature, is not an established unity but must be created by acts human and divine. "Generally speaking," Swaim observes, "the classical attaches to the prelapsarian and to Raphael, and the biblical attaches to Michael." Yet Swaim insists that these "directly oppositional complexes of imagery and thought" are complementary and not "exclusive or excluding alternatives." They "participate in a cumulative design that reflects the complex reality of the human condition."[11]

Here is a characteristic gesture of Milton scholarship: it conceives *Paradise Lost* as a design on the analogy of a building. Thus, Swaim astutely identifies "directly oppositional complexes of imagery and thought" yet treats them as balanced and complementary. When she writes of *Paradise Lost* as a "cumulative design," she emphasizes the "design" and not the "cumulative." Like most Miltonists, she assumes that "Milton" stands as much behind the parts of the poem as he does the whole. This assumption entails the language of complementarity and balance, with the architectural analogy it implies. Granted, the analogy is traditional (*condere carmen,* "to build the lofty rhyme"), but it necessarily scants the poem's *movement* from one oppositional complex to another.

My argument emphasizes precisely this movement. Where Swaim finds a "cumulative *design,*" I see a "*cumulative* design," and the later oppositional complex I see as not simply balancing the earlier: it may also counter, qualify, and even correct it. Swaim rightly argues that "the classical" attaching to Raphael and "the biblical" to Michael "do not function as exclusive or excluding alternatives," but she then incorrectly assumes that they prove of equal value. This assumption is implied in the ambiguity of "Milton" as the voice of every part of the poem.

In my view, however, they are not of equal value, not within the poem and not for the historical Milton. First, *Paradise Lost* is not a static entity. It must be read in time, and it presents itself in a certain sequence. The poem thus read, Swaim's later oppositional complex receives greater emphasis simply by being later. Plots function this way; temporal sequence is designed to emphasize the climax. Milton designed the poem to move *from* the classical and Raphael *to* the biblical and Michael. The contrasts are not merely complementary: the later one receives emphasis precisely because it is later.

When we consider the historical Milton, it is not hard to understand why. He thought Scripture of greater value than the classics, Michael's lessons on moral choice more important than Raphael's ladder of Nature. To be sure, he knew and loved the classics and alluded

11. Kathleen M. Swaim, *Before and After the Fall: Contrasting Modes in "Paradise Lost"* (Amherst, Mass., 1986), 10, xiii. Pages ix–xiii give a prospective summary of the book.

to them often, but he believed that classical knowledge alone could not lead one to salvation, the ultimate goal of human life, whereas the knowledge of Scripture could. Although these are not exclusive alternatives, one of them, for Milton, proved clearly superior. He constructed the resoundingly biblical ending of *Paradise Lost* to emphasize it. Even if Raphael's discourse were longer and more classical than it is, it would be outweighed by Michael's, simply because Books XI and XII conclude the poem.

This critique may be made less formally and more substantially. Swaim correlates, in fine detail, the similarities and differences between Raphael's ladder of Nature and Michael's typological discourse. Yet her assumption that "Milton" authorizes both equally establishes these oppositional complexes as merely complementary. But Michael's discourse, I contend, does not merely complete Raphael's; it counters and corrects that lesson. In the world we live in, the ladder of Nature can no longer be climbed, for it has been ruptured by the Fall.

Although Raphael's ladder is often said to be "Milton's," *Paradise Lost* as a whole shows us that the historical Milton did not endorse the doctrine. True, he wrote Raphael's speech and clearly felt the charm of the subject, but the poem as a whole declares the ladder of Nature an error, false to the world in which we live. Book X records the disruptions in Nature caused by the Fall: Raphael's ladder is no longer a viable way to Heaven. The only viable way is expounded in Michael's biblical discourse, with which the fallen poet concludes his poem. The poem as a whole, then, reveals Raphael's Neoplatonism to be erroneous, a nostalgic fiction, a yearning for a natural harmony that had been ruptured for millennia before the Neoplatonists lived. Raphael's speech constitutes not a prelapsarian vision but only the fallen poet's aspiration to one, inspired by pagan writers and revealed as vain in the final books of the poem. For Milton, as for Augustine, the Neoplatonic ascent was not a valid way to the vision of God (*Confessions,* VII, 10–21). Only the right understanding of Scripture could lead one to that vision. The principles of that understanding are conveyed in Michael's discourse. In this regard, the later speech does not complement Raphael's but corrects it.

To sum up the traditional view, then, the ambiguity of "Milton" implies that the historical Milton expressed his views in every part of

Paradise Lost, and since every passage is held to bear Milton's authority, parts of the poem recognizably oppositional are considered to be complementary, giving the epic a static design. In my view, however, distinguishing Milton from his Bard proves true to the poem and provides greater clarity than the ambiguity of "Milton" can. It emphasizes the poem as a design in movement, a work unfolding in time. It attends to the self-presentation of *Paradise Lost* as being composed "now," in the ongoing present of our reading. It thereby allows oppositions to be felt fully as oppositions: they may be found complementary, but the later can also be seen to qualify or correct the earlier. The issue is thus not prejudiced by the ambiguity of "Milton." Similarly, distinguishing Milton from his Bard does not necessarily sunder them. We are free to see Milton's anguish in the Bard's complaint on his blindness, if we wish. But we are not bound to think that Milton uttered his own theology, simply and absolutely, in God's first speech, though we may. The relation between the historical Milton and his Bard's utterance on any point is not prejudged; instead it is left to be established by argument. That argument, however, must consider Milton in relation to the poem as a whole, progressive entity: later passages may qualify or correct earlier ones, but earlier ones can, at best, only condition later ones.

This position strikes directly against the ambiguity of "Milton," and it proves simply the consequence of two unobjectionable principles. First, Milton wrote the whole poem and designed its sequential order to achieve certain ends. Second, in the sequential order of a work, what comes later can modify something earlier, whereas something earlier cannot modify something later. Miltonists have not fully appreciated this point. Intent on an ambiguous "Milton," they have sought to smooth out differences and oppositions within the poem. They have thereby ignored what we might call "the sequential principle": later utterances on any point modify earlier ones and so have greater weight.

The movement of the poem is emphasized by a prominent school of Miltonists whose leading expositor is Stanley Fish. My view of the poem has much in common with his, especially with his appreciation of Milton's didactic aims, but we differ fundamentally on the voice of *Paradise Lost.* For Fish, Milton was an author who stood at a distance from the movement of his poetry as he designed interpretive traps for his readers. In other words, Fish corrects the ambiguity of "Milton" by ignoring the narrator of *Paradise Lost* and identifying Milton solely with the author of the poem.[12] In my view, however, Milton created a narrator who is imagining his poem in an ongoing present. What Fish identifies as Milton's interpretive traps I understand as the Bard's being pulled in different directions by various sympathies, traces of which are evident in his composition. A brief instance may illustrate these differences:

> *Thammuz* came next behind,
> Whose annual wound in *Lebanon* allur'd
> The *Syrian* Damsels to lament his fate
> In amorous ditties all a Summer's day,
> While smooth *Adonis* from his native Rock
> Ran purple to the Sea, suppos'd with blood
> Of *Thammuz* yearly wounded: the Love-tale
> Infected *Sion's* daughters with like heat,
> Whose wanton passions in the sacred Porch
> *Ezekiel* saw, when by the Vision led
> His eye surveyed the dark Idolatries
> Of alienated *Judah.*
>
> (I, 445–57)

A reader-response critic would see in these verses an interpretive trap set by Milton: the liquid beauty of the first seven lines lulls the reader into sympathy with the demonic-pagan ritual, while the following six lines rebuke that sympathy, as much by their harsh rhythms as by explicit statement. In contrast, I see a Bard who enjoys his lore, his skill, and the traditions of erotic poetry he evokes. The reader feels sympathy for the Adonis ritual because the Bard feels it, too, and the reader is chastened because the Bard chastens himself. He is, after all a Christian poet and should not be evoking this demonic history and experience sympathetically. Of course, he does so repeatedly, for demons are his only characters in Books I and II, and his bravura use of the classical apparatus of epic often lends them a heroic aura that he comes to regret. Thus, we often find him criticizing or undermining his own representations in various ways in these books.

A. J. A. Waldock attacked Milton for this self-criticism within the poem, calling it "inconsistent" and the poet "incompetent." Waldock,

12. Stanley Eugene Fish, *Surprised by Sin: The Reader in "Paradise Lost"* (New York, 1967), 1–35.

it seems to me, was a victim of the ambiguity of "Milton" and disastrously confounded the narrative voice with the author of the poem. Fish defends Milton by locating the author beyond the movements of the poem, designing its interpretive traps. In general, where Waldock found an inconsistency in "Milton," Fish finds Milton designing a didactic device.[13] My view envisions this aspect differently. Milton created an imperfect narrator, the Bard, who composes the poem in an ongoing present. Therefore, he must correct any wrong impressions he feels himself giving as he sings because, as an oral poet, he cannot revise his utterance. Milton intended readers to respond to the Bard's flow of sympathies as he elaborates his song. That is why Milton's readers have never felt harassed or hectored by the poet, though they have been instructed. The Bard mediates Milton's instruction for readers, not because the author set interpretive traps, but because the Bard is learning from the experience of inventing the details of his poem as he sings it in the ongoing present.

Thus far, my view of *Paradise Lost* has been presented partially and negatively by treating its differences with representative works in Milton criticism. Now I shall put disagreements aside to articulate my thesis more directly and to suggest the story of Milton's Bard more fully.

The felt quality of Milton's verse in *Paradise Lost,* not merely as elaborate but as being elaborated in the now of composition, has often received attention. Centering on the poet within the poem calling his verse "unpremeditated" (IX, 24), Louis L. Martz argues that "in the act of creation the poet discovers the true, developing nature of his own response" to what he sings. Martz sees this poet "interpreting the discoveries of his 'unpremeditated Verse,' and encouraging us to read the poem as the progress of an interior journey." Martz praises as discoveries what Waldock and John Peter criticized as inconsistencies, the same felt quality but perceived in a different light. Perhaps the reader-response critics prove the keenest students of this quality. They, too, find the poetry full of discoveries, yet they see these discoveries not as the poet's but as those he has designed his readers to make. Charles Martindale also finds this quality in Milton's poetry

13. For A. J. A. Waldock's critique of the poet's handling of Satan, see *"Paradise Lost" and Its Critics* (Cambridge, Eng., 1947), 65–96. Stanley Fish begins *Surprised by Sin* as an extended reply to Waldock on Satan; see especially pp. 1–17.

as a brilliant imitation of Homer's oral song. Although the verse of *Paradise Lost* is obviously not oral-formulaic, its "sense variously drawn out from one Verse into another" evokes the full, rolling movement of Homer's verse-periods. Martindale suggests that Milton designed his verse to evoke the spontaneity of oral composition.[14]

This quality of the poetry suggests a certain relation between the narrator and his poem, which Berger illuminates by contrasting it with Dante Alighieri and the *Divine Comedy.*[15] Dante's poem narrates a remembered journey: experience *then,* narrative *now.* Dante the pilgrim-character and Dante the poet-narrator stand in a dialectical relationship; the poet-narrator has completed the journey that the pilgrim-character is still making. Dante the poet knows the end of the journey, and he recollects it all in relative tranquility compared to Dante the pilgrim, who is frequently anxious or astounded and who is always being taught. The *Divine Comedy* presents itself as an autobiographical tale, so it tells the story of how Dante the pilgrim journeys to become Dante the poet, who can then narrate the completed journey. This self-presentation, of course, is a fiction. We must postulate a third figure, Dante the maker or author, who made the whole thing up.

In *Paradise Lost,* however, there is no difference between a present of narration and a past of visionary journeying. The Bard is experiencing now the events of his poem as he sings them. Implied throughout the poem, he states this explicitly in the proems: "Thee I revisit now with bolder wing, / Escap't the *Stygian* Pool, though long detain'd / In that obscure sojourn" (III, 13–15) and so on. The Bard is recalling a past experience, but it is not, like Dante's, an autobiographical past being recollected in a contemplative present. Rather, the Bard is feeling the immediacy of what he is imagining now and responding to it as he elaborates his song. Milton, as author, stood beyond these urgencies. That is not to say he did not feel them, for he designed them for his Bard, but he did not feel them as urgencies, because he was not an oral poet. In other words, the Bard feels the continuous pressure of his visionary experience as he imagines and sings it in an ongoing present,

14. Louis L. Martz, *The Paradise Within: Studies in Vaughan, Traherne, and Milton* (New Haven, 1964), 109–10; John Peter, *A Critique of "Paradise Lost"* (New York, 1960); Charles Martindale, *John Milton and the Transformation of Ancient Epic* (London, 1986), 113–16.

15. Berger, "*Paradise Lost* Evolving," 483–87.

responding to it, making discoveries in it, and modifying it, even with "inconsistencies," as he goes along. Milton felt the pressure of this experience not directly, like the Bard, but mediately, as an artistic problem—the problem of imagining and recreating the Bard's experience as he sings.

These notions may be clarified by an illustration, the poet's first imagining of Adam and Eve, with his apostrophe against "guilty shame." These verses have received considerable comment in recent years, but the perspective I wish to offer cuts across the bias of current debate. The sentiments in this passage cannot simply be ascribed to the historical Milton. Rather, he designed these lines to reveal the character of the oral Bard as the Bard imagines his poem and responds to his imaginations in his singing. The indecorousness of the apostrophe against shame reveals the historical Milton's distance from these verses, for he composed a deliberate indecorum to point up the Bard's involvement in what he is imagining.

> For contemplation hee and valor form'd,
> For softness shee and sweet attractive Grace,
> Hee for God only, shee for God in him:
> His fair large Front and Eye sublime declar'd
> Absolute rule; and Hyacinthine Locks
> Round from his parted forelock manly hung
> Clust'ring, but not beneath his shoulders broad:
> Shee as a veil down to her slender waist
> Her unadorned golden tresses wore
> Dishevell'd, but in wanton ringlets wav'd
> As the Vine curls her tendrils, which impli'd
> Subjection, but requir'd with gentle sway,
> And by her yielded, by him best receiv'd,
> Yielded with coy submission, modest pride,
> And sweet reluctant amorous delay.
> Nor those mysterious parts were then conceal'd,
> Then was not guilty shame: dishonest shame
> Of Nature's works, honor dishonorable,
> Sin-bred, how have ye troubl'd all mankind
> With shows instead, mere shows of seeming pure,
> And banisht from man's life his happiest life,
> Simplicity and spotless innocence.
> So pass'd they naked on. . . .
>
> (IV, 297–319)

The Bard has already treated the human pair together as "The image of their glorious Maker" (293), shining with "Truth, Wisdom, Sanctitude severe and pure" (294). In this passage, he imagines them as individuals, with different qualities in different bodies. He spends four lines on Adam and twice as many on Eve. Nor is it hard to see why.

The Bard's description of Eve begins with her hair, but shortly after he imagines her "wanton ringlets" (306), he is imagining her relationship with Adam ("Subjection, but requir'd with gentle sway," 308), even their lovemaking ("sweet reluctant amorous delay," 311). By a series of subtle movements, his envisioning of Eve's hair turns into an explicit appreciation of her erotic charms. The passage moves as though by inadvertence: the Bard seems to be, in Martz's phrase, "interpreting the discoveries of his 'unpremeditated Verse.' " Or we might simply say that the Bard cannot help himself. Although he is a Christian who admires Eve's "Sanctitude severe and pure," he is also a heterosexual male imagining the most beautiful woman imaginable ("the fairest of her Daughters *Eve*," 324) naked in the Garden of "blissful Paradise" (208). Nor does his appreciation of her severe sanctitude quench his appreciation of her beauty. Quite the opposite: what she yields amorously is reluctant and delayed and, therefore, sweet.

At this point, the Bard reminds us that Eve is naked ("Nor those mysterious parts were then conceal'd," 312), and he bursts into a six-line apostrophe against "guilty shame" (313–18) before returning to his narrative. His insistence that "Then was not guilty shame" implies that now is and that he is clearly feeling it. The fallen poet, having imagined unfallen sexual intercourse with Eve and observed the nakedness of her pudendum, bursts into an apostrophe against shame that shatters, momentarily, the decorum of his song. He doth protest too much. His audience does not need to be chastened nearly as much as he does, for he is imagining directly as he sings, while we imagine only mediately, through his utterance.

Milton's cue for the Bard's apostrophe may be found in Augustine's examination of the first punishment of the Fall, shame at being naked, displayed when Adam and Eve seized fig leaves "to cover their *pudenda*, their 'organs of shame.'" Augustine explains: "These organs were the same as they were before, but previously there had been no shame attaching to them. Thus they felt a novel disturbance in their disobedient flesh, as a punishment which answered to their own disobedience."[16] The Bard's indecorous outburst begins immediately after he imagines Eve's unconcealed pudendum. At this, he feels an all-too-familiar "disturbance in [his] disobedient flesh," and he lashes out against "guilty shame."

The sentiments in these lines have often been ascribed to "Milton," but to this ambiguous "Milton" anything in the poem may be attributed. When we distinguish Milton, as author, from his Bard, as narrator, these sentiments appear differently. For Milton, by the definition of *author,* comprehended the whole of this passage, as he did the whole of *Paradise Lost.* What the Bard utters and feels successively, Milton embraced simultaneously, in principle. Since we do not know the sequence of operations by which the historical Milton composed this passage, we cannot rightly say that his feelings changed as he wrote it. He may well have written the apostrophe to shame before he elaborated his description of Eve. Although the sequence of Milton's operations remains unknown, the sequence of the Bard's is evident in the self-presentation of the poem. We must say, therefore, that the Bard swings from erotic fascination to moral alarm, whereas Milton designed this movement for his narrator. As the Bard describes Eve, he is not aware of any moral difficulty in a fallen poet's imagining of unfallen sexuality. But he becomes aware of that difficulty as he sings, and he then attacks "guilty shame." We cannot say with certainty that the historical Milton felt either erotic fascination for Eve or guilty shame at imagining her naked, only that he created this movement for his narrator. The author of the whole and the narrator of every part of *Paradise Lost* cannot be identified simpliciter, as they are in "Milton."

Perhaps another illustration will clarify this point. Miltonists agree that Satan degenerates in *Paradise Lost* after Books I and II, where he sometimes appears heroic. For Milton, as the author of the whole poem, Satan was never heroic, but for the Bard, as the narrator of its parts in succession, Satan sometimes is. For Milton as author, by definition, the "apples of Sodom" passage in Book X exists simultaneously with Satan's most heroic moments in Books I and II. In fact, he may have actually composed Books I and II rather late in his labor on the poem, as Allan Gilbert thought. The Bard, however, composes *Paradise Lost* in the order of its self-presentation. When he gives Satan

16. Augustine, *City of God,* trans. Henry Bettenson (London, 1972), XIII, 13.

some heroic moments in Book I, Satan's degeneration is still hundreds of lines in the future. The mature Milton was never a satanist, though the Bard sometimes is, early in *Paradise Lost.* In the course of his singing, the Bard works his way to Milton's understanding.

The sequence of the epic as a whole, then, reveals the Bard's story as he changes in the course of his singing. Significant change in the matter and manner of the poem implies significant change in its poet, not in Milton, who designed this movement, but in his Bard. This change appears most clearly when we contrast the first two books of the poem with its last two.

Books I and II swell with the matter and manner of classical epic. They are filled with epic topoi and classical allusions. Heroic speeches, an epic catalog, an *ekphrasis,* a council of the gods, an Elysian fields, and an odyssey are set forth in exalted diction and elaborate syntax. The narrative passages are crowded with epic similes, and the poetry alludes constantly to the great works of antiquity. In Books XI and XII, in contrast, the matter is biblical and the style simpler. Adam's visions in Book XI, with but one exception, are taken from Genesis 4–9; Michael's discourse in Book XII telescopes the rest of salvation history, down to the Redemption and Last Judgment. Classical allusions and epic topoi appear hardly at all, and they are handled more distantly or more critically. When Michael leads Adam to a mountain top to give him visions of his descendants, for example, the poem recalls Anchises' leading Aeneas up a hill to view the pageant of the Roman heroes. But it also recalls passages from Scripture about Moses and Ezekiel. The allusion to a pagan epic does not force itself on our awareness, as do the classical precedents for the catalog of the demons, the description of armies, or the epic similes in Book I. When the matter of epic appears explicitly in Michael's discourse (XI, 638–99), the archangel attacks the martial virtues celebrated in it. In the last two books of *Paradise Lost,* the matter of classical epic has a different status than it did in Books I and II.

So, too, does the epic manner. Books I and II contain thirty-six epic similes; Michael's discourse contains none. The style of the last two books is tuned to a lower pitch than that of the first two, the diction and syntax simpler and more direct. Some complaints against the style of the last two books are famous. Joseph Addison thought that Book XII suffered because "in some Places the Author has been so attentive to his Divinity, that he has neglected his Poetry," and C. S. Lewis found Michael's discourse "an untransmuted lump of futurity" in which the writing is "curiously bad."[17] Yet the ultimate lessons of the poem are presented in this clear and direct manner, one appropriate for didactic poetry. The biblical survey proves conspicuously lower in style than that employed for the demons in Books I and II. The higher subject, in the Christian poem, receives a lower treatment.

These differences have long been recognized. They are closely related to differences between the two halves of the epic. The narrative models for Books I through VI are largely extrabiblical. Although passages from Scripture refer to a war in Heaven, imply councils between God and the angels, and suggest certain characteristics of a physical Hell, none of these are treated at any length. And though Adam and Eve in the Garden comprise a fully biblical subject for poetry, Genesis does not describe Paradise in detail or Adam and Eve at all, nor does it narrate Eve's first moments. The poet ambitious enough to treat these subjects must look for matter outside of Scripture. The Bible provides the source for the poet's treatment of these themes, but the models for that treatment are extrabiblical.[18] Significantly, the poet of Books I through VI looks repeatedly to classical poetry. He has declared his intention "to soar / Above th' *Aonian* Mount" (I, 14–15) in his song, and he cannot overgo classical poetry unless he evokes its matter and manner.

Where classical models of narrative dominate the first half of *Paradise Lost,* scriptural paradigms govern the second. Genesis 1 provides the model for the story of creation in Book VII; Genesis 2, for Adam's narrative in Book VIII; Genesis 3, for the Fall in Book IX and judgment in Book X; Genesis 4–9, for Michael's discourse in Book XI;

17. Joseph Addison, *The Spectator,* No. 369, in *The Works of the Right Honourable Joseph Addison,* ed. Richard Hurd (6 vols.; London, 1811), IV, 202; C. S. Lewis, *A Preface to Paradise Lost* (London, 1942), 125. Christopher Ricks agrees with these judgments in *Milton's Grand Style* (Oxford, 1963), 16. Stanley Fish offers an insightful history of the modern reevaluation of Book XII in "Transmuting the Lump: *Paradise Lost,* 1942–1982," in *Literature and History: Theoretical Problems and Russian Case Studies,* ed. Gary Saul Morson (Palo Alto, Calif., 1986), 33–56.

18. For an opposing view, see Leland Ryken, Introduction to *Milton and Scriptural Tradition: The Bible into Poetry,* ed. James H. Sims and Leland Ryken (Columbia, Mo., 1984), 3–30. Yet Ryken does not distinguish a biblical "model" from a biblical "source."

and the rest of the Bible for his teaching in Book XII. In Book VII, the poet turns away from imaginative flights into Hell and Heaven as he begins to sing "More safe" (24) a song "narrower bound / Within the visible Diurnal Sphere" (21–22). The poem makes a new beginning, one founded in Scripture and in its story of the beginning. The narrative sequence of Books VII to XII is largely governed by the scriptural sequence. Where the poet adds to his biblical source, he draws primarily on Christian materials. Classical motifs do appear in the second half of the poem, but they prove less prominent and are governed more fully by the biblical paradigm of the plot.

Beginning in Book VII, then, the balance between the classical and the biblical begins to shift in *Paradise Lost.* In its first half, because the plot is largely extrabiblical, the matter and manner of classical epic inform the poetry more fully than in the second half. Classical models guide the narrative, and the style is as lofty as any theorist of epic could wish, for it tells "Great things, and full of wonder" (VII, 70) in the grand style. Beginning in Book VII, however, biblical materials come increasingly to occupy the foreground. Classical allusions continue to be made, but they are less prominent than in the first six books, except when Satan occupies the stage. Also, the stylistic register is more inclined to a lower key. The *sermo humilis* of Scripture informs the style of Books VII through XII more fully than it does Books I through VI and nowhere more than in Books XI and XII.

This shift of balance between the classical and the biblical in *Paradise Lost* does not occur all at once, nor is there a uniform increase of the biblical over the second half of the poem. Yet if we could weigh the felt presence of these in each half, the scales would tip in opposite directions. The differences between the first two books of the poem and the last two are analogous, yet more extreme.

These differences point to the change in Milton's Bard. In Books I through VI, he embarks on visionary adventures, for he aspires to ambitious revelations. In Books VII through XII, however, he submits himself increasingly to Scripture and sings a narrative exegesis of the Bible. In Books I and II, he asserts his own greatness as a poet; he overgoes classical precedents in a song that "intends to soar / Above th' *Aonian* Mount, while it pursues / Things unattempted yet in Prose or Rhyme" (I, 14–16). But in Books XI and XII, he asserts not himself but his subject, the truths of Scripture. In Books I and II, he asserts his own greatness, in part, stylistically, singing in the grand style. In Books XI and XII, he composes in a simpler style, for he is concerned to edify his audience, not to achieve greatness for himself.

These contrasts may be summed up in a formula: where the Bard begins by singing a Christian *epic,* he ends by singing a *Christian* epic. This formulation does not imply that the first half of *Paradise Lost* is more classical than Christian, for Christianity governs the poet's aims from beginning to end. But the matter and manner of classical epic prove less prominent in the second half of the poem, where biblical paradigms for the narrative not only dominate but predominate. The shift from Christian *epic* to *Christian* epic occurs gradually, and the formula implies merely a shift of balance. Miltonists have traditionally emphasized the balance in the poem, whereas I emphasize the shift—a shift that represents the Bard's changed understanding of what his Christian epic truly requires. It reveals the growth of his mind as he comes to maturity in his vocation as a Christian poet.

Milton represented this poetic progress as an improvement, simultaneously moral and aesthetic, in the Bard. The Bard's visionary adventures in Books I through VI generate wonderful poetry, but they falter theologically in certain respects, as we shall see in subsequent chapters. More to the point, the Bard turns away from adventurous visions in Book VII, where he explicitly recognizes their danger, and never embarks on them again. Having explored the limits of his visionary powers, in Book VII he takes the sequence of Scripture as his guide for the rest of the poem. Gradually, he realizes his original calling to didactic poetry, no longer asserting his superiority over earlier epic poets but, instead, asserting his biblical subject to edify his audience. Without repudiating the earlier parts of his poem, he manages to modify some of them by subsequent assertions. He cannot retract his epic war in Heaven, for example, but he does have Michael criticize the epic glorification of war, just as Michael's typological discourse serves to correct Raphael's Neoplatonic ladder of Nature. The later books of the poem, therefore, are presented as morally better than its first books, but not only that. Milton understood them also to be aesthetically better because more coherent artistically. Michael's discourse, for example, lacks the absurdities evident in Raphael's war.

To be sure, these assertions run counter to the taste of the ages, which has preferred Milton's grand style to his lower, more didactic flights. Nevertheless, this argument about the Bard's progress in *Paradise Lost* is supported by *Paradise Regained,* which Milton presented as the Bard's subsequent song. *Paradise Regained* continues in the stylistic and didactic vein of Books XI and XII, and it reflects, in various ways, on the earlier books of the earlier poem. Arnold Stein notes an allusion in its opening lines, where Milton implies that "*Paradise Regained* is the real epic, not *Paradise Lost,*" which proves mere "apprentice-work."[19] He finds in that implication both irony and challenge, for he understands "Milton" as the poet of both. Still, he reads the allusion correctly for Milton's Bard. I intend to show why Milton presented *Paradise Regained* as a poem superior to *Paradise Lost,* for it proves the culmination of the Bard's progress.

These conclusions perhaps seem unpalatable because they do not answer to our taste, but they are implied in the self-presentation of Milton's epics as the sequentially unfolding performance of an oral Bard. His changed manner between the first half of *Paradise Lost,* on the one hand, and Books XI and XII and *Paradise Regained,* on the other, indicates a changed conception of Christian epic. Moreover, this change in the poet and his poetry represents Milton's effort to reform the taste of his readers: to lead them from the pleasures of the grand style to a more austere and biblical poetry. To be sure, he failed in this effort, and he was confronted with his failure while he lived. He wrote the later epic, in part, to underscore his Bard's movement away from the exalted visions of *Paradise Lost,* Books I through VI, to the simpler and more didactic poetry of Michael's discourse and *Paradise Regained.* In the later poem, all the visionary adventures are Satan's, and Jesus explicitly repudiates the matter and manner of classical poetry and rhetoric, so prominent in the first half of *Paradise Lost.* Even while Milton lived, however, as Edward Phillips tells us, *Paradise Regained* was "generally censured to be much inferior" to the earlier work, "though [Milton] could not hear with patience any such thing when related to him."[20] In my view, he was vexed at his readers' failure to see the progress of these two works and its significance. His attempt to reform his readers' taste in poetry was wrecked on the rock

19. Arnold Stein, *Heroic Knowledge: An Interpretation of "Paradise Regained" and "Samson Agonistes"* (Minneapolis, 1957), 6–7.

20. Edward Phillips, "The Life of Milton," in Milton, *Complete Poems and Major Prose,* 1036.

of that taste, and the progress of his Bard was not even misunderstood: it was simply invisible.

The preceding pages offer an outline of my argument. Although eccentric to the tradition of Milton studies, it emerges from two unobjectionable principles: the distinction between author and narrator, and an emphasis on the movement in Milton's design. Where Miltonists have treated the poem as a static design by Milton, I emphasize its movement as evidence for a changing Bard. Scholars have long understood how later books in *Paradise Lost* recall earlier ones, and they have treated the similarities in these passages as evidence for Milton's consistent positions. But the present work explores the differences as evidence for the Bard's growth as a Christian epic poet. To be sure, Milton and his Bard share the same concerns, but they do not always share them in the same way. Since scholars have long explored Milton's presence in the work, I dwell on those points that reveal change in his Bard.

I intend to show that the Bard changes by demonstrating how and why he changes. This is the Bard's story, and the following chapters treat it with regard to the proems, Satan, the colloquy in Heaven, and the war in Heaven. Characteristically, a passage from the later books is shown to modify significantly a passage from the earlier ones. Once the Bard's story has been set forth, I consider what Milton gained by conceiving *Paradise Lost* in this way. The final chapter carries the Bard's story forward into *Paradise Regained* to show why Milton presented it, not *Paradise Lost,* as his true Christian epic.

These chapters argue an unfamiliar thesis, and the burden of that task may be felt throughout. Although certain texts are treated rather closely, they are used only to argue my thesis, and much of their poetry is thereby ignored. Furthermore, certain parts of the poem are neglected, especially those concerning Adam and Eve. Since human beings change more readily than supernatural ones, it proves easier to reveal a changing Bard with respect to his supernatural characters than with respect to Adam and Eve. His changing relation to them is subtler, and exploring it would not alter his story in *Paradise Lost.* To show that the Bard changes, and how and why he changes, to tell his story in Milton's epics for the first time, proves task enough for one book.

ONE

The Four Proems of *Paradise Lost*

Miltonists have often treated the four proems of *Paradise Lost* together in order to explore Milton's attitude toward his poetic inspiration, his understanding of sacred poetry, his sense of vocation, and so on. They have assumed that the mature Milton wrote each of the proems in propria persona, and they endeavor to weigh the various statements on the issues in order to arrive at Milton's position. In this manner, they have arrived at several different positions, which can be divided into two major groups. Some argue that Milton took up the mantle of the highest prophets, and they tend to see the first two proems as primary.[1] Others argue that Milton's sense of divine inspiration was more mediated, and these see in the last two his ultimate position.[2] All of these views, however inconsistent with one another they are, find warrant in the poem—a warrant founded on the assumption that all of the proems are equally "Milton's."

This assumption my argument denies, holding, in contrast, to the self-presentation of *Paradise Lost:* each of the proems is uttered by

1. See, among others, John Broadbent, *Some Graver Subject: An Essay on "Paradise Lost"* (London, 1960); William Kerrigan, *The Prophetic Milton* (Charlottesville, Va., 1974); Joseph A. Wittreich, *Visionary Poetics: Milton's Tradition and Its Legacy* (San Marino, Calif., 1979); and John Guillory, *Poetic Authority: Spenser, Milton, and Literary History* (New York, 1984).

2. See Ferry, *Milton's Epic Voice,* and Lewalski, *"Paradise Lost" and the Rhetoric of Literary Forms,* among others. Lewalski criticizes those who place Milton's "Bard on a par with the Biblical prophets" (*"Paradise Lost" and the Rhetoric of Literary Forms,* 7, 26).

Milton's narrator, the Bard, at that point in his original composition of the epic. Each represents, not one view of Milton's attitude, but the Bard's attitude at that point in his composing. Milton wrote them all, of course, but not to present various aspects of his consistent position. Rather, he wrote them to point up the *changing* attitudes of his Bard, the movement of his narrator from one sense of poetic vocation to another. Hence, the four proems should be considered with "the sequential principle" in mind: later utterances can modify earlier ones, but earlier ones cannot modify later ones. Because a poem is a design *in movement,* later utterances enjoy authority simply by being later. Milton structured the movement of *Paradise Lost,* and if we wish to argue for Milton's position from his Bard's four proems, we should give priority to the fourth and the third, in that order. The ambiguity of "Milton" is resolutely denied, but that denial does not sunder the mature Milton from his Bard. Distinguishing the two does not separate them, and what the Bard utters at any point may be argued to be the mature Milton's view. But it must be argued. It may not be assumed, as it is in the ambiguity of "Milton."

Since Miltonists have preferred to keep this ambiguity, I would like to illustrate my view by considering the poet's lament on his blindness in the second proem, often considered Milton's most personal utterance in *Paradise Lost.* Its felt relation to the historical Milton has led scholars to discount Anne Ferry's distinguishing Milton from his Bard, even while they accept her treatment of the blind Bard's symbolic significance. That figure, they counter, proves more than a symbol, though symbolic it is: it is Milton presenting himself in his own voice.[3]

This I deny, and my evidence comes from the poet's subsequent presentations of his blindness. Granted, the mature Milton drew on his experience of blindness in writing the second proem. It is even possible that he wrote it in the grip of the anguish it expresses, though not likely. Probably the emotion was recollected for writing, and it may have been remembered from many years earlier, when his

3. See William G. Riggs, *The Christian Poet in "Paradise Lost"* (Berkeley, 1972), 7–10, on how modern Milton studies have come to understand the narrator as a central figure in the epic, especially p. 10, n. 17, for his criticism of Ferry.

blindness was new and the anguish fresh. Yet though it proves the poet's longest comment on his blindness, it is not his last. The third and fourth proems refer to his blindness, more briefly and sternly. Moreover, the third proem points not only to his suffering from blindness but to the danger of death: the poet is "In darkness, and with dangers compast round" (VII, 27), threatened by "*Bacchus* and his Revellers" (33). Graver dangers threaten him, yet he faces them more sternly.

Furthermore, the extent of his blindness is treated differently in different proems. In the second, he laments it as total: "but not to me returns / Day, or the sweet approach of Ev'n or Morn" (III, 41–42). In the third proem, though, he reveals that his blindness is not really that severe, for the Muse is said to visit him "Nightly, or when Morn / Purples the East" (VII, 29–30). The anthimeria of "Purples" and the enjambment linking it to "Morn" emphasize the verb, and we see that the poet still enjoys some perception of color, not to speak of light. In truth, then, Day does return to him and so, too, the "sweet approach" of Morn, though he denies this when in the grip of his anguish in the second proem. On this score, the third proem corrects the second.

For this reason, I deny that the second proem was the mature Milton's self-presentation in his own voice. Rather, he designed a movement for his Bard: from anguish at his blindness, when his ambitions are highest, to a firmer wrestling with greater adversity as his song "descends," in the second half of the poem. This interpretation simply argues what *Paradise Lost* asserts about itself. Miltonists usually consider the proems as a set of prefaces by Milton to a poem already completed, but *Paradise Lost* presents them as the Bard's self-presentations in the course of composing his epic. Milton designed the proems as a series revealing the Bard's growth as he sings his poem. If we wish to find in them the mature Milton's public attitude toward his blindness, we must look to the fourth and third proems for evidence.

Clearly, then, I treat the proems as evidence for my argument about *Paradise Lost*. They reveal, not different aspects of Milton's purportedly consistent position, but a coherent movement in his Bard, the growth to poetic maturity and self-understanding. Miltonists already understand how the proems are fitted into the poem, how the latter two descend with the descending song, and I draw on this understanding to reveal the Bard's progress.[4] The four proems move from one written in the high style with a bold invocation to one that has no invocation at all, a verse epistle and somewhat casual in tone. In the first, the Bard invokes God himself; in the third, only Urania. He represents himself through three classical figures, beginning with Icarus, a high-flying figure for the poet, and ending with Orpheus, "Standing on Earth, not rapt above the Pole" (VII, 23). With this descending movement comes a changed sense of the poem he is composing. In the first proem, he aspires to overgo the ancient epics with his "advent'rous Song" (I, 13); in the fourth, he understands that his Christian argument is already "higher" than the subjects of classical epic and that all he needs is an "answerable style." In the first proem, the Bard asserts himself, as he intends to sing "Things unattempted yet in Prose or Rhyme" (I, 16), whereas in the fourth he asserts his Christian subject. In short, where the first proem emphasizes what he will achieve, the last concentrates on what he has received, on that to which he aims to be answerable. To be sure, this change proves, in the end, a shift of balance in the poet's conception of his poem, from a Christian *epic* to a *Christian* epic. Nevertheless, the shift is crucial.

The first proem of *Paradise Lost* features the extraordinary ambition of its poet. He sets forth his Christian argument with allusion to the classical epics as he declares his aim of surpassing them. Composing in the grand style, he invokes the God of Moses to sing his epic, which aspires to the heights of theodicy. The ambition of the first proem is well understood, and I shall simply highlight some aspects of it that have not been fully explored. My discussion emphasizes the Bard's use of Icarus as a classical figure for himself, the Muse he invokes, and the theodicy he promises.

4. See Michael Fixler, "Plato's Four Furors and the Real Structure of *Paradise Lost,*" *PMLA,* XCII (1977), 952–62, and Lee M. Johnson, "Milton's Epic Style: The Invocations in *Paradise Lost,*" in *The Cambridge Companion to Milton,* ed. Danielson, 65–78. Two scholars have found that the poems dramatize changes in Milton's narrator: Rollin, "*Paradise Lost:* 'Tragical-Comical-Historical-Pastoral,' " and Rosenblatt, "The Mosaic Voice in *Paradise Lost.*"

The first proem, following classical theory, is not the preface to a work already written but the *initium* to a work still to be sung.[5] Scholars intent on Milton tend to adjust the first proem to the rest of the work, for they assume that Milton declared in it what the epic fulfills. For example, the "Heav'nly Muse" (I, 6) of the first invocation is sometimes said to be Urania, simply because she is invoked by name in the third proem. But when we consider the first proem by itself, the "Heav'nly Muse" that inspired Moses "on the secret top / Of *Oreb,* or of *Sinai*" (6–7) can hardly be Urania. The poet is invoking God himself and so ambitiously that Miltonists have often muted it, for Homer's "Sing, Goddess" (*Iliad* I, 1) is deliberately echoed in what proves tantamount to "Sing, God." The invocation should not be muted, however, and the exultant ambition it reveals in the Bard should be fully felt and weighed.

The self-presentation of *Paradise Lost* should be honored: it is an epic being composed "now," in the ongoing present of our reading. When we read the first proem, we should not be thinking about the third, for it has not yet been sung. When, however, we read the third proem, we may recall the first in order to see what is different and why. The sequential principle functions for the composing Bard and for his audience, and to insist on it is simply to insist on the artistic integrity of *Paradise Lost.*

The first proem, then, begins an epic that is still to be composed. We must take the Bard at his word about his aims in the work, for aims are all we have, and all he has, at the beginning of the poem. Without weighing his ambitions against his subsequent achievements, we should allow ourselves to feel the height of those ambitions as he declares and implies them. When he proclaims that his song intends to soar "Above th' *Aonian* Mount," we should judge the height of his ambitions by what he says. Some scholars treating Milton's use of the classics argue that Milton did not actually overgo the ancient epics and did not think that he did.[6] We may agree with their

5. For the rhetorical functions of a poem according to classical literary theory, see R. W. Condee, "The Formalized Openings of Milton's Epic Poems," *Journal of English and Germanic Philology,* L (1951), 502–508.

6. For recent studies on Milton's use of ancient poetry, see Francis C. Blessington, *"Paradise Lost" and the Classical Epic* (Boston, 1979); David J. DuRocher, *Milton and Ovid* (Ithaca, 1985); and Martindale, *Milton and the Transformation of Ancient Epic.*

judgment about Milton yet preserve our sense of the Bard's ambition in his first proem. To aim is not necessarily to achieve. Having rejected the ambiguity of "Milton," we can see any discrepancy between the Bard's aspiration and his achievement as part of Milton's plan for the poem.

This discrepancy lurks in the Bard's allusion to Icarus, which comes at the end of his first invocation:

> I thence
> Invoke thy aid to my advent'rous Song,
> That with no middle flight intends to soar
> Above th' *Aonian* Mount, while it pursues
> Things unattempted yet in Prose or Rhyme.
> (I, 12–16)

"With no middle flight" alludes to Ovid's story of Daedalus and Icarus in the *Metamorphoses,* where the father advises his son to "shape his course in a middle flight" ("medio ut limite curras").[7] Anthony Low has noted the allusion, arguing that it declares the difference between Milton's inspired Christian poetry and the merely human achievements of the pagan poets.[8] To be sure, the Bard intends precisely this, but the allusion has ominous undertones. Icarus is a traditional figure for the poet who fails through excessive ambition and, in Christian allegory on Ovid, a figure for Satan. I shall establish these traditions briefly and then explore their relevance to the first proem.

The *locus classicus* for Icarus as a failed poet is Horace's *Odes.* In IV, 2, Horace addresses a *recusatio* to Iullus Antonius, who had urged him to celebrate Augustus' victories in the west in Pindaric strains. This he politely refuses to do, insisting that whoever would rival Pindar is an Icarus, drawn by ambition into catastrophe (IV, 2, 1–4). When, in another poem (II, 20), Horace celebrates his poetic inspiration and the spread of his fame, he describes his metamorphosis into

7. Ovid, *Metamorphoses,* ed. Frank Justus Miller, rev. G. P. Goold (2 vols.; Cambridge, Mass., 1977), Vol. I, Bk. VIII, 203. All quotations from the *Metamorphoses* in Latin are taken from Vol. I of this edition; all English translations are mine, unless otherwise noted.

8. Anthony Low, " 'No Middle Flight': *Paradise Lost,* I.14," *Milton Newsletter,* III (1969), 1–4. My discussion of Milton's figures for the poet owes its inspiration to Robert M. Durling, *The Figure of the Poet in Renaissance Epic* (Cambridge, Mass., 1965).

a swan and his subsequent flight. He will be "more renowned than Daedalean Icarus" ("Daedaleo notior Icareo," I, 20, 13), because his flight will be successful.[9] Icarus gave his name to the Icarian Sea, into which he fell. But Horace's name will be heard beyond the borders of the Roman empire while, within it, his verses will live in the mouths of the learned (17–20). Hence, he will be immortal (21–24).

Ovid's story of Daedalus and Icarus is, on one level, a fable on the dangers of excessive boldness and filial disobedience. After Daedalus successfully tests the wings he has made, he advises his son: "I warn you, Icarus, to shape your course in a middle flight, lest, if you go too low, the sea weighs down your wings, or if too high, the heat melts them. Fly between the two!" (*Metamorphoses,* VIII, 203–206). He also tells the boy not to fly too far to the north or to the south. After this brief sermon on *mediocritas,* the pursuit of the mean, Daedalus urges Icarus to follow him in flight. In the event, however, "the boy begins to rejoice in his bold flying" (223), deserts his father's path, and, "drawn by a lust for heaven," seeks a loftier course ("caelique cupidine tractus / altius egit iter," 224–25). The wax melts from his wings, and he plummets into the sea, frantically beating his now-naked arms. Having dared too high a flight, he perishes.

Ovid's treatment of Icarus' rash disobedience also suggests that art itself is the source of danger.[10] Daedalus "devotes his mind to unknown arts and transforms nature" (188–89); his teaching Icarus to fly is described as instruction in "harmful arts" (215); and the story closes with Daedalus cursing "his own arts" (234). Characteristically, Ovid is exploring the ambivalence of artistic skill: the greater one's power to transform nature, the greater the danger. Indeed, he suggests that Icarus' excessive boldness in flight emerges from Daedalus' bold excess in invention. Ovid has taken Horace's application of the myth to poetry and developed it for artistic skill in general.

These are the sources of the tradition on Daedalus and Icarus as figures for the poet. If the tradition today seems obscure, known only through James Joyce's *Portrait of the Artist as a Young Man,* it was by no means arcane in Milton's day. Sir Philip Sidney alludes to it frankly

9. I quote from Horace, *Odes and Epodes,* ed. Paul Shorey, rev. Paul Shorey and Gordon J. Laing (1919; rpr. Pittsburgh, 1960). The translations are mine.

10. See the commentary by William S. Anderson in his edition of *Ovid's Metamorphoses: Books 6–10* (Norman, Okla., 1972), 350–53.

in his *Defense of Poetry* when he considers why the English, so gifted in all else, should lack contemporary greatness in poetry: "Yet confess I always that as the fertilest ground must be manured, so must the highest-flying wit have a Daedalus to guide him. That Daedalus, they say, both in this and in the other [*i.e.,* in poetry and oratory], hath three wings to bear itself up into the air of due commendation: that is, art, imitation, and exercise."[11] Sidney elaborates the allusion with familiar metaphors: genius is always "high-flying" and seeks "to bear itself up" into praise. His casual "That Daedalus, they say" suggests that the myth was a familiar figure for poetic aspiration.

The allusion to Icarus in "With no middle flight," then, was familiar to Milton's audience, but it also had special relevance for religious poetry, for Guillaume de Salluste, Seigneur du Bartas, used it in his *Divine Weeks and Works.* Having scolded the atheist for asking what God did in eternity before he created (51–72), du Bartas meditates on God's self-contemplation and the Trinity (73–96), but he cautions himself rather to adore that mystery than to explore it in his poem (97–118). He intends to treat God's splendor in his created works. Du Bartas does not presume to contemplate God directly, and he refuses to consider creatures apart from their creator. He charts a middle flight for his poem:

> Climbe they that list the battlements of Heav'n,
> And with the Whirle-wind of ambition driven,
> Beyond the Worlds walls let those Eagles flie,
> And gaze upon the Sunne of Majestie;
> Let other-some (whose fainted spirits doo droope)
> Down to the ground their meditations stoope,
> And so contemplate on these Workmanships,
> That th' Authors praise they in themselves eclipse.
> My heedfull Muse, trayned in true Religion,
> Devinely-humane keeps the middle Region:
> *Least, if she should too-high a pitch presume,*
> *Heav'ns glowing flame should melt her waxen plume;*
> Or, if too low (neere Earth or Sea) she flagge,
> Laden with mists her moisted wings should lagge.
> (I, 1, 127–40; emphasis added)[12]

11. Philip Sidney, *A Defense of Poetry,* ed. Jan Van Dorsten (Oxford, 1966), 63.

12. Guillaume de Salluste, Seigneur du Bartas, *The Divine Weeks and Works of Guillaume de Saluste, Sieur du Bartas,* ed. Susan Snyder, trans. Joshua Sylvester (Oxford, 1979).

The passage begins by alluding to Capaneus, who defies Jove and storms the battlements of Thebes, where he is struck down by lightning. He is a classical exemplum against theological presumption; Dante locates him among the blasphemers in Hell.[13] The imagery of poetic flight governs the rest of the passage: the poet-eagles who would soar to the divine sun and the birds who would "stoope" to alight on earth, directing their visions downward. Du Bartas' "heedfull Muse," however, will not have her wings melted in too high a flight, as does Icarus, nor weighed down with moisture from too low a flight. She follows the advice Icarus fails to take: "fly between the two" (*Metamorphoses,* VIII, 206). Du Bartas assures himself that his middle flight allows an expansive view of creation illuminated by the divine sun. Just as important, it will prove safe and successful.

This tradition on Icarus, then, was a commonplace in Milton's day. "With no middle flight" evokes a figure of poetic failure shunned by du Bartas, and does so in lines recording great religious-poetic ambition. The Bard, it seems reasonable to say, knows what he is doing here. Confident of his powers, he evokes the tradition in defiance of du Bartas. He dares disaster as he proclaims his ambition; sure of his strength, he trusts he will not fail. This confidence has ominous undertones, however, for Icarus was also a well-known allegory for Satan.

This tradition may be found in any number of sources. The *Ovide Moralisé* links Icarus to the fallen angels.[14] Dante's *Inferno* implies that both Icarus and Phaeton are analogous to Satan: the sons of the great maker and of the sun, respectively, they aspire to heavenly heights beyond their natures and so fall headlong into the sea.[15] Whether Milton knew this allegory need not be debated, for Satan is linked unambiguously to Icarus twice in Book II of *Paradise Lost.* The first allusion occurs as Satan begins his journey out of Hell:

> Meanwhile the Adversary of God and Man,
> *Satan* with thoughts inflam'd of highest design,

13. P. Papini Stati, *Thebais et Achilleis,* ed. H. W. Garrod (Oxford, Eng.), Book X, and Dante Alighieri, *La Divina Commedia,* ed. C. H. Grandgent, rev. Charles S. Singleton (Cambridge, Mass., 1972), *Inf.* XIV.

14. C. D. De Boer, ed., *Ovide Moralisé: Poème du commencement du quatorzième siècle* (5 vols.; Amsterdam, 1966), Vol. III, ll. 1811–68.

15. Dante refers to Icarus and Phaeton in a double simile at *Inf.* XVII, 106–14. Three figures in the lower Hell imitate the ambitions and the headlong falls of Ovid's characters: the simoniac pope Nicholas III, Ulysses, and Satan.

> Puts on swift wings, and towards the Gates of Hell
> Explores his solitary flight; sometimes
> He scours the right hand coast, sometimes the left,
> Now shaves with level wing the Deep, then soars
> Up to the fiery concave tow'ring high.
>
> (II, 629–35)

That a seraph, even though fallen, must put on wings should alert us to possible allusions. The gesture suggests Mercury, but the subsequent actions declare Icarus. Satan does precisely what Daedalus warns his son not to do. Daedalus tells Icarus not to go too far to either the north or the south; Satan "scours" both coasts of Hell. Icarus is warned against flying too close to the sea, lest his wings grow heavy with moisture, or too high, lest they melt. Satan flies farther in both directions: he "shaves with level wing the Deep" and then soars aloft into the "fiery" sky of Hell.

The second allusion occurs as Satan begins his flight into Chaos:

> At last his Sail-broad Vans
> He spreads for flight, and in the surging smoke
> Uplifted spurns the ground, thence many a League
> As in a cloudy Chair ascending rides
> Audacious, but that seat soon failing, meets
> A vast vacuity: all unawares
> Flutt'ring his pennons vain plumb down he drops
> Ten thousand fadom deep. . . .
>
> (II, 927–34)

Satan's vain beating of his wings clearly recalls Icarus frantically moving his arms as he plummets. The boy's arms can take no hold on the air ("non ullas percipit auras," *Metamorphoses,* VIII, 228), nor can Satan's wings take hold when they encounter a "vast vacuity." Both falls come after a bold soar: the Bard's "audacious" (931) in this context recalls Ovid's "audaci volatu" (223).

But how conscious is the Bard of the satanic undertones in his aspiration to poetic soaring "with no middle flight"?[16] Hardly at all. He

16. Steven Blakemore explores the Satanic implications of the phrase in " 'With No Middle Flight': Poetic Pride and Satanic Hubris in *Paradise Lost,*" *Kentucky Review,* III (1985), 23–31. I am grateful to Ethan Gilsdorf for this reference. Rollin, "*Paradise Lost:* 'Tragical-Comical-Historical-Pastoral,' " 31–32, treats the issue, as does Riggs, *Christian Poet in "Paradise Lost,"* 17–20.

adopts the figure of Icarus in deliberate defiance of du Bartas, confident of greater poetic powers and deeper religious learning. Given the density of biblical allusions in the first invocation, he seems unaware that his confidence has satanic undertones. He seems to think that his lofty subject is unproblematically joined to his lofty ambition. He feels himself the perfect poet for Christian epic: his exultant powers are suited to the most exalted subject, the story of the Fall and Redemption. He seems not to recognize that the poet as Icarus risks being what the allusion implies, the poet as Satan.

By the end of Book II, though, he has been singing of Satan for many hundreds of lines. Hence, the Bard cannot fail to understand how his two allusions to Satan as Icarus reflect on himself as an Icarus-poet. Indeed, he makes explicit the connection between himself and Satan in his second proem: "Thee I revisit now with bolder wing, / *Escap't* the *Stygian* Pool, though long *detain'd* / In that obscure sojourn" (III, 13–15; emphasis added to "Escap't" and "detain'd"). The poet as Icarus, at the beginning of Book I, and Satan as Icarus, in the second half of Book II, are here closely, if momentarily, identified.

This discussion of "with no middle flight," then, aims simply to clarify the danger in the Bard's extraordinary ambition. It is of a piece with his first invocation. Familiarity has perhaps dulled our sense of how bold that invocation is, and its boldness is muted additionally by two ambiguities in critical practice. One of these, the ambiguity of "Milton," I have already criticized, insisting that the "Heav'nly Muse" of the first proem cannot be Urania.[17] The second is the ambiguity of "invocation."

The term is used indiscriminately to cover the classical invocation of a Muse and the Christian prayer for divine inspiration, but these two gestures are grammatically different and categorically distinct.[18] With regard to *Paradise Lost,* I shall reserve *invocation* for the classical

17. David Daiches argues that the poet invokes "God himself" and then, a few pages later, says that he invokes "Urania." See "The Opening of *Paradise Lost,*" in *The Living Milton: Essays by Various Hands,* ed. Frank Kermode (London, 1960), 55–69, esp. 60, 64.

18. See Lily B. Campbell, *Divine Poetry and Drama in Sixteenth-Century England* (Berkeley, 1959), 74–92. Her examples of Salluste du Bartas' influence on English invocations are all Christian prayers, that is, petitions, not invocations on the classical model. For a more recent study, see E. R. Gregory, "Three Muses and a Poet: A Perspective on Milton's Epic Thought," *Milton Studies,* X (1977), 35–64.

gesture and *prayer* for the Christian. The classical poet invokes with the imperative "Sing, goddess." To be sure, it may have been felt as a request rather than a command, but a command it remains grammatically. The Christian prayer, in contrast, makes verbal gestures of request, petition, supplication. The Christian God, properly speaking, should not be invoked. Yet the Bard does precisely that in the first sentence of *Paradise Lost.* The God who gave the Decalogue to Moses "on the secret top / Of *Oreb,* or of *Sinai*" and who there inspired the story of creation is called a "Heav'nly Muse" and is commanded to "Sing" the Bard's poem. Such audacity should startle us. It was certainly designed to shock Milton's contemporaries. For whether Christian poets should invoke their God had become a matter of contemporary discussion. In his preface to *Gondibert,* published in 1650, William Davenant inveighed against the practice as "saucy familiarity with a true God." Thomas Hobbes agreed and added this scathing judgment: "But why a Christian should think it an ornament to his Poeme, either to profane the true God, or invoke a false one, I can imagine no cause, but a reasonlesse imitation of custome; of a foolish custome; by which a man enabled to speake wisely from the principles of nature, and his owne meditation, loves rather to be thought to speake by inspiration, like a bagpipe."[19]

The first sentence of *Paradise Lost,* published not long after these remarks, dares failure of decorum in this regard. The Bard features the highest mode of divine illumination: the direct impression of the divine upon the human intellect that occurred to Moses on Mount Sinai.[20] Furthermore, the Bard does not supplicate the inscrutable God of Moses but invokes him as though he were a classical Muse.

The contrast between invocation in the classical manner and the Christian prayer for divine inspiration is made clear within the first proem, for the Bard's second sentence is just such a prayer: "And chiefly Thou O Spirit, that dost prefer / Before all Temples th' upright heart and pure, / Instruct me, for Thou know'st" (I, 17–19). The rev-

19. William Davenant, *Sir William Davenant's "Gondibert,"* ed. David F. Gladish (Oxford, 1971), 22 (for Davenant's remark) and 49 (for Hobbes's agreement).

20. Lewalski, *"Paradise Lost" and the Rhetoric of Literary Forms,* 25–27. She cites John Smith, "Of Prophesie," *Select Discourses* (London, 1660), 169–83. Broadbent, *Some Graver Subject,* 68, uses Smith to emphasize the height of inspiration being invoked.

erent address comes before the verb, which is understood as an optative: "May Thou instruct me." The contrast to "Sing, Heav'nly Muse," where command comes before address, could not be clearer, yet this Christian prayer actually serves to soften the boldness of the previous invocation. The Bard is already responding to what he sings, as he elaborates his poem.

The Bard's audacity in invoking the God of Moses as though he were a classical Muse is almost equaled by the Bard's promise to sing biblical themes yet pursue "Things unattempted yet in Prose or Rhyme." David Daiches asks the pertinent questions: "Does he mean unattempted even in the Bible? Is he going to overgo Moses as Spenser intended to overgo Ariosto? Or does he mean 'unattempted in modern poetry' or 'unattempted in English literature'?" Daiches quotes from *The Christian Doctrine* to illustrate Milton's belief that "the Bible tells all the truth about ultimate things that men know or need to know." He concludes that Milton intended the poem as "a complete retelling, under new plenary inspiration deriving from the same divine source as Moses' inspiration, of the whole story of the mutual relations of God and man."[21] In my view, Daiches interprets the purport of the sentence correctly, not for Milton, but for the Bard. Clearly, the Bard does aspire to overgo Moses, not by having a higher inspiration, for there is none, but in telling the full story of salvation. He aspires to equal the Bible in the scope of his epic and the height of his inspiration. There can be no more daring ambition for a Christian poet. In the Bard's first proem, though, it proves only an ambition, not an achievement.

The Bard also aspires to an ambitious theodicy, to "justify the ways of God to men" (I, 25). The extraordinary intention of these words has not been fully understood, because it has been weighed against what the poem actually achieves. To be sure, *Paradise Lost* contains a theodicy, rather fully elaborated, albeit indirectly, as Dennis Danielson has shown.[22] Whether the poem accomplishes *this* theodicy depends on how we interpret these lines in context. For one thing, they seem to promise a more direct theodicy than the poem actually gives

21. Daiches, "The Opening of *Paradise Lost*," in *The Living Milton*, ed. Kermode, 63.

22. Dennis Richard Danielson, *Milton's Good God: A Study in Literary Theodicy* (Cambridge, Eng., 1982).

us. In this respect, a small discrepancy is already visible between what the poet aspires to in his first proem and what he eventually does.

The extraordinary ambition of this theodicy lies in its use of two plurals: "And justify the *ways* of God to *men*." Danielson comments on the significance of the plural "men."[23] "Man" would have been less ambitious, implying that all human beings are subsumed in Adam and Christ, as the declared subject of the poem implies. "Men" seems to refer to every human being in every time and place. "Ways" proves an equally significant plural. Had the Bard said, "And justify the *way* of God to men," he would have suggested a single pattern in God's dealing with every human being. This pattern would imply the Fall, whose effects all feel, and the redemptive grace open, in theory, to all. It might suggest God's providential plan for all humanity and the plan's fulfillment in Christ, "the way, the truth, and the life." But the plural "ways" implies, not a single pattern, but all the various ways God uses with human beings.

In short, "And justify the ways of God to men" aspires to much more than justifying either "the ways of God to man" or "the way of God to men." The resounding ambition of the first proem gives warrant for interpreting these words to their fullest extent. His words thus understood, the Bard aspires to prove the justice, here and now, of all God's ways with every single human being. Even the suffering of the innocent and the persecution of the righteous will be vindicated in this poem.

This interpretation of the line has not heretofore been given, and there is no wonder why, for it implies an impossible theodicy. At the Last Judgment, God will justify all his ways with all human beings; only God can do this, and Christian theology asserts that he will do it only when he establishes his kingdom forever. Although Miltonists have long recognized the lofty ambition of the first proem and of this line, they have not found this meaning in it because they have understood it to be "Milton"'s. Its meaning is thereby muted to something reasonable, something consonant with what is achieved in *Paradise Lost*.

Yet, given the climactic movement of the first proem, the two plurals in "And justify the ways of God to men" do not mean less than I have said, and they could hardly mean more. This interpretation accords with the Bard's extraordinary ambition at the beginning of his epic: his overgoing aspiration, which extends even to Moses; his clas-

23. Danielson, *Milton's Good God*, 10, 235 n. 10.

sical invocation of the Christian God; his intention to soar above the achievements of all previous poets. When the first proem is read, not as the preface to a completed work, but as the *initium* of a poem still to be sung, the ambition of its Bard emerges with greater clarity and force. Miltonists have always recognized the boldness of this proem. My interpretation of a few points finds it even bolder than they have seen. The Bard, exultant in his powers, begins his song with the loftiest ambitions a Christian poet can have. To what extent he achieves them can be answered only by the poem he goes on to sing.

Scholars intent on "Milton"'s meaning in this proem will object to these interpretations, but I must ask them to suspend their critical disbelief. Differences of local interpretation between us cannot readily be debated, because there is no ground where they can meet: they emerge from different assumptions about the poem. Miltonists understand the voice of the poem to be Milton's. This assumption demands that the first proem be balanced against the rest of *Paradise Lost*. Thus, Miltonists naturally feel that "Sing, Heav'nly Muse" is more like a prayer than a classical invocation. Their assumption leads them to seek a unified and consistent poem under Milton's authorial consciousness, so they labor to resolve differences and (seeming) inconsistencies in the poem as a whole.

My argument, in contrast, distinguishes the Bard's narratorial voice from Milton's authorial consciousness. Inconsistencies in what the Bard asserts at many points are well established in scholarly debates, yet they may be resolved in the coherent story of the Bard's development. In my view, then, "Sing, Heav'nly Muse" is what it appears to be in its context, before the Bard prays to the Holy Spirit or sings the rest of the poem. Thus isolated according to its own self-presentation, it enacts the classical invocation of the Christian God, something bold and even shocking. This interpretation, unnatural though it may seem to Miltonists, proves wholly consistent with the Bard's ebullient sense of his own powers. If Miltonists are to consider my argument fairly, they must check their tendency to balance early assertions in the poem by later ones. For when the poem is treated according to its self-presentation as an oral song unfolding now, these later utterances do not yet exist.

Because the Bard's extraordinary ambitions do not begin to change until the third proem, the second is not essential to his story. Nevertheless, I should like to attend briefly to the invocation in Book III, to the Bard's identification with Satan, and to his lament on his blindness as it leads to his final prayer.

An old debate about the invocation in Book III is illuminated by the distinction between Milton and his Bard. Scholars have asked precisely who or what is being addressed in these splendid lines:

> Hail holy Light, offspring of Heav'n first-born,
> Or of th' Eternal Coeternal beam
> May I express thee unblam'd? since God is Light,
> And never but in unapproached Light
> Dwelt from Eternity, dwelt then in thee,
> Bright effluence of bright essence increate.
> Or hear'st thou rather pure Ethereal stream,
> Whose Fountain who shall tell? before the Sun,
> Before the Heavens thou wert, and at the voice
> Of God, as with a Mantle didst invest
> The rising world of waters dark and deep,
> Won from the void and formless infinite.
> . . . .
> . . . thee I revisit safe,
> And feel thy sovran vital Lamp; but thou
> Revisit'st not these eyes, that roll in vain
> To find thy piercing ray, and find no dawn.
> (III, 1–12, 21–24)

At the end, the poet is clearly addressing physical light. At the beginning, he is speaking either to the *lux increata* of the Son or the *lux effusa* of God's glory. In between, his language points to the light created on the first day of Genesis. All are addressed as a single "Thou."

Scholarly debate on this issue assumes that Milton composed these lines in his own voice to address a clear and consistent "Thou."[24] Yet Book III clearly features an inconsistency of address. The failure of Miltonists to agree on what this passage is doing suggests either a lapse by the poet or an error in their assumptions.

24. See Alastair Fowler's long note on the debate in his edition of *Paradise Lost* (London, 1971), at III, 1–55, and Lewalski's discussion and notes, *"Paradise Lost" and the Rhetoric of Literary Forms,* 31–33, 292–94. See also Kathleen M. Swaim, "The Mimesis of Accommodation in Book III of *Paradise Lost,*" *Philological Quarterly,* LXIII (1984), 461–75, rpr. in Swaim, *Before and After the Fall.*

These lines become coherent when understood as the Bard's elaborating on his invocation in the present. They do not address a single, consistent entity. Rather, they reveal his desire to address the highest "holy Light" he can and remain "unblam'd." Hence, the opening lines vacillate in emphasis between the Son and God's glory, before the poet modulates downward to the physical light of the first day of creation and, finally, to the place of physical light in the sun ("thy sovran vital Lamp," 22). The tension in the Bard's address may be felt in its opening ambiguities. In "offspring of Heav'n first-born," "Heav'n" suggests something less than God and so points to his glory, whereas "first-born" implies the Son. Similarly, "of th' Eternal Coeternal Beam" could refer to either, depending on whether one emphasizes "Coeternal" (the Son) or "Beam" (glory). Likewise, in "Bright effluence of bright essence increate," "effluence" suggests God's glory, while emphasizing that it is "increate" implies the Son. Yet the Bard, it seems, does not feel that he can address spiritual light "unblam'd," so he then adjusts his invocation downward, to created light. Eventually he asserts his own powers with respect to the physical light of the sun: "thee I revisit safe." He can hardly assert his power to visit the highest "holy Light" at will. For that, he would certainly be blamed.

In short, these lines feature inconsistency of address in order to reveal the movement of their speaker as he elaborates his second proem. They do not present themselves as written by Milton, and the scholarly debate on them is generated by neglecting the self-presentation of *Paradise Lost*.

The poet's identification with Satan in the second proem has been much noticed and much excused. Miltonists who take the voice of the poem to be Milton's want naturally to distance him from Satan. They rightly contrast his invoking divine aid with Satan's determination to stand or fall on his own power.[25] But his prayer for aid occurs almost forty lines after his identification with Satan. In its context, therefore,

25. See Walter Schindler, *Voice and Crisis: Invocation in Milton's Poetry* (Hamden, Conn., 1984), 50. He cites Galbraith Miller Crump, *The Mystical Design of "Paradise Lost"* (Lewisburg, Pa., 1975), 37. See also Riggs, *Christian Poet in "Paradise Lost,"* 20–23, and Stephen Wigler, "The Poet and Satan Before the Light: A Suggestion About Book III and the Opening of Book IV of *Paradise Lost*," *Milton Quarterly*, XII, (1978), 59–64.

the link with Satan cannot be discounted so easily. It is underscored both by the genre it contravenes and the Bard's attitude toward his Muse.

The genre has been treated by Barbara Lewalski. She points out that the second proem is "a Christian version of the third kind of hymn in [Joseph] Scaliger's classification (those celebrating the *numen* of a god)." These hymns have three parts: an *exordium* addressing the god through his attributes, a narrative myth of the god's action, and a closing peroration.[26] After the address to light, then, the Bard was expected to relate a story celebrating its activity and power. Instead, he celebrates his own activity and power. This contravening of the genre emphasizes the Bard's linking himself to Satan, another figure who prefers to praise himself, rather than God:

> Thee I revisit now with bolder wing,
> Escap't the *Stygian* Pool, though long detain'd
> In that obscure sojourn, while in my flight
> Through utter and through middle darkness borne
> With other notes than to th' *Orphean* Lyre
> I sung of *Chaos* and *Eternal Night,*
> Taught by the heav'nly Muse to venture down
> The dark descent, and up to reascend,
> Though hard and rare: thee I revisit safe,
> And feel thy sovran vital Lamp. . . .
>
> (III, 13–22)

The Bard's praise of his own powers in these lines is further underlined by his attitude toward his "heav'nly Muse." Syntactically, she is relegated to a distant second place in the Bard's achievement: she appears in a participial phrase after six lines describing his own bold deeds. Nor does that phrase grant her much. He does not say that she "guided" or "led" him. "Taught by the heav'nly Muse to venture down / The dark descent" does not even assert that she taught him *how* to descend, merely that she told him he ought to do so. Syntactically and semantically, then, the Muse here is a secondary figure and appears only as a convention. This can hardly be the "Heav'nly Muse" of the first invocation, the divine inspirer of Moses on "the secret

26. Lewalski, *"Paradise Lost" and the Rhetoric of Literary Forms,* 28–31.

top / Of *Oreb,* or of *Sinai.*" Here the Bard insists on his flight and his song: "I revisit" (13, 21), "my flight" (15), and "I sung" (18) grant the Muse little part in his achievement.

The Bard's slighting of the Muse, combined with his contravening of the hymnic convention, emphasizes his similarity to Satan. How are we to evaluate the connection? The Bard acknowledges that he has been with Satan for over fifteen hundred lines, as it were: "long detain'd" in Hell, both have "Escap't the *Stygian* Pool" (14) and have come to the light after a "flight / Through utter and through middle darkness" (15–16). The Bard's having been "borne" through the darkness even suggests that Satan has carried him. Granted, the Bard must fly with Satan in vision in order to sing of his journey. The similarity to Satan thus emerges, in some sense, from the visionary requirements of the Bard's song: he must be with Satan in Hell now, in imagination, in order to sing of him. Yet words like "detain'd" and "Escap't" suggest something more than mere similarity. The Bard identifies himself with the character who has dominated his song in his first two books. And that verbal identification is made more ominous by his celebrating his own achievements where he should be praising those of the "holy Light" already invoked.

At the same time, the identification marks a growth in the Bard's self-awareness, for he now acknowledges the Satanic undertones of his Icarian aspiration. Perhaps he feels he can do so safely because he is leaving Satan behind for the first time in his poem. The danger of imagining Satan's experience at length may be explicitly felt because as Satan "hies" himself to the physical light of the universe, so the Bard intends to journey to the spiritual light of the Empyrean. Although the ascents are analogous, one even a repetition of the other, leaving Satan behind removes the danger from recognizing their Icarian affinities.

After the Bard's address to "holy Light," with its celebration of his own achievements, comes his lament on his blindness. Its substance is well understood, and I want only to remark on how it functions in the proem for the Bard elaborating his song now.

First, there is no literary necessity for the Bard's confession of blindness. In classical epic, no poet ever confesses so intimate a detail, and the Bard's first proem accords with this tradition, giving no acknowledgment of his blindness. He invokes the Muse twice in Book I (1–26, 376–80), and both times he maintains the impersonality that tradition requires, as he does also in his hymn to "holy Light." His personal confession of blindness violates the conventions not only of the epic but also of the hymnic form in his second proem. It comes as a literary surprise.

Second, this absence of literary necessity is underscored by the length and tone of the confession. It is no mere acknowledgment of blindness but a lament. It contravenes the convention of impersonality, not only by being a confession, but by the Bard's confessing with such feeling and at such length. It comprises twenty-eight lines (III, 23–50) and so is longer than the whole first proem.

Third, when those lines are read as the utterance of an oral Bard, they reveal him struggling to comfort himself and not entirely succeeding. After admitting his blindness in lines 22–26, he dwells for some fifteen lines (26–40) on his poetic activity. Here he refers to his blindness three times, each reference longer than the previous one: "Nightly I visit" (32), the blind classical poets and prophets (34–35), and the nightingale (37–40). His joy in poetic composition is gradually overwhelmed by his anguish at his blindness, and ten lines of unrelieved lament follow (40–50). Having failed to solace himself, he prays to God for comfort in a closing address to "Celestial Light," and the proem ends.

Finally, the confession seems to be torn from him. It has no literary necessity, and it runs on at a surprising length, as the Bard struggles to comfort himself. Ironically, the confession is motivated by his assertions of poetic achievement (13–21) and of his success in returning to the light: "Thee I revisit," uttered twice (13, 21). Then suddenly he modifies his declaration, confessing that his power with respect to the light is not as great as he would wish: he can "feel" (22) but not see it. His self-assertion falters into lament. From being the poet who celebrates his own achievement, he falls to the blind man lamenting his own weakness. The change in him is sudden and drastic: "thee I revisit safe, / And feel thy sovran vital Lamp; but thou / Revisit'st not these eyes" (21–23). For us, it appears over these last six words, but for him it occurs in the pause of a semicolon.

The Bard's lament on his blindness, however, generates a shift of attitude in the proem. He begins by trying to address the highest "holy Light" he can and still remain "unblam'd." He gradually modulates downward to physical light and then asserts his power with respect to it. But this assertion fails: he is blind, and a confession of his blindness is wrung from him. After experiencing his weakness at length, he prays to the highest holy Light there is:

> So much the rather thou Celestial Light
> Shine inward, and the mind through all her powers
> Irradiate, there plant eyes, all mist from thence
> Purge and disperse, that I may see and tell
> Of things invisible to mortal sight.
>
> (51–55)

The proem as a whole, then, unfolds the Bard's movement from invocation to prayer and from self-assertion to humility. The lament on his blindness proves crucial to that movement. Only after failing to comfort himself does he turn to God for comfort. He confronts his failure to assert his power with regard to physical light and finally prays for insight from "Celestial Light." What begins as a hymn to light that turns into self-celebration becomes, in the end, an ardent and humble petition.

The Bard's poetic aspirations, nevertheless, remain exalted. If he has soared "Above th' *Aonian* Mount" already in Books I and II, he aims now to soar into the Empyrean to sing "Of things invisible to mortal sight" (55). He aspires to revelation, no longer of things invisible "below," but of those "above." His poetic ambition remains as exalted as ever, and it aims at a higher subject. He will not begin to curb it until his third proem, after he has given it its head and explored the range of his abilities.

Miltonists have long understood that the third proem initiates a downward movement in *Paradise Lost*.[27] The poet declares that the second half of his poem will be "narrower bound / Within the visible Diurnal Sphere" (VII, 21–22) and that he will therefore sing "More safe" (24), "Standing on Earth, not rapt above the Pole" (23). His second half is set largely within the created universe, whereas his first half was largely outside it. The poet's style, too, is tuned to a lower pitch in Book VII than in Book VI, and it will prove lower still in Books XI and XII. These changes in the poem are well understood. I

27. Isabel Gamble MacCaffrey first remarked the downward course of the last half of the poem in *"Paradise Lost" as "Myth"* (Cambridge, Mass., 1959), 58–59.

shall simply interpret them as evidence for change in the poet, Milton's Bard. My treatment of the third proem will dwell on the implications of the two classical figures for the poet, Bellerophon and Orpheus. First, however, I want to make some remarks about the invocation of Urania and the Bard's treatment of his blindness, comparing these to what we have seen in the second proem.

The Bard has a different attitude toward his Muse in the third proem than he did in the second. There, as we saw, he slighted her role in his achievement. Both syntactically and semantically, he relegated her to a secondary place. In the third proem, in contrast, he addresses her by name and features her role in his singing. The following excerpts reveal clearly how the Bard comes to acknowledge his reliance on the Muse more and more as the proem progresses:

> Descend from Heav'n *Urania,* by that name
> If rightly thou are call'd, whose Voice divine
> Following, above th' *Olympian* Hill I soar,
> Above the flight of *Pegasean* wing.
> . . . .
> . . . Up led by thee
> Into the Heav'n of Heav'ns I have presum'd,
> An Earthly Guest, and drawn Empyreal Air,
> Thy temp'ring; with like safety guided down
> Return me to my Native Element:
> . . . .
> . . . still govern thou my Song,
> *Urania,* and fit audience find, though few.
> (VII, 1–4, 12–16, 30–31)

In the first of these excerpts, the Bard features his own activity as he follows Urania's "Voice divine" (2). In the second, he moves from acknowledging that he has been "led" (12) by her to asking her to "Return" (16), not merely lead, him to earth. In the third, "still govern thou" is a prayer, a verbal gesture humbler than the request in "Return," and it recognizes that she has been governing his song all the while. Finally, after he asks her to "drive far off the barbarous dissonance / Of *Bacchus* and his Revellers" (32–33), his prayer becomes imploring: "So fail not thou, who thee implores" (38). As the Bard acknowledges an ever greater role for Urania in his singing, his verbal gestures toward her grow humbler.

What begins as a classical invocation, "Descend from Heav'n *Urania,*" becomes, at the end, a Christian prayer, yet the movement from the one to the other is so nicely modulated that the contrast is hardly felt. The harmony of classical and Christian in the figure of Urania comes gradually to suffuse the Bard's style.[28] He is learning a middle flight for his song. The third proem declares a descent and enacts it beautifully in subject and in style.

This lower stylistic pitch affects the Bard's sense of himself in the third proem. Where in the second he lamented his blindness at length, in the third he faces even greater dangers more firmly and sternly. He now confronts the danger of death from "*Bacchus* and his Revellers"; he is not only "In darkness" but "with dangers compast round" (27). When we compare the two proems in this regard, a pattern emerges. With the lofty ambition and self-celebration of the second proem came anguish at his blindness. In the third, his lowered ambitions and willingness to celebrate his Muse bring him increased fortitude. Lowered ambitions, evident in a lower style, make for a morally stronger poet.

They also make for a poet who has a changed sense of his blindness. In the second proem, the Bard lamented his blindness as total: the world was "a Universal blanc / Of Nature's works to me expung'd and ras'd, / And wisdom at one entrance quite shut out" (III, 48–50). In the third, we see that he knows "when Morn / Purples the East" (VII, 29–30), indicating he sees not only light but color. His lamenting their utter loss to him in Book III was a piece of self-indulgence in despair, born out of his self-assertion that he could revisit the light at will (III, 13–21). The Bard in Book VII asserts less for himself, so he sees more of what there is for him to see. Compared to Book III, he proves saner and sterner with himself, though conscious of greater adversity.

The Bard's increased self-control emerges from his lower ambitions. Since he is no longer straining toward extraordinary heights in

28. For Milton's use of the figure of Urania, see Michael Fixler, "Milton's Passionate Epic," *Milton Studies,* I (1969), 167–92, esp. 182–85, and Gregory, "Three Muses and a Poet," esp. 54–61.

his song, he can sing with greater assurance and in a steadier key. This lowering of ambitions is evident in his movement from Bellerophon to Orpheus, and the allusion to Bellerophon marks his reappraisal of the Icarian poetry in Books I through VI. For Icarus symbolizes a poet whose wings of inspiration are his own, whereas Bellerophon rides a beast whose energy and will are not wholly in his control.

The Bard's new understanding proves too important to be left to the single reference "Above the flight of *Pegasean* wing" (4). He elaborates the allusion in his first prayer to the Muse. Here he both accuses and excuses himself, recognizes the danger in his daring and appeals to the Muse for safety:

> Up led by thee
> Into the Heav'n of Heav'ns I have presum'd,
> An Earthly Guest, and drawn Empyreal Air,
> Thy temp'ring; with like safety guided down
> Return me to my Native Element:
> Lest from this flying Steed unrein'd, (as once
> *Bellerophon,* though from a lower Clime)
> Dismounted, on th' *Aleian* Field I fall
> Erroneous there to wander and forlorn.
> Half yet remains unsung, but narrower bound
> Within the visible Diurnal Sphere;
> Standing on Earth, not rapt above the Pole,
> More safe I Sing with mortal voice, unchang'd
> To hoarse or mute. . . .
>
> (VII, 12–25)

The Bard recognizes the danger in having sung of the Empyreal heaven in Books III, V, and VI. He terms the act presumption toward the divine ("I have presum'd, / An Earthly Guest"), though qualified and excused by the Muse's guidance. When he prays to be guided down "with like safety" (15), he implies that he has sung safely of Heaven, but he quickly grants that he will sing "More safe" (24) "Standing on Earth, not rapt above the Pole" (23). "Rapt" does not refer to the Muse's guidance. That he describes as his following her voice (2–3) and as his being "Up led" by her (12). The sweeping force of *raptus,* to the contrary, refers to an experience of inspiration that the poet figures in Pegasus, "this flying Steed unrein'd" (17).

"Unrein'd" implies his lack of control over this inspiration, a wild force that he rides without bit, bridle, or saddle.

Pegasus is a figure of violence from his birth and, hence, far different from Icarus, whose wings are fashioned by human art. The horse is conceived from the rape of Medusa by Poseidon and born from the Gorgon's blood after she is slain by Perseus. The stroke of his hoof on Mount Helicon creates the Hippocrene, a fountain sacred to the Muses, so Pegasus' violence is traditionally associated with the rapture of poetic inspiration. He is given by the gods to Bellerophon so that the hero can slay the Chimera and conquer the Amazons. He is a half-wild, semidivine flying horse: a fierce supernatural energy without reason, controllable only by the gods or by their aid.[29] Icarus' wings, in contrast, are fashioned by human artifice for a peaceful purpose, to escape Crete. Icarus controls the movement of his wings to direct his flight; he fails only to govern his ambitions. The poet choosing Icarus as the figure for his art asserts mastery over his flight, but the poet who rides a Pegasus acknowledges that his imagination has wings of its own, not of his fashioning and beyond his full control. "Above the flight of *Pegasean* wing" (4), then, proves a double-edged allusion. On one side, as Miltonists have seen, it implies the poet's overgoing the inspiration of classical poetry. On the other, a supra-Pegasean flight also implies theological presumption.

Natalis Comes understood Bellerophon precisely as a figure of theological presumption. The hero is so elated by his successes that he decides to ascend to heaven. Jupiter deems this an arrogance (*arrogantia*) and a daring (*temeritas*) that require divine vengeance: he sends a gadfly against Pegasus, and Bellerophon is unhorsed, falling headlong (like Icarus) to earth. Comes goes on to draw the moral: it is not fitting to sorrow too greatly in adversity or to glory too much in success. Rather, we should know from experience that God is the governor (*moderator*) of all these things. He both aids us in calamity and chastens our elation at success, as he did to Bellerophon.[30]

29. See Natalis Comes, *Mythologiae* (1567; rpr. New York, 1976) VII, xi, p. 221b, ll. 35–39, and IX, vi, p. 270b, ll. 41*ff.* Poseidon's rape of Medusa is told by Ovid in *Metamorphoses,* IV, 790–803; his being the father of Pegasus, in VI, 119–20; Pegasus' hoof creating the spring sacred to the Muses, in V, 256–59.

30. Comes, *Mythologiae,* IX, iv, p. 271a, ll. 9–12, 28–33.

The Bard's likening himself to Bellerophon proves a distancing gesture, as he reappraises the Icarian poetry of Books I through VI. In the allegorical tradition, both Bellerophon and Icarus symbolize the pride and daring of theological presumption, for both would ascend into the heavens at will. Icarus, however, is a figure for Satan, both outside *Paradise Lost* and within it; I have found no such allegory for Bellerophon.[31] When the Bard compares himself to the latter, then, he recognizes the danger of his poetic daring yet distances himself from its Satanic implications. Although both Icarus and Bellerophon fall headlong for their excesses, only Icarus perishes. The Bard also acknowledges, through the figure of Pegasus, that his imagination in Books I through VI seemed to have an energy and will of its own. He admits that he could not control at all points its movements. This admission seems directed at his narrating of events in the "Heav'n of Heav'ns" (13), though it might also apply elsewhere. Having embarked on the unreined flying steed of his imagination, he had to ride it wherever it carried him and hope in the Muse's guidance.

In the allusion to Bellerophon, then, the Bard reflects on what he has finished singing and chastens his aspirations. As he begins the second half of his song, he elects a new classical figure for himself as poet. In its immediate context, the allusion to Orpheus represents the poet in peril, but it also proves apt for the subjects of Books VII and VIII. According to tradition, Orpheus sings the origins of the world and the movements of the heavens. He thus proves an apt figure for the poet soon to treat these very subjects.

Yet there is more to the tradition of Orpheus that makes him an apt figure of the poet of all of *Paradise Lost.* First, Orpheus experiences irrevocable loss through excessive love for his wife Eurydice, so he proves a fit symbol for the poet of the Fall. That loss teaches a lesson about moderation similar to the one Michael conveys in Books XI and XII. In addition, the Bard's turn from Icarus or Bellerophon to Orpheus represents a change in his poetry: no longer does he strive toward visionary height for himself but rather seeks to teach his audi-

31. Riggs, *Christian Poet in "Paradise Lost,"* 29, asserts that Bellerophon was a figure for Satan, but he does not cite his sources. Broadbent, *Some Graver Subject,* 235, relates the myth to the theme of presumption in Books VI through VIII. Joseph H. Summers contrasts the poet's presumption with Satan's in *The Muse's Method* (Cambridge, Mass., 1962), 137.

ence. Finally, Orpheus is a poet of encyclopedic learning. He proves the ultimate classical figure of the Bard for good reason.

The Bard alludes to Orpheus as he appeals to the Muse for assistance in his song and protection from dangers:

> . . . still govern thou my Song,
> *Urania,* and fit audience find, though few.
> But drive far off the barbarous dissonance
> Of *Bacchus* and his Revellers, the Race
> Of that wild Rout that tore the *Thracian* Bard
> In *Rhodope,* where Woods and Rocks had Ears
> To rapture, till the savage clamor drown'd
> Both Harp and Voice; nor could the Muse defend
> Her Son. So fail not thou, who thee implores:
> For thou art Heav'nly, shee an empty dream.
> (VII, 30–39)

The allusion emphasizes the peril of the virtuous poet in a vicious age, as is well understood.[32]

Less well understood is the Bard's emphasis on his audience, both just before and within the allusion. In its context, "fit audience" is contrasted with the unfit revellers of Bacchus. The latter not only lack the moral disposition to heed the Bard but even threaten him. "Fit audience" implies those who have ears to hear the Bard's message, the pious and, perhaps, those not determinedly impious. Primarily, moral disposition, not intelligence or learning, makes an audience fit. This is a Christian commonplace: the right orientation of the will is crucial to the understanding of the Gospel.[33] Also, at the center of the allusion, the Bard refers to the transforming power of Orpheus' "Harp and Voice" (37) "where Woods and Rocks had Ears / To rapture" (35–36). Just as the ancient singer could move trees and stones to

32. See George Sandys, *Ovid's "Metamorphoses": Englished, Mythologized, and Represented in Figures,* ed. Karl K. Hulley and Stanley T. Vandersall (Lincoln, Nebr., 1970), 519. See also Lewalski, *"Paradise Lost" and the Rhetoric of Literary Forms,* 34–36, and Schindler, *Voice and Crisis,* 86–87. Some comments on Milton's use of the Orpheus figure may be found in Don Parry Norford, "The Sacred Head: Milton's Solar Mysticism," *Milton Studies,* IX (1976), 37–75, esp. 41–43.

33. Out of many classic texts in the New Testament, see esp. II Corinthians 3–4. My formulation is Augustinian. The classic treatment of the problem is in Augustine's *On Christian Doctrine,* trans. D. W. Robertson, Jr. (Indianapolis, 1958), III, 5–25; the classic portrayal, in Augustine's *Confessions.*

attend his song but not the Thracian Bacchantes, so the Bard would quicken the hearts of those who hear him, if the Muse will ward off the clamor of the corrupt "Revellers" (31). He is using a traditional allegory here: the Orpheus story represents the civilizing power of poetry, which teaches the minds and cultivates the manners of the rude and ignorant, represented as woods and rocks.[34] Although the allusion ends by dwelling on the poet's peril, it begins with and centers on the Bard's desire to teach his audience. He has become a self-consciously didactic poet.

The Bard is thus reasserting the vocation to instruct his audience evident in the first proem yet absent in the second. In the former, his use of "man," "our," "us," and so on implies his addressing an audience involved in the story he would tell. His promised theodicy is explicitly didactic. But the latter conveys no concern for his audience at all. The Bard is occupied with his exalted ambition and so also with his weakness in being blind. In the third proem, however, he reasserts his vocation to instruct what "fit audience" the Muse may find for him in a corrupt age. No longer straining for lofty visions, now "Standing on Earth" and so "More safe," the Bard again considers his mission to instruct and edify.

The Bard's didactic mission is implied in his choice of Orpheus as his ultimate classical figure of the poet. According to Comes, Orpheus sings the origins of the universe, "the mutual generation of the elements among themselves, the force of love in natural things," and also "the order and motion of the stars."[35] The Bard treats the same subjects in Books VII and VIII. Orpheus also proves an apt figure for the poet of the Fall. He loses Eurydice a second time because he loves her so much he forgets to heed Prosperina's rule not to look back at her until they have reached the upper world. Orpheus is like Adam: excessive love for his wife leads to irrevocable loss. The parallel is not

34. The *locus classicus* for this interpretation is Horace, *Epistles, Book II; and, Epistle to the Pisones ("Ars Poetica")*, ed. Niall Rudd (Cambridge, Eng., 1989), 391–401. Both Sandys, *Ovid's "Metamorphoses,"* 476, and Comes, *Mythologiae*, p. 228a, quote the relevant verses. The tradition is so well known that even Shakespeare's Lorenzo refers to it: "Therefore the poet / Did feign that Orpheus drew trees, stones, and floods; / Since naught so stockish, hard, and full of rage / But music for the time doth change his nature" (*The Merchant of Venice*, ed. Brents Sterling [New York, 1970], V, i, 79–82).

35. Comes, *Mythologiae*, VII, xiv, p. 227a, ll. 38–39, 45–46.

adventitious. Comes and George Sandys draw a moral allegory from the Orpheus story similar to the one often ascribed to Genesis 3. Orpheus and Adam are both figures of reason (*ratio*) overwhelmed by emotions (*affectus*) arising from the lower parts of the soul, associated with Eurydice. Comes draws a stern moral in terms applicable to the Fall: "Therefore the good man should always be attentive (*vigilare*) and never surrender even to honorable desires (*honestis cupiditatibus*), which induce the gravest perturbations of soul. For if anyone should yield to such desires, he will soon slide into the greatest calamities or fall into the most wretched kind of death. Therefore these events regarding Orpheus were handed down for our remembrance by the ancients, so that we might govern our affections with moderation, and that we might understand not to desire anything beneficial too wholeheartedly."[36]

Adam's desire for Eve in *Paradise Lost* is nothing if not honorable, and, indeed, it does induce in him the gravest perturbations. He yields to his desires and suffers calamity as a result. In the Bard's allusion, Orpheus has already suffered the loss of Eurydice and, hence, has learned the consequences of excessive desire. Orpheus knows the moral of the Fall from hard experience. He proves a fitting classical figure for the Bard who will soon sing the events of Genesis 3.

In this light, Orpheus is another figure for the Bard chastening his ambitions. The moral allegory on all his figures for himself urges reliance on reason and moderation: Icarus, Bellerophon, and Orpheus all suffer loss through their failure to check desire by reason. Yet the sequence of these figures represents the possibility of increased understanding. Icarus loses his life; Bellerophon, his sight; Orpheus, his wife. As a figure for the Bard, then, Orpheus looks not only forward but backward, not only to the Fall but to the Bard's "honorable desires" in Books I through VI. To "justify the ways of God to men," to represent in song celestial "things invisible to mortal sight," might induce piety, though they risk presumption. The figure of Orpheus, "Standing on Earth, not rapt above the Pole," represents, in part, the Bard's chastening these laudable desires in his poetry.

Orpheus also proves an apt figure for the poet of *Paradise Lost* as a whole because he is an encyclopedic religious poet. Orpheus treats

36. *Ibid.*, VII, xiv, p. 228a, l. 45 to p. 229b, l. 3. Sandys, *Ovid's "Metamorphoses,"* 476, elaborates a similar moral.

"the beginnings of the gods, and universal theology"; he also writes of "the giants warring with Jove, and of the rape and mourning of Proserpina." These stories have their Christian analogues in *Paradise Lost.* Orpheus also sings of all the religious practices of paganism, including sacrifices, various forms of prophecy, and the processes for placating angry gods. Milton's Bard sings biblical forms of all these. Sandys has such respect for the Orphic hymns that he considers Orpheus a pagan Moses: "Orpheus begins the song (containing the rest of this booke) with the praises and omnipotency of Jupiter: it being the true and original use of Poetry, to sing the praises of the Highest, and to inflame the mind with zeale and devotion. Such Moses among the Hebrewes, among the Grecians, Orpheus."[37] With so rich a tradition implied in Orpheus, he is the perfect classical figure for the Bard in *Paradise Lost,* so he is the last.

Orpheus proves an expansive figure for the Bard, who is descending to a song "narrower bound." To combine contraction in the scope of the poem with expansion in the figure of the poet seems contradictory. Here, the Bard introduces an innovation into the epic tradition.

Barbara Lewalski observes that the third proem recalls Vergil's invocation in Book VII of the *Aeneid.* The Latin poet seeks the Muse's aid because he is beginning the Iliadic half of his epic, a higher subject (*maior rerum ordo*).[38] The Bard of *Paradise Lost,* to the contrary, seems to be declaring a lower one. He is contravening not only Vergil but the whole tradition. After the invocation at the beginning of the work, poets only call on the Muse again for one of two reasons: either they happen upon a difficult passage for which they need aid, like the catalog of the ships, or their poems are moving to higher levels, which require greater inspiration. The Vergilian pattern becomes standard for all heroic song. Dante's invocations in the *Purgatorio* and the *Paradiso* refer to the higher subjects he is about to sing; Torquato Tasso's later invocations in the *Gierusalemme Liberata* occur as the narrative moves to more climactic junctures.[39] Since a well-constructed

37. Comes, *Mythologiae,* p. 227a, ll. 26–47; Sandys, *Ovid's "Metamorphoses,"* 479.

38. See Lewalski, *Paradise Lost,* 33–34. I quote from *The Aeneid of Virgil,* ed. R. D. Williams (2 vols.; London, 1972–73), Bk. VII, 43. All quotations from the *Aeneid* in this book come from this edition, and all translations are my own, unless otherwise stated.

39. For Dante, see *Purg.* I, 1–12, and XXIX, 37–42, and *Par.* I, 1–36, XXX, 97–99, and XXXIII, 67–75. For Torquato Tasso, *Gierusalemme Liberata,* ed. Lanfranco Caretti (Milan, 1979), see IV, 19, VI, 39, and XVII, 3.

narrative proceeds climactically, later invocations normally seek higher inspiration for greater subjects. In *Paradise Lost,* however, the high flight is over and the song is descending.

The Bard's progress unfolds as a Christian paradox: the humble shall be exalted. In Augustinian terms, those who would ascend to heaven at will are prideful and fall. The saint urges us to follow not Adam but Christ: "But where do you ascend when you have set yourselves on high and have placed your mouth against the heavens? Descend, so that you may ascend to God. For you have fallen by ascending against God" (*Confessions,* IV, 12, 19). The Bard's song in the second half of *Paradise Lost* is lower than in the first half, but greater. Although it begins "narrower bound" in space, it expands to include all human history. Because it is less ambitious, it proves more assured. By descending to Earth, the Bard comes to treat human beings making choices in time; these are easier to represent than supernatural beings enduring the eternal consequences of a choice already made. The Bard also finds the true subject for his poem, "the better fortitude / Of Patience and Heroic Martyrdom" (IX, 31–32). He ceases to be the poet of epic self-assertion and becomes the poet of Christian patience and obedience. In going lower, he rises higher.

The fourth proem differs from its predecessors in ways well understood by Miltonists, and I need touch on these but briefly to adapt them to my argument. The burden of my discussion falls elsewhere: on the poet's changed understanding of the relation between his Christian poem and the classical epics. Because the proems have been read as Milton's utterances, scholars have assumed that they present different aspects of his consistent position about *Paradise Lost.* Hence, the poet's discussion of his "higher Argument" (IX, 42) in the fourth proem is taken to be a nonmetaphorical treatment of what is implied by his soaring "Above th' *Aonian* Mount" (I, 15) in the first. In my view, this proves a misreading that emerges from a mistaken assumption. I argue, in contrast, that the fourth proem articulates the Bard's new understanding of what his Christian epic requires of him. In the first proem, he asserts that his song will overgo the ancient epics; in the last, he argues that his Christian subject, in and of itself, surpasses them. In the first, he emphasizes what he will achieve; in the last, what he has received.

The fourth proem differs from its predecessors in both genre and style. Most obviously, it lacks an invocation of the Muse, either in the classical manner or in Christian prayer. The poet merely refers to her in the third person, albeit in tones of admiration and gratitude (20–24, 46–47). Lewalski identifies its genre as the verse epistle and notes its "rather unusual placement here."[40] For one thing, verse epistle is not traditionally found in epic, and for another, the poet of *Paradise Lost* is just now reaching the crux of his subject, "Man's First Disobedience," which he announces in solemn tones: "I now must change / Those Notes to Tragic" (IX, 5–6). Here, if anywhere, aside from the beginning of the poem, one would expect an appeal to the Muse for inspiration. Instead, we have a verse epistle on the Christian epic that the poet is singing.

As a verse epistle, its style is lower than that of the earlier proems, whose invocations demand a lofty style. Its tone is rather casual, by comparison, and so is its structure, as Lee M. Johnson has shown.[41] The poet is no longer aspiring to height of vision, so he need not strain for his Muse. He also evinces no concern about presumption or safety, as in the third proem, and no identification with questionable figures, like Satan in the second. The Bard is confident enough of his inspiration not to invoke his Muse, and his verse epistle addresses his audience without ever explicitly doing so. His manner proves almost conversational.

The "rather unusual placement" of this verse epistle can be explained by the Bard's justifiable confidence. He has already sung eight books of poetry. In the previous two books, he has turned away from aspiring to exalted visions and has begun to organize his plot on the sequential model of Scripture, using Genesis 1 for Book VII and Genesis 2 for the second half of Book VIII. In other words, the proem does not represent Milton's having commented on *Paradise Lost* at this point. Rather, it explicitly presents a Bard composing his poem in the sequence of its self-presentation, having sung eight books of poetry and about to embark on the subject he originally announced. He has reason to trust his Muse, who, for several thousands of lines already, has inspired his "unpremeditated Verse" (24). More

40. Lewalski, *"Paradise Lost" and the Rhetoric of Literary Forms,* 36.

41. Lee M. Johnson, "Milton's Epic Style: The Invocations in *Paradise Lost,*" in *The Cambridge Companion to Milton,* 65–78, esp. 69–76.

to the point, his turning away from the aspiration to exalted vision and his increased reliance on Scripture make it easier for him to compose. His ambitions no longer compel him to invent "Things unattempted yet in Prose or Rhyme." Rather, he is taking the Bible and Christian commentary as guides for his singing. For these reasons, even though he is arriving at the crux of his poem, he need not invoke his Muse. He trusts in her inspiration, his ambitions are not exalted, and he has the Bible to guide his invention. He is confident but not self-confident.

His confidence is also born, in part, from his new understanding of what his Christian epic requires. It can be seen by contrasting what the first and fourth proems assert about the relations between this Christian epic and its classical predecessors. Both assert that *Paradise Lost* is higher than the classical epics, but they interpret that "higher" in two different ways. The first sees it as overgoing, as "greater but in the same sort of way," whereas the last conceives it as utterly different.

As is well known, *Paradise Lost* begins with the Bard declaring his subject in a way that challenges comparison with the great pagan epics. The poet's "Man" evokes the openings of the *Odyssey* and the *Aeneid* and implicitly argues that his story is greater than Homer's or Vergil's. His story of Adam and Christ, Fall and Redemption, comprehends and exceeds their stories, as Christian truth surpasses whatever the ancients achieved. This traditional line of Christian thinking was commonplace long before the seventeenth century. When the Bard goes on to declare his aims as poet of this exalted subject, he seems simply to make explicit what is already implied. In fact, though, he confounds his exalted subject, which is given to him, with the exalted song he intends to make of it. When he declares "no middle flight" for a song that "intends to soar / Above th' *Aonian* Mount, while it pursues / Things unattempted yet in Prose or Rhyme" (I, 14–16), he mixes his lofty ambition together with his exalted subject.

The fourth proem, in contrast, dwells only on his subject. The Bard insists, not that his song is more heroic than the classical epics, but that his subject is. He does not claim, here, that he has soared "Above the flight of *Pegasean* wing" (VII, 4), for he has plumbed the danger of such ambition. Rather, he insists that the biblical story he will recount proves an "argument / Not less but more Heroic" (IX, 13–14) than those of classical epic. Later, he reiterates the point: his "higher Argument" (42) alone is "sufficient of itself to raise / That name" (43–44) of epic. In short, in the first poem, the Bard asserts the greatness of his song; in the fourth, the greatness of his subject.

The contrast may also be felt in the stylistic aspirations of the two proems. In the first, the Bard aims at "no middle flight," for he intends to overgo the pagan epics. In the fourth, he seeks only a style answerable to his higher argument. Even though the argument is higher, a style answerable to a biblical story is not necessarily exalted, as is evident from a glance at books of the Old and New Testaments. At the beginning of his poem, the Bard, confounding his subject with his ambition, assumes that a more exalted subject than pagan epic demands a more exalted style. By the fourth proem, he understands the distinction between matter and style clearly, because he has lowered his ambitions and taken Scripture as his guide since Book VII. Hence, the Bard does not merely assert that his subject is greater than those of classical epic in the fourth proem. Rather, he labors to distinguish the two. Dennis Burden developed a point made by Thomas Newton to distinguish God's "anger" at the Fall from the passions felt by the heroes and gods of pagan epic:[42]

> I now must change
> Those Notes to Tragic; foul distrust, and breach
> Disloyal on the part of Man, revolt,
> And disobedience: On the part of Heav'n,
> Now alienated, distance and distaste,
> Anger and just rebuke, and judgment giv'n,
> That brought into this World a world of woe,
> Sin and her shadow Death, and Misery
> Death's Harbinger: Sad task, yet argument
> Not less but more Heroic than the wrath
> Of stern *Achilles* on his Foe pursu'd
> Thrice Fugitive about *Troy* Wall; or rage
> Of *Turnus* for *Lavinia* disespous'd,
> Or *Neptune's* ire or *Juno's,* that so long
> Perplex'd the *Greek* and *Cytherea's* Son.
> (IX, 5–19)

42. Dennis Burden, *The Logical Epic: A Study of the Argument of "Paradise Lost"* (Cambridge, Mass., 1967), 11ff., cited in Fowler's note on Book IX, 10–11.

The disobedience of "Man" is characterized as "foul" and "disloyal," and the divine response is "just rebuke, and judgment." The Christian poet contrasts this with the unjust and excessive passions of the classical figures. Achilles' *menis* proves unassuageable even by Hector's death and the violation of his corpse; Turnus' *furor* rages uncontrolled in the second half of the *Aeneid* until his death in its final lines. Neptune hunts Odysseus for merely defending himself and his men against the Cyclops, while Juno pursues Aeneas simply because of her hatred for Troy and for Venus. The wrath possessing these figures is not properly measured to its cause, so all of them fail in their revenge. The "anger" of the Christian God, in contrast, is both right and successful.

More telling, still, is the Bard's contrast between the preeminent Christian and classical virtues. Whereas the classical hero asserts himself through victory in battle, the Christian hero enacts "the better fortitude / Of Patience and Heroic Martyrdom" (31–32). This Christian heroism is "Unsung" (33) because it proves unimaginable in martial epic, where a man may die nobly, but his death is not good, and he goes down fighting. The classical hero asserts himself in words and deeds, and death can never be a victory, even if victory should be won in death. The model for Christian heroism is Christ, who proves victor precisely because he willed to be victim. The Christian hero asserts, not himself, but the truth of God, so he discovers what no hero of classical epic ever could, "that suffering for Truth's sake / Is fortitude to highest victory, / And to the faithful Death the Gate of Life" (XII, 569–71).

By the fourth proem, the Bard has become the poet of "the better fortitude" in two related senses. The first is explicit: he will celebrate this virtue in his Christian epic. "Unsung" in previous epics, this "better fortitude" will be inculcated as the central didactic aim of his song. The Bard has arrived at his realization of the importance of fortitude because he has rejected epic self-assertion for himself as a poet, by lowering his ambition and submitting himself more fully to the guidance of Scripture. This is the second sense. In previous proems, he boasts of his own achievement, what he will do or what he has done. But in the fourth proem, he praises, not himself, but the Christian truth given to him in Scripture, and not merely does he assert its superiority but he argues for it. In Books I through VI, he struggles to invent "Things unattempted yet in Prose or Rhyme." Now he seeks only an "answerable style" for the higher argument of Scripture. The Christian hero does not assert himself but humbles himself; the Christian epic is not, properly, in the grand style but in a lower one, imitating the *sermo humilis* of Scripture; and the Christian poet does not assert his own ambition but submits himself to the guidance of Scripture in order to instruct his audience.

Although the Bard becomes the poet "Of Patience and Heroic Martyrdom" only in Book IX, he is, of course, aware of these virtues in Books I through VI. As Miltonists have shown, Abdiel proves a figure of patience in Book V, and the Son, of martyrdom in Book III. But the Bard presents these virtues imperfectly in the early books because he aims too intently to achieve greatness for himself through his song. He gives little space to their portrayal, nor does the style he uses—the grand style—correspond to them. Humility portrayed in the grand style lacks something of humility. For this reason, the Bard is not fully the poet "Of Patience and Heroic Martyrdom" in Books I through VI even when he portrays them. Rather, the poem as a whole reveals a movement in the poet: the Bard gradually realizes what his vocation to Christian epic truly requires. His growth is not a transformation but a self-discovery: what has been present earlier, but imperfectly, comes to be more fully understood. His realization effects a shift of balance in the poem, from Christian *epic* to *Christian* epic, proving decisive in the development of both poet and poem. Yet, at heart, it is still only a change of balance. Where Miltonists have always emphasized the balance in the poem, I stress the change in the Bard.

How the Bard changes over the course of his epic should now be clear in outline. The third proem stands at the crux of his development. There he turns away from the soaring visions and ambitions of Books I through VI to sing a song "narrower bound" in matter and in manner. Yet as this humbler song refuses visionary flights, it embraces Scripture for the sequence of its plot, and it eventually unfolds the course and meaning of human history, from Creation to Redemption and the New Jerusalem. The Bard's progress thus enacts a Christian paradox: the stylistically lower song of Books VII through XII turns out to be higher than the visionary flights of Books I through VI. The poet's epic ambitions in the first six books gradually give way in the second six books to his Christian desire to edify his audience. As the Bard gives up his ambition to overgo the ancients, he discovers more profoundly the true Christian height of his "higher Argument." Hence, as he gives up his ambitions, he fulfills them in singing a more fully Christian song of greater scope and depth. This progress marks his increased understanding of his vocation to Christian epic: not the height of his song but the height of his subject "gives Heroic name / To Person or to Poem" (IX, 40–41).

TWO

Satan and the Bard

Miltonists have generally agreed that Satan, or the portrayal of Satan, changes over the course of *Paradise Lost,* but they describe this change in different ways. C. S. Lewis, on the one hand, understands it as a moral deterioration, the consequence of Satan's "self-intoxication" evident in Book I. A. J. A. Waldock, on the other hand, sees it as Milton's degradation of a character often heroic in Books I and II. Whereas Waldock finds the degradation poetically incompetent, Lewis sees it as morally astute and artistically compelling. Other Miltonists describe the change in Satan in different ways, but they would agree with Waldock that "the Satan of the first two books stands alone" and after them "he is never as impressive again."[1]

Satan's sometime heroic stature in Books I and II has raised the question of Milton's sympathy with him. It is an old question, for Dryden considered Satan the hero of Milton's epic, and he was not alone. Long before the Romantics, what we call "Milton's Satanism" was bruited about, and the topic has enjoyed a vigorous debate in our

1. Lewis, *Preface to "Paradise Lost,"* 96–98; Waldock, *"Paradise Lost" and Its Critics,* 65–96, esp. 81. For a position similar to Lewis', see Lewalski, *"Paradise Lost" and the Rhetoric of Literary Forms,* 55–78; for one close to Waldock's, see Peter, *Critique of "Paradise Lost,"* 31–62. For a counterargument, see Jules David Law, "Eruption and Containment: The Satanic Predicament in *Paradise Lost,*" *Milton Studies,* XVI (1982), 35–60. For a theologically synoptic treatment of Satan's deterioration, see Gale H. Carrithers, Jr., and James D. Hardy, Jr., *Milton and the Hermeneutic Journey* (Baton Rouge, 1994), 74–79.

century.[2] In my view, the issue is largely created by confounding in "Milton" both the author of the poem and its narrator, the Bard. When we distinguish these two figures, the question, as it is usually addressed, disappears.

Milton I take to be a writer, the author of *Paradise Lost* as a whole: he planned and wrote the whole poem, working on its various parts whenever he pleased. Hence, from Milton's perspective, when Satan acts heroically in Books I and II, his moral degeneration later in the poem has already occurred in principle and perhaps did occur in fact. It already occurred in principle according to the definition of *author.* It perhaps did occur in fact because Milton may have written Books I and II after he had already composed Satan's degeneration in the later books. We know, for instance, that several lines from Satan's soliloquy in Book IV were composed many years before Milton decided to write an epic on the Fall, and Allan Gilbert thought Books I and II among the parts of the poem written late.[3] Since we know little about how Milton actually wrote the poem, Satan's heroism in Book I and his metamorphosis into a serpent in Book X prove contemporaneous from the authorial perspective. Whatever sympathy for Satan Milton may be said to have had must incorporate Book X in its consideration of Books I and II. We must also regard the sequential principle: when assessing Milton's view of Satan, later books must be given greater weight.

For the Bard, on the other hand, Satan's heroic moments in Books I and II prove a genuine temptation. This oral narrator does evince sympathy with Satan at many points, and it often alarms him so much that he checks himself and undermines what he has said. The metamorphosis of Satan into a serpent in Book X does not exist for the Bard in Book I, as it did for Milton the author, for the simple reason that the narrator has not yet sung it. Nor will he be able to sing it until

2. John M. Steadman studies the history of the notion in "The Idea of Satan as the Hero of *Paradise Lost,*" *Proceedings of the American Philosophical Society,* CXX (1976), 253–94. For further bibliography on this issue and a sensible treatment of it, see John Carey, "Milton's Satan," in *The Cambridge Companion to Milton,* ed. Danielson, 131–45.

3. See Gilbert, *On the Composition of "Paradise Lost,"* 90–142, 154–55. See also John T. Shawcross, *With Mortal Voice: The Creation of "Paradise Lost"* (Lexington, Ky., 1982), 173–75.

he distances himself more fully from Satan. This he does rather dramatically by composing the colloquy in Heaven in Book III, when, for the first time, he turns away from demonic subjects. There he finds a genuine hero for his Christian epic, the Son, whose redeeming love has saved him and all humanity. When he turns back to Satan after that break, Satan "is never as impressive again," as Waldock puts it, because the Bard's sympathy with him is decisively broken. Eventually, by Book X, the poet acquires the distance to dispatch grotesquely his sometime hero of Books I and II. But in those early books, he proves unable to treat Satan with such critical consistency. There is too much of the Bard in Satan because there is too much Satan in the Bard.

In short, the sympathy for Satan often felt in Books I and II comes from the Bard, not from Milton the author. Distinguishing Milton from the Bard thereby preserves both Milton's integrity as a Christian poet and our responses to the heroic aura often cast around Satan by the poetry. What sympathy Milton may be said to have had for Satan cannot be inferred directly from the narrator's utterance, as Miltonists have sometimes done, though it may be argued on other bases. One of these bases, to be sure, could be the Bard's fitful Satanism. But "Milton's Satanism" is fully qualified by the rest of the poem, and it may not be simply assumed from the narrator's voice in Books I and II.

The changing portrayal of Satan is the first indication of a change in the poet of *Paradise Lost,* not Milton, but his Bard. Miltonists have responded to this portrayal with a debate mirroring the different attitudes toward Satan featured in the poem. The story of the Bard's attraction for his character in Books I and II is drawn largely from this scholarship; his distancing himself from Satan is evident in Satan's degeneration over the rest of the poem. In Book I, the demons are the Bard's only characters, and the singer of epic gives them an epic aura, with motives and doubts we shall presently explore. Composing in the ongoing present, he becomes increasingly involved with Satan, who occupies the center of his imagination in the first two books. The Bard's singing of the colloquy in Heaven displaces Satan from that center, however, and when the poet brings him to earth and Eden in Book IV, the proximity of "our first parents" enables him to reduce Satan to a schemer torn by doubt and self-contempt. Satan's degeneration from that point on proves readily intelligible. Where in Books I and II Satan sometimes achieves heroic stature, after Book III he does little more than strike heroic postures. This change in a putatively sempiternal character reflects a changed attitude in the Bard.

But the Bard's relations with Satan in these first two books are more complicated. The overgoing poet is attracted by his overgoing character. As an epic poet, the Bard finds in Satan and the demons innumerable opportunities to overgo the ancients, and these he seizes. The heroic apparatus, when applied to the demons, often lends them a heroic aura that a Christian poet can only regret and try to correct. From this conflict flow the inconsistencies that Milton's critics have found in Books I and II—inconsistencies that emerge, not from Milton switching loyalties, but from the essential incompatibility of the Bard's project in these books: a Christian epic with demons as central figures. The epic poet must give the demons epic qualities for the sake of his poem, but the Christian poet often regrets the heroic aura cast about his reprehensible characters. The Bard's epic aspirations, in short, frequently conflict with his Christianity in Books I and II. What failures of Christian perspective we find in "Satan as hero" emerge from the poet's struggle with the essential tensions of Christian epic.

In this chapter, I propose to examine the Bard's story in Books I and II. Although complicated, it follows a broadly intelligible course, from fitful sympathy with Satan and fitful critique early in Book I to a largely uncritical treatment of Satan's heroism in the journey of Book II. Throughout the discussion I draw from scholarship on these books, adapting remarks about "Milton"'s meaning and aims to those of the Bard. To tell the Bard's story in these books, we must begin again at the beginning, Book I.

As several scholars have observed, the poet's ambition in the first proem is ominously echoed in Satan.[4] The echoes begin early and continue throughout the first six books. The Bard's Icarian aspirations to "no middle flight," the adventurousness of his song, his daring "Things unattempted yet," the "height" of his "great Argument" all have Satanic echoes. Miltonists usually distinguish the poet from Satan, in this regard, by insisting that the former prays for divine inspiration, whereas the latter rebels against God. Yet this crucial distinction does not go as far as is sometimes thought. William G. Riggs

4. See Riggs's first chapter in *Christian Poet in "Paradise Lost,"* "The Poet and Satan," 15–45, esp. 15–20; Blakemore, " 'With No Middle Flight' "; and Stocker, *Paradise Lost,* 78–85.

reminds us that the poet may pray for divine inspiration, but he must not presume to receive it. What is more, neither the poet nor we ourselves can tell to what extent Books I and II represent his prophetic vision of Hell or his epic ambitions projected through the demons. Are these books "inspired," and if so, are they inspired from above or from below? The poem raises these questions, but it gives no answers.

One thing the Satanist controversy makes clear: the Bard has enough sympathy with Satan to give him some heroic moments. These moments are well treated in scholarship on Satan's speeches and acts, so I need say little about them. Instead, I shall treat a few neglected aspects of that sympathy. These lie in the Bard's use of verb tenses and his point of view.

Little attention has been paid to the historic present in *Paradise Lost,* but its use is often dazzling, especially in the early books, as the Bard competes with his epic predecessors.[5] Narrative poetry in English is normally written in the past tense, as were Homer's epics, but the Roman poets found the perfect tense metrically awkward, and they came to use the historic present as the standard tense for narration. In Vergil's hands, as Kenneth Quinn has shown, the variations in verb tense became an instrument for subtle poetic effects.[6] Quinn calls the movement from an imperfect or perfect to a present tense "tracking forward" and its opposite, "tracking backward." The cinematic metaphor aptly suggests the effect of the change in tenses: a shift from past to present tense moves the reader "forward" into the action, close-up and now. In *Paradise Lost,* where an oral Bard is composing his poem in an ongoing present, the poet's shift to the historic present represents his own, as well as our, "tracking forward" into the action. This shift suggests his greater sympathy with his characters or

5. K. W. Gransden makes some astute remarks on verb tenses in the poem in "*Paradise Lost* and the *Aeneid,*" *Essays in Criticism,* XVII (1967), 281–303, esp. 296–302. Although Milton's verb tenses are little studied, his manipulation of time has received considerable attention. See Fish, *Surprised by Sin,* 30–37; Elizabeth Jane Wood, " 'Improv'd by Tract of Time': Metaphysics and Measurement in *Paradise Lost,*" *Milton Studies,* XV (1981), 43–58; and Malabika Sarkar, " 'The Visible Diurnal Sphere': Astronomical Images of Space and Time in *Paradise Lost,*" *Milton Quarterly,* XVIII (1984), 1–5. For chronology in the poem, see Fowler's edition of *Paradise Lost,* 25–28, and the works he cites.

6. See Kenneth Quinn, *Virgil's "Aeneid": A Critical Description* (Ann Arbor, 1968), 77–97.

his involvement in their actions, which is then communicated to us. In other words, the Bard is not a writer who can manipulate the perspective and point of view of his audience from a contemplative distance that allows for the reconsideration and revision of what he has written. Rather, he is envisioning his characters and action now, and his tracking forward and backward imply the flow and ebb of his own sympathy and involvement.

With these principles in mind, let us consider the first vision of Satan in the poem. The Bard, following epic precedent, considers the "cause" (I, 28) of the Fall, "Who first seduc'd them to that foul revolt?" (33). Twenty lines of narrative summary follow, uniformly in the past tense. But as the Bard isolates Satan from his army, he tracks forward, with historic presents and not without some nervousness, into Satan's consciousness:

> But his doom
> Reserv'd him to more wrath; for now the thought
> Both of lost happiness and lasting pain
> *Torments* him; round he *throws* his baleful eyes
> That *witness'd* huge affliction and dismay
> Mixt with obdúrate pride and steadfast hate:
> At once as far as Angels' ken he *views*
> The dismal Situation waste and wild,
> A Dungeon horrible, on all sides round
> As one great Furnace flam'd, yet from those flames
> No light, but rather darkness visible
> *Serv'd* only to discover sights of woe,
> Regions of sorrow, doleful shades, where peace
> And rest *can never dwell,* hope never *comes*
> That comes to all; but torture without end
> Still *urges,* and a fiery Deluge, fed
> With ever-burning Sulphur unconsum'd:
> Such place Eternal Justice *had prepar'd*
> For those rebellious. . . .
> (I, 53–71; emphasis added)

There are several movements of tracking forward and back in this passage. Up to the "now" of line 54, Satan and the demons have been viewed externally and in the past. Then suddenly the Bard projects himself and us into the present tense and into Satan's thought, simultaneously. For two verbs, "torments" and "throws" (56), he lingers briefly in the present before he tracks backward for a single verb, "witness'd" (57), governing two lines. The ambiguity of "witness'd," joined with the abstractions that follow it, keeps us in Satan's consciousness. As Harry Berger notes, " 'witness'd' means both 'saw' and 'reveal'd.' "[7] The "huge affliction and dismay" that Satan "witness'd" are not only outside him but also within him: his eyes gave witness to his feelings, and the poet suggests that Satan is projecting his inner bale onto the outer Hell. In his next verb, the Bard tracks forward into the present of what Satan "views" (59) for four lines, presenting an external description of a "Dungeon" (61) like a "Furnace" (62). Then he tracks backward into a past tense, "Serv'd," that nevertheless reveals inner experience, "sights of woe, / Regions of sorrow" (64–65). The Bard is nervously fascinated by Satan. He enters Satan's consciousness and retreats, tracks forward and back, and even tracks backward with a past tense while yet dwelling on Satan's feelings. The Bard's sympathy with Satan and his anxiety about it are betrayed in these complex movements.

The last sustained use of the historic present in Book I evinces that sympathy in a different way. Satan has called the demons from the lake and "gently rais'd / Thir fainting courage" (529–30). Then they march to martial music until "they stand, a horrid Front" (563) before their leader. The Bard describes Satan's perceptions and feelings in the present tense:

> He through the armed Files
> Darts his experienc't eye, and soon traverse
> The whole Battalion views, thir order due,
> Thir visages and stature as of Gods;
> Thir number last he sums. And now his heart
> Distends with pride, and hard'ning in his strength
> Glories: For never since created man,
> Met such imbodied force, as nam'd with these
> Could merit more than that small infantry
> Warr'd on by Cranes. . . .
>
> (567–76)

7. Berger, "*Paradise Lost* Evolving," 499. Marshall Grossman makes the same point in *"Authors to Themselves": Milton and the Revelation of History* (Cambridge, Eng., 1987), 29.

The overgoing topos continues, for fifteen lines all told, before the poet turns back to his narrative.

In this passage, the overgoing angel and the overgoing Bard meet as they both glory in their strength. The passage begins by narrating Satan's perceptions as though from the outside, and even when it describes his feelings, the Bard's attitude seems critical. Although the historic present projects us into the now of Satan's experience, a Christian reader cannot but look askance when Satan's "heart / Distends with pride." Yet Satan's glorying in the size of his army coalesces with the Bard's ebullience in the strength of his invention. Satan's army comes to be the Bard's army, as the poet elaborates its size until it overgoes the combined armies of classical and romance epic. The Bard implies, here and elsewhere, that his ability to imagine a more magnificent army magnifies his achievement over his predecessors'. He is showing himself to be the "strong poet" of Harold Bloom's critical imagination.[8] In doing so, however, he links himself with Satan's feelings, though how conscious the oral Bard may be of it one can hardly say.

Shortly thereafter, the Bard enters Satan's consciousness even more deeply, though in the past tense. When he returns to his narrative, he describes Satan from the demons' perspective: they "observ'd / Thir dread commander" (588–89), and he "appear'd" not "Less than Arch-Angel ruin'd" (592–93). In the following lines, Satan's eyes mark the shift of perspective from what they see to how Satan feels:

Dark'n'd so, yet shone
Above them all th' Arch-Angel: but his face
Deep scars of Thunder had intrencht, and care
Sat on his faded cheek, but under Brows
Of dauntless courage, and considerate Pride
Waiting revenge: cruel his eye, but cast
Signs of remorse and passion to behold
The fellows of his crime, the followers rather
(Far other once beheld in bliss) condemn'd
For ever now to have thir lot in pain,
Millions of Spirits for his fault amerc't
Of Heav'n, and from Eternal Splendors flung

8. Harold Bloom, *A Map of Misreading* (New York, 1975), 125–43.

> For his revolt, yet faithful how they stood,
> Thir Glory wither'd.
>
> (599–612)

In this beautiful passage, the Bard dares to take up Satan's terms in his own voice. He enters through Satan's cruel eye to mark "Signs of remorse" (605) within him, and he goes on to follow Satan's silent thoughts. He projects himself and us into Satan's self-correction in "The fellows of his crime, the followers rather" (606). He imagines Satan's brief repining at having led these "Millions of Spirits" (609) to forfeit "Eternal Splendors" (610). We are almost in interior discourse. "His" in lines 606, 609, and 611 can be changed to "my" with no distortion of perspective, and Satan's egotism, even in remorse, emerges clearly. The Bard adopts not only Satan's perspective but even his words. This is evident especially in "faithful how they stood" (611). For a Christian poet, the rebel angels can never be "faithful," nor, being fallen, can they truly be said to stand. Yet Satan sees them as faithful to him precisely because they are fallen, and the Bard imagines Satan's perspective and inner speech in his own narrative voice.

The Bard's sympathy with Satan, then, is evident not only in heroic moments of speech or action but in the subtler movements of verb tense and point of view. Sympathy, of course, proves only part of the Bard's story. As Miltonists have long noted, he also resists that sympathy and checks, undermines, or counters it in various ways. The most obvious of these Waldock calls "allegation or commentary" by the poet, as distinct from "demonstration or exhibition" in the narrative and in the speeches of the characters.[9] Since Satan's first speech has become the critical *locus classicus* on this issue, I will treat it first.

Waldock criticizes "Milton" for giving to Satan splendid speeches "at the level of demonstration" and then undermining them "at the level of allegation." Stanley Fish defends Milton by finding, in this practice, an interpretive trap as a didactic device.[10] Waldock and Fish agree about how the poem progresses in this regard, but they disagree about Milton because they are talking about two different figures under the same name. Waldock attacks "Milton," the Bard within the poem, and Fish defends Milton, the author beyond it. Fish

9. Waldock, *"Paradise Lost" and Its Critics,* 78.

10. Fish, *Surprised by Sin,* 1–37.

ignores the narrator as a persona distinct from the author, whereas Waldock confounds the two. But when we consider Satan's first speech as the Bard's oral composition, we find him responding to Satan's heroism within the speech itself, even before the "allegation" after it. I begin quoting in the middle of the speech, at what is often considered its most heroic moment:

> What though the field be lost?
> All is not lost; the unconquerable Will,
> And study of revenge, immortal hate,
> And courage never to submit or yield:
> And what is else not to be overcome?
> That Glory never shall his wrath or might
> Extort from me. To bow and sue for grace
> With suppliant knee, and deify his power
> Who from the terror of this Arm so late
> Doubted his Empire, that were low indeed,
> That were an ignominy and shame beneath
> This downfall; since by Fate the strength of Gods
> And this Empyreal substance cannot fail,
> Since through experience of this great event
> In Arms not worse, in foresight much advanc't,
> We may with more successful hope resolve
> To wage by force or guile eternal War
> Irreconcilable to our grand Foe,
> Who now triúmphs, and in th' excess of joy
> Sole reigning holds the Tyranny of Heav'n.
> So spake th' Apostate Angel, though in pain,
> Vaunting aloud, but rackt with deep despair.
>
> (I, 105–26)

Our responses to these lines, of course, follow the movements of the narrative voice. Yet in a poem that presents itself as being composed now, the speaker is also responding to his imagining as he elaborates his poem. The conflict that Waldock and Fish see between "demonstration" and "allegation" is real, but it is muted by the Bard's responding to Satan's heroism within the speech, before the concluding comment. The Bard does indeed give Satan some heroic-sounding lines, but he recognizes this sympathy with Satan and begins to draw away from it. At the beginning of this passage, Satan appears like a stoic Roman general, unbowed even in disaster. His heroism is perhaps darkened by his touching on "the study of revenge, immortal hate" (107), but the touch is slight. The heroism of these opening lines (105–10) rings for us because the Bard feels them as heroic. Nevertheless, he recognizes the danger in this sympathy with Satan and begins to distance himself and us from it. This withdrawal can be heard in Satan's refusal to "deify" God's power and his insistence that God "Doubted his Empire," frightened by the "terror" of Satan's "Arm." Here the plausible heroism of the Stoic general is undercut by Satanic bluster. The defiant general, who seems heroic, is once again the contumelious Satan, who does not. The final lines of the speech so obviously represent Satan's view of God that the Christian reader, and the Christian Bard, can hardly sympathize with him. Calling God "our grand Foe, / Who now triúmphs, and in th' excess of joy / Sole reigning holds the Tyranny of Heav'n" (122–24) is pure Satan, and the poet is imagining his words at a critical distance.

There follows the "allegation" that Satan is merely "Vaunting aloud, but rackt with deep despair" (126). As Fish argues, it chastens the reader. But this chastening is mild, because it has actually begun some fifteen lines earlier and because, in it, the Bard is also chastening himself. It is neither sudden nor harsh, unless one is too enthralled by Satan to attend to the movements of the poetry.

In sum, my view of this passage moderates the conflict that Waldock sees between "demonstration" and "allegation"—a conflict that Fish places in Milton's didactic hectoring of the reader.[11] The Bard's mediating voice changes this conflict into a tension present throughout the passage quoted above. This tension is entailed in a Christian epic that has demons at its center. If Satan is not sufficiently epic, the poem fails in its very beginning. If he is too persuasively heroic, the Christian Bard misrepresents the truth of his faith and misleads his readers. The poet's epic aspirations lend Satan some heroic moments in his first speech and elsewhere, but the poet's Christian vocation soon leads him to undercut Satan's heroism. In Books I and II, Satan is the protagonist of the Bard's Christian epic, and what the epic poet

11. For criticism of Fish's method, see Burton Jasper Weber, "The Non-Narrative Approaches to *Paradise Lost:* A Gentle Remonstrance," *Milton Studies,* IX (1976), 77–103, and Ferry's Preface to *Milton's Epic Voice,* xiii. Fish describes Milton's didactic method as harrassing and hectoring the reader in *Surprised by Sin,* 4.

gives with one hand, the Christian poet must, sooner or later, take away with the other.

This tension is unavoidable because it comes with the territory that the Bard has staked out for himself. He does not have to sing of Satan in Hell. His proem commits him only to "Man's First Disobedience," and he could have begun his poem with Satan in the Garden or about to arrive there. In other words, he could have begun his epic where Milton had once planned to begin his tragedy on the Fall, with Satan's first soliloquy in Book IV. If he had, the problems involved with singing a Christian epic about demons could have been avoided. Once he pursues his treatment of the "cause" (I, 28) of the Fall into Satan's consciousness in Hell, however, he is committed, and the tension between Christian truth and epic achievement proves unavoidable. It inheres in the Bard's genre and subject.

Nor is the tension easily governed in either the poem or its poet. The first we have glanced at: the epic apparatus tends to glorify Satan, and this tendency the Christian poet must counter or undercut. But this unavoidable conflict in the poem is complicated by the epic aspirations of the poet. He intends to sing the greatest epic ever. His aspirations have led him to begin his narrative with Satan in Hell, something his declared subject does not require. The Bard is fascinated by the overgoing angel, for Satan gives him wonderful opportunities to surpass his predecessors. More powerful than Achilles, craftier than Odysseus, having suffered a fall worse than Aeneas, more fratricidal than the Theban brothers, Satan offers the overgoing epic poet all he could want. What the epic poet enjoys in Satan, though, the Christian must suspect and perhaps criticize. In short, the tension between Christianity and epic in Books I and II is found in the poem because it exists first in the poet, Milton's Bard. It is never finally resolved because it cannot be resolved.

These remarks are intended to supercede the criticism of Books I and II by Waldock, John Peter, and others. These critics point to inconsistencies in the poem once famous (or infamous), now largely ignored. These inconsistencies emerge from the tension between Christianity and epic in Books I and II. Hell, for example, is said to be a place where "hope never comes" (66), but soon Satan is encouraging Beelzebub and the other demons, who march, build Pandemonium, plan for the future, and feel "hope" (I, 190; II, 522, 568). Satan is said to be bound to the lake with "Adamantine Chains" (I, 48), but he rises from it as though the chains did not exist. And though he is supposed to be experiencing "torture without end" (I, 67), he speaks in periods of Ciceronian complexity. As Peter comments, "Satan's composure makes the flames of Hell seem tepid, while the flames make his composure seem absurd."[12] Waldock and Peter criticize the poet for trying to accomplish "two incompatible things at the same time."[13] The Christian Hell is a place of endless torture, yet the poet must make Satan active enough to rouse the demons, or his poem fails. A more effectively Christian Hell would have made a much less interesting epic. What the Christian poem requires of Hell the epic poem must refuse or founder in its very beginnings.

Waldock's analysis of these difficulties, though often perceptive, proves limited in at least two ways. First, he implies that a poet of greater talent or skill could have avoided them. In my view, the Bard possesses great skill, and his problems arise, not from lack of talent, but from attempting a task with unresolvable tensions. A Christian epic cannot be composed about demons, for the epic poet tends to magnify his subject, and this the Christian poet must counter. Second, Waldock taxes Milton for these difficulties. In my view, Milton anticipated them and composed Books I and II to feature them. He did not attempt to resolve the unresolvable himself, in propria persona, because he understood their incompatibilities more profoundly than Waldock. Rather, he created an epic narrator who encounters these difficulties, not through any lack of talent, but through a failure of judgment—a failure emerging from his epic ambition, which is attracted to Satan. The singer of Christian epic narrates Satan's waking in Hell, and this commits him to extensive treatment of the demons. Thus committed, he must labor in the strain caused by the tension between his genre and his demonic subjects.

Granted, Miltonists generally agree that Satan is presented as a debased version of a classical hero.[14] This well-established point coun-

12. Peter, *Critique of "Paradise Lost,"* 33. See his whole chapter on "Satan and His Angels," 31–62, and Waldock, *"Paradise Lost" and Its Critics,* 65–96.

13. Waldock, *"Paradise Lost" and Its Critics,* 94. See Peter, *Critique of "Paradise Lost,"* 31–34.

14. See C. M. Bowra, *From Virgil to Milton* (London, 1944); Lewis, *Preface to "Paradise Lost";* and especially two works by John M. Steadman, *Milton and the Renaissance Hero* (Oxford, 1967) and *Milton's Epic Characters* (Chapel Hill, N.C., 1968).

ters the arguments for a "Satanist Milton," which rely on Satan's sometime epic grandeur in Books I and II. The very principles of my argument refute the Satanist interpretation, as I have shown. Yet they also acknowledge the grounds for it in the poem and locate them in the Satanist temptation in the Bard.

Distinguishing Milton from his Bard enables us to embrace two different yet equally true critical perceptions. As Charles Martindale points out, Satan proves an unsatisfactory hero by Homeric and Vergilian standards. Nevertheless, "what we have is in certain respects a glittering portrayal," for "Satan comes enmeshed in echoes of some of the finest passages in Homer and Virgil, and he is more closely associated with epic values and activities than any of the poem's major characters."[15] In *Paradise Lost,* Satan turns out to be a debased version of a classical hero, for he degenerates over the course of the poem. At the same time, he achieves moments of epic stature in Books I and II, where he often enjoys "a glittering portrayal." Both perceptions are true, inconsistent with one another though they are. That inconsistency is rendered coherent, however, when we distinguish Milton from his Bard and examine the Bard's story in *Paradise Lost.*

Although the tension between Christianity and epic in a poem about demons cannot be finally resolved, the Bard often handles it more subtly than I have suggested, especially later in Book I. Milton's Satanist critics have enabled me to state my case clearly and on familiar ground, albeit at the risk of oversimplifying. Now I should like to explore two uses of the classical tradition late in Book I, the building of Pandemonium and the assembling of the demons for the great consult. Even though both have been well studied, I shall point to allusions that have not been noticed and treat the Bard's handling of the Christian-epic tension in them.

The building of Pandemonium is an epic *ekphrasis* containing many classical allusions, and its praise for the swift construction of magnificence proves rich with irony, as many have noted.[16] But it is also an elaborate parody of digestion. In it, the Bard combines high achievement with concealed low humor, lofty verse with latent sarcasm.

15. Martindale, *Milton and the Transformation of Ancient Epic,* 38.

16. See Fowler's notes for *Paradise Lost,* I, 710–12, 713–17. See also Julia Bolton Holloway, "Not *Babilon* nor Great *Alcairo,*" *Milton Quarterly,* XV (1981), 92–94, and Steven Blakemore, "Pandemonium and Babel: Architectural Hierarchy in *Paradise Lost,*" *Milton Quarterly,* XX (1986), 142–45.

The poet's model of digestion is appropriately classical, that is, Aristotelian.[17] In this understanding, food is assimilated by three digestions. The first occurs in the stomach and the small intestine, and it is called "concoction." The natural heat of the body cooks the food in the stomach and breaks it down into "chyme." This heat is supplied by the blood, which moves to the stomach area from the heart, understood as a lake or reservoir. (Our model of the heart as a pump was developed by Milton's contemporary, William Harvey.) After food is concocted into chyme in the stomach, it moves to the small intestine, where the waste matter is separated and kept, while the chyme is passed through the mesenteric veins into the liver. There the second digestion takes place, refining the chyme into "chyle." This is further refined in the third digestion, which takes place in the heart (or, some said, in the veins). Only then can nourishment be assimilated by the members of the body.

The building of Pandemonium enacts an elaborate parody of the first two digestions. There is no third because Pandemonium is fundamentally unassimilable. First, the food for the building is taken from the bowels of Hell. Mammon, who taught humankind to rifle "the bowels of thir mother Earth" (I, 687), leads his crew to open "a spacious wound" (689) in Hell and to dig out "ribs of Gold" (690). These ribs are then concocted "in many cells prepar'd, / That underneath had veins of liquid fire / Sluic'd from the Lake" (700–702). This lake is analogous to the "lake of the heart," from which "veins" convey its heat. Once the ore is melted, a "second multitude" (702) of spirits acts analogously to the small intestine: "Severing each kind" of metal, they scum "the Bullion dross" (704). The bullion itself is then sent to a third group of spirits, who "had form'd within the ground / A various mould, and from the boiling cells / By strange conveyance fill'd each hollow nook" (705–708). "Strange conveyance" suggests the passage of the chyme to the liver by means of the mesenteric veins, a process that ancient physiology inferred rather

17. The association of Hell with the bowels is traditional. For a treatment of these issues in Dante, see Robert M. Durling, "Deceit and Digestion in the Belly of Hell," in *Allegory and Representation: Selected Papers from the English Institute, 1979–80,* ed. Stephen J. Greenblatt (Baltimore, 1981), 61–93. The chief Aristotelian source is the *Parts of Animals,* trans. A. L. Peck (Cambridge, Mass., 1937), Book I, 646–50.

than observed. The Bard's diction throughout the passage sustains the digestive underside of the narration. "Veins" (701) provide the heat for concocting the ore; "cells" (700, 706) could also mean enclosed places or sacs in an organic body; and the work is done by "spirits," analogous to the "vital spirits" of Aristotelian physiology, one of whose functions is digestion.[18] And all this labor is conducted in cells "within the ground" (705), that is, in the bowels of Hell.

The Bard's description of this process suggests two things about Pandemonium. On the one hand, it is built of the noblest metals highly refined. On the other, it rises as a work of incomplete digestion on base materials. It ascends, therefore, like flatulence:

> As in an Organ from one blast of wind
> To many a row of Pipes the sound-board breathes.
> Anon out of the earth a Fabric huge
> Rose like an Exhalation, with the sound
> Of Dulcet Symphonies and voices sweet.
> (708–12)

The classical allusions are well known.[19] Like Thebes, the fratricidal city, Pandemonium is built to music. But Amphion uses a lyre, whose seven strings betoken the seven planets, while the music of flatulence is of a lower sort. Pandemonium, "Built like a Temple" (713) with a roof of "fretted Gold" (717), proves a microcosmos. The music of its building is thus like the music of the spheres. Yet the metaphor of digestion implies all this in the mode of infernal parody. Plato's *Timaeus* (44a–45b) asserts that the curvature of the heavens is like that of the human head because both are lofty and represent order and reason. The Bard's parody turns on the popular correlation of the head with the buttocks. The classical music of the spheres becomes, in Pandemonium, the music of the hemispheres, emitted by an "Organ" (708) through "Pipes" (709). Ultimately, of course, its construction proves

18. For *cell* as a technical term in physiology, see the definition in the *Shorter Oxford English Dictionary: On Historical Principles* (3rd ed.; Oxford, 1980). The "vital spirits" of ancient and medieval medicine are usually divided into three categories, according to Aristotle's hierarchy of souls: vegetative (or nutritive), sensitive, and rational. For a brief discussion, see C. S. Lewis, *The Discarded Image: An Introduction to Medieval and Renaissance Literature* (Cambridge, Eng., 1964), 166–69.

19. See Fowler's notes for *Paradise Lost,* I, 710–12, 713–17, and 717–22.

a parody of God's creating through words, spoken as though through a mouth.[20]

In the verses on Pandemonium, then, the Bard's lofty *ekphrasis* has a low comic underside. He uses classical tradition to magnify and debase the demons at the same time. What the epic poet grants to demonic achievement seems not to conflict with what the Christian poet takes away from it, and the resolution is beautifully handled. It does require some obscure medical learning to be appreciated, however. To be sure, the Bard's irony tips us to suspect Pandemonium, but without the medical learning, Miltonists have found in the passage allusions to Amphion and the "music of the spheres," which, while true, gild Pandemonium and so misrepresent it. The Bard's deftness thereby defeats his parodic purpose.

Still, his subtle skill at evoking the classical tradition compels admiration. It can be seen not only in verbal or thematic allusion but in what Martindale calls "manner of writing."[21] One instance occurs in the profusion of epic similes concluding Book I, the gathering of the demons for the great consult. The summons for the consult is issued at line 757, and thirty of the final forty lines are taken up with epic similes. In all classical literature, only one passage packs so many similes so closely together: Homer's description of the Greek army marching to battle (*Iliad,* II, 455–73). The Bard is trying to overgo Homer's achievement, for he uses, with equal density, longer and more complex similes in order to describe the movement of a large host. Homer's host, of course, marches to battle, whereas the demons assemble for council. This proves a difference without a distinction, however, for both are going to war.

The Bard's epic manner here serves to magnify the demons even though his images literally belittle them, describing them as bees (768–76) or pigmies and elves (778–88). The demons possess extraordinary powers, yet they are only as extraordinary as the Bard's power of invention. His bravura necessarily affects their performance. We are moved "with joy and fear" (788) at them only because the

20. For other scatological undertones in Books I–II, see Michael Lieb, *The Dialectics of Creation: Patterns of Birth and Regeneration in "Paradise Lost"* (Amherst, Mass., 1970), 28–30. See also John Wooten, "The Metaphysics of Milton's Burlesque Humor," *Milton Studies,* XIII (1979), 255–73.

21. Martindale, *Milton and the Transformation of Ancient Epic,* 159.

Bard is moved first, and they prove wondrous only as the poet is wonderful. In other words, the Bard achieves greatly as a poet only insofar as the demons achieve greatly as his subjects. The two achievements prove distinguishable, to be sure, and the Bard may use various means to denigrate the demons. But he may go only so far in that direction without defeating his poem and himself. The vitality of his poem here depends upon the vitality of his demons. If the poet aims to be admired for his achievement, he cannot help but make his demons *admirable,* "to be wondered at."

The Bard's success in resolving the unresolvable tension between Christianity and epic in poetry featuring the demons is dazzling. I have suggested that his handling of it improves over the course of Book I. If there is some warrant for Waldock's seeing a clash between "demonstration" and "allegation" in Satan's first speech, there is no clash between Christianity and epic in the passages on Pandemonium and the assembling of the demons. The tension remains, though. The Bard's achievement is too closely tied to Satan's for him to reduce Satan too drastically, and it remains tied until he finds his way to characters of a different sort.

The inextricable tie between the achievements of the Bard and of Satan in these books may be seen in the former's changing portrayal of the latter in Book II. The Bard's treatment of Satan in the great consult manages to be both splendid and critical. Satan's style, we may say, proves of more-than-epic grandiosity and ironically debases him. When the poet narrates Satan's subsequent journey, however, he becomes more involved with Satan's character, for he cannot narrate a great journey without lending some of its greatness to the voyager. What appears as grandiose posturing at the great consult thus comes to seem more like real greatness during Satan's odyssey to the light.

Satan's grandiosity at the great consult is emphasized by the Bard at its beginning and its end. Book II opens with Satan enthroned "High" (II, 1) on a seat of barbaric splendor, "by merit rais'd / To that bad eminence" (5–6). The Bard uses rhetorical splendors to make his poetry magnificent and undercut Satan at the same time. By the end of the consult, we know how Satan and Beelzebub have rigged the results (378–80), and Satan's exit, carefully calculated to forestall objection to his hazarding the journey alone (466–73), shows the demons servilely adoring him. His courage to attempt a passage alone through "The dark unbottom'd infinite Abyss" (405) is thereby both obscured and undercut. The Bard controls the tension between Christianity and epic beautifully: he displays his imaginative power while bestowing only a specious grandeur to Satan.

After the consult concludes, he spends well over a hundred lines narrating the demons' *divertissements.* Many of these are heroic occupations in classical epic, like athletic contests (528–38) and martial poetry (546–55), but the whole passage rings with classical echoes as the Bard displays his learning and talent at length. The Christian Hell of "torture without end" is relegated to the background, for the vitality and interest of the poem here depend completely on the vitality and interest of the demons.

When the Bard turns back to Satan, he begins with "Meanwhile" (629), and his narrative syntax deserves attention. The poet takes us back to Satan just after the great consult and shows him as he "Puts on swift wings" (631) to begin his flight. The Bard intends to narrate Satan's journey from its very beginning. He does not have to do that. The consult was "dissolv'd" (506) over 125 lines before, and the poet could have returned to Satan in midflight. Thus he could have abbreviated his narrative of Satan's journeying and so maintained a reduced stature for his character, but the Bard is too attracted by the overgoing opportunities in Satan's journey to abbreviate it. A short or easy journey would reduce Satan's achievement at the cost of reducing the Bard's. To magnify his own achievement, the poet must magnify Satan's. This he does, seemingly without question.

The Bard's narrative syntax follows Satan's journey in detail, with hardly a break, for Satan occupies the center of his imagination. When Satan encounters Sin and Death (648–73), so does the Bard and we through him. When Satan moves on, we witness his experience in detail: the sight of chaos (890–918) and its sounds (920–27). Even his departure is told us, when "At last his Sail-broad Vans / He spreads for flight" (927–28). We follow Satan's plummeting, Icarus-like, through a "vast vacuity" (932) and his "chance" (935) escape, his struggle through chaos (939–50), his decision to ply "Undaunted" (955) toward whatever "Spirit of the nethermost Abyss" (956) he might meet, and his encounter with Chaos and Night (959–1009). When Satan moves on from there, his "glad" (1011) feelings are conveyed, and we even see his hopeful departing as he "Springs upward"

(1013). The Bard attends him very closely, looking away only for a moment to describe Sin and Death "Following his track" (1025). After this brief interlude, he turns back to Satan, who sees the light of our world appear in the distance, and we follow his journey there through the end of Book II. Satan's experience is narrated from beginning to end, in detail and without abbreviation. The extent and difficulty of his journeying display, at the same time, both his adventurous powers and the Bard's.

In contrast stands the narrative syntax of Satan's journey after the colloquy in Heaven in Book III. The story of his journeying is now abbreviated, for the Bard often turns away from him to describe something else, and each time the poet returns to him, Satan is farther along. For instance, he alights and walks (III, 422, 441) on the outside of our universe throughout the passage on the Paradise of Fools (444–97), during which "long he wander'd" (499). Then he descries the stairway to Heaven "far distant" (501). After the stairway is described (502–39), Satan suddenly appears "now on the lower stair" (540). Clearly, he has traveled throughout the previous description, and the Bard is abbreviating his narrative of Satan's odyssey. Again, after Satan "throws / His flight precipitant" (562–63) into our world, the Bard describes the panoply of the stars and then the sun (565–86), where Satan suddenly "lands" (588), the narrative of his flight having been replaced by the poet's description.

In short, Satan occupies the center of the Bard's imagination during his odyssey in Book II, as the Bard follows his every move from beginning to end. Not so after the colloquy in Heaven in Book III. The poet's narrative syntax proves different because his attitude toward Satan is different. He is abbreviating the narrative of Satan's journey and reducing Satan's stature at the same time. He tells of Satan's journey but does not narrate his journeying; he points to completed stages in Satan's progress, but he no longer narrates that progress itself. Hence, Satan's journeying in Book III quite lacks the heroic glamor it enjoyed in Book II. The poet grants it neither extent nor difficulty, and when Satan finally sees another spirit, he transforms himself into "a stripling Cherub" (636) to accost Uriel. Satan's odyssey is no longer heroic, and its bold adventurer is now but a skillful "Impostor foul" (692). The Bard's narrative syntax reduces the voyage and the voyager at the same time, for the poet has found, in the divine colloquy, a new imaginative center, a new hero.

In the course of singing Satan's odyssey in Book II, however, the Bard comes increasingly to sympathize with his character. Although Satan merely affects heroic stature in the great consult, he achieves it in his odyssey to our world, and this change marks the Bard's deepest involvement with his character. The Bard's achievement and Satan's achievement become all but indistinguishable. The success of the poet's "advent'rous Song" requires a successful adventurer, and Satan becomes, for several hundred lines, the hero of a Christian epic. This irony emerges inevitably from the tension inherent in the Bard's genre and subject. Greater poetic talent or skill, if such could be imagined, would not resolve the Christian Bard's difficulties. A lesser voyage for Satan necessarily means a lesser poetic achievement. In this event, the Bard's epic ambitions overmaster whatever Christian hesitations he may have had, and the sly manipulator of the great consult becomes a heroic voyager. The Bard brings great imaginative energies to his narrative, and these necessarily infuse the actions of his character. With the Bard's success linked so intimately with Satan's, he naturally sympathizes with his character. Where early in Book I the Bard often countered or undercut Satan's heroism, he is now caught up in narrating it, with hardly any critique.

That sympathy grows nearly to identification in the second proem, as we have seen. At the end of Book II, Satan is hastening toward the light of our world. In the beginning of Book III, the Bard addresses the light as he hastens toward the Empyrean to sing the divine colloquy. He explicitly links himself with Satan, for both have "Escap't the *Stygian* Pool, though long detain'd" (III, 14) there, and the poet even suggests that Satan has "borne" him "Through utter and through middle darkness" (16). The narrative syntax of Book II implies as much: Satan goes only where the Bard imagines him to go, and the Bard is with him for every perception along the way. This momentary identification in the second proem proves brief but telling: the Bard and Satan are very close here, as they never will be again. For the colloquy in Heaven displaces Satan from the center of the Bard's imagination, and when the Bard turns back to him to sing the rest of his journey, both Satan and his flight are much reduced.

Such is the Bard's story in Books I and II and the difficulties besetting his Christian epic about the demons. The story is new, but the critical perceptions guiding it are not. Clarifying the ambiguity of "Milton" enables us to grasp coherently the truth of seemingly inconsistent critical perceptions. Satan does indeed prove heroic at times yet not really at all after Book II. When we try to resolve these inconsistencies for "Milton," we have a critical debate lasting centuries. But when we distinguish the Bard from Milton, the narrator's inconsistencies have authorial coherence, for the Bard's inconsistency emerges from the tension between his Christian epic genre and his demonic subjects. Composing his poem in an ongoing present, he is pulled by this tension in various directions as he invents his plot, and he resolves these pulls as best he can. This process has been examined in some of its detail and variety, largely through long-established, if conflicting, interpretations. Miltonists, it may be said, have explored the Bard's story in *Paradise Lost* without quite knowing that they did so.

What, then, may be said about Milton in relation to Satan in Books I and II? This issue has been admirably explored by Riggs, and I will simply point to his conclusions. For Riggs, Milton was fully conscious of the Satanist temptation implied in his ambitious Christian epic, and he featured, rather than hid, the similarities between the poet and Satan so that he could explore and define the differences. Milton understood "the satanic potential of his poetic act," that pride and presumption haunt it from the very beginning. The poet's praying for divine assistance, of course, stands in contrast to Satan's rebellion against God, but as Riggs rightly insists, the poet can only pray for inspiration and hope that it is granted. He can neither command it nor presume that it has been granted, for the danger of self-delusion in this regard is great. Hence, Milton objectified the similarities between his poetic ambition and Satanic presumption so as to weigh and explore the differences. He also featured instances of infernal creativity, such as Pandemonium, dangerously close to his own attempt "to build the lofty rhyme." In this way, Milton continually exposed "the satanic aspect of his poetic posture" so as to distinguish and explore the differences between his audacity and Satan's.[22] The more clearly Milton could project the similarities, the surer he could be that he had not been blinded by pride.

22. Riggs, *Christian Poet in "Paradise Lost,"* 15–45, esp. 45, 20.

Riggs finds that *Paradise Lost* raises the question of its inspiration but does not answer it. Berger also argues the point: "*If* the muse descends, then the poem may be a symbol of what is substantially real, more real than itself; it will be, for all its size, like a sacramental ark. If the muse does not descend, the poem may be a vast and glittering Pandemonium, an externalization of the satanic forces within the poet's soul."[23] The poet seeks the highest divine inspiration in his first two proems, but nowhere does he claim to have received it. He does claim, in the third proem, to have been guided by Urania, yet to be guided is not the same as to be divinely inspired, and Urania, even "The meaning, not the Name" (VII, 5), is hardly the Spirit brooding at the Creation or the Celestial Light itself. Miltonists, however, often write as though the poet of *Paradise Lost* were granted the divine inspiration he prays for in Book III. They assume that the poem has answered the question of its own inspiration. As Riggs and Berger remind us, though, the poem features the problem of its inspiration, and it proves more troubling than Miltonists have customarily assumed.

One source for their assumptions lies in the ambiguity of "Milton." What the poem sings of Heaven is felt to be properly Milton's own song, and when various aspects of Books III, V, and VI are criticized, Milton's honor as a great Christian poet seems at stake. Hence, not only have Miltonists defended, for example, God's first speech and the war in Heaven, but they have also argued that Milton presented these as divinely inspired. Moreover, these books present an exalted Christian subject in an exalted style, and this exaltation of matter and manner, they feel, shows that "Milton"'s prayer for revelation has been granted.

But Riggs reminds us that exaltation does not prove the truth of a vision. Indeed, in Eve's dream and elsewhere, the poem features exalted vision and language as a problem: does the inspiration for it come from above or from below?[24] The colloquy in Heaven, for example, presents divine subjects in beautiful and moving poetry, but does that mean it is true? Miltonists often assume that it does. Yet Riggs shows how the poem poses the problem and refuses to answer

23. Berger, "*Paradise Lost* Evolving," 492.

24. Riggs, *Christian Poet in "Paradise Lost,"* 85–93.

it definitively. The poet prays for illumination from the Celestial Light, but he never asserts that he has received it. He can never be sure that he has.

The problem may also be put this way: are the colloquy and the war in Heaven inspired by divine vision or by epic ambition? Is the poet merely asserting what has been granted to him by God, or is he asserting the greatness of his own powers? Granted, there need not be a strict opposition between these in the Bard's production: divine inspiration may use the poet's epic ambition to good effect. The moral tension between the poet's assertion of his vision and his assertion of himself proves troubling, however, because only God can know, at any point, which is primary. Yet Miltonists often write as though this tension either hardly exists or is easily resolved. Riggs and Berger argue that it was Milton's genius to pose the problem of inspiration and authority in *Paradise Lost* without answering it. Milton left that problem for us to grapple with. If we decide too quickly that it is already answered, his genius is slighted and we fall short of what his poem would demand of us.

THREE

God, the Son, and the Bard

Few characters in English literature have provoked such varied responses as "Milton's God." Critics' religious sympathies might seem a reliable index to their responses, but here nothing is predictable. William Empson admires "Milton's God" because the character proves so unlikable, whereas Stanley Fish upholds him as the voice of truth. C. S. Lewis defends the great Christian poem, but its God makes him almost as uneasy as God's critics, while Burton Jasper Weber finds that God transcends the plot of the epic, giving an authoritative view of its story.[1] The scholarship on "Milton's God" reveals a variety of positions. To write about God in *Paradise Lost* is to enter a critical melee.

Part of the problem with "Milton's God" lies in its very formulation. Because the Christian God is understood to be eternal and immutable, God in *Paradise Lost* is generally assumed to be an unchanging character.[2] He is thought to possess not merely the consistency we look for in any character but that consistency in an eminent degree. Miltonists' assumptions about God in *Paradise Lost* are joined to their sense that "Milton" sings the poem in his own voice, the voice of an author consistent, or aspiring to consistency, on all the issues he

1. See William Empson, *Milton's God* (London, 1961); Lewis, *Preface to "Paradise Lost,"* 125–27; Fish, *Surprised by Sin,* 59–87; and Burton Jasper Weber, *The Construction of "Paradise Lost"* (Carbondale, Ill., 1970), 1–2.

2. For an argument that Milton presents "an evolving God," see Joan Webber, "Milton's God," *English Literary History,* XL (1973), 514–31.

treats. God in *Paradise Lost* is thus held to be the consistent character of a consistent Milton articulating his theology in the epic, insofar as that can be done. These assumptions are made equally by those who defend and by those who attack "Milton's God."

In my view, however, "Milton's God" is neither God nor Milton's, neither an eminently consistent character nor the product of a consistent consciousness. Rather, God in *Paradise Lost* is presented differently in Books III through VII than he is in Books X through XII, and this difference emerges from a change in Milton's narrator, the Bard. The present chapter endeavors to show that God changes, how he changes, and why the Bard changes his way of presenting him.

The argument proceeds in three sections. The first contrasts God's first speech in the poem with his first speech after the Fall, in which he explicitly recalls his first speech. I argue that the Bard has anticipated the critical remarks made by Lewis and A. J. A. Waldock, for in the late books of the poem he presents a God less self-assertive and defensive than in Book III, both milder and more mysterious. The second section explores why God's first speech goes wrong: the Bard attempts to overgo Vergil, and his classical paradigm distorts his Christian representation. The third section treats the theology of the Redemption in the poem and shows how and why Book XII differs from Book III. As in the previous chapters, the argument draws on conflicting views about "Milton's God" as evidence for distinguishing Milton from his Bard. That distinction resolves, in part, conflicting interpretations of Book III, which are seen to be correct when applied appropriately to the Bard and to Milton.

God's first speech in *Paradise Lost* has its defenders as well as its critics. The defenders are motivated largely by their belief that Milton himself is impersonating God: in defending the speech, they are defending Milton. I have been arguing, to the contrary, that Milton designed the self-presentation of his poem as the song of a Bard composing now and that he thereby distances himself as author from the Bard's narratorial voice. Hence, I join the critics of God's first speech, yet without attacking Milton. On the contrary, the very limitations of the speech testify to Milton's genius in creating the persona of his Bard. In general, those who defend the speech reveal the Bard's aims and hopes in composing it, whereas those who criticize point to his actual achievement. The speech fails in signal respects, and this failure is marked in the poem by the Bard's resinging it in Book X. Milton designed all this to reveal his great innovation in epic: a Bard who matures through the experience of singing his poem.

Since the criticisms and defenses of God's first speech are well known, I shall present my position with regard to them. One way of defending the speech is to insist that it is above criticism. Weber, for example, argues that it stands above the rest of the poem as God's authoritative commentary on the action. Similarly, Fish insists that the speech states the truth about the angelic and human falls. Readers who fault God's speech are thus really defending themselves against its truth and thereby evincing their own fallenness.[3] Both of these reasonably represent the Bard's aims in the speech.

In my view, the speech fails in both respects, because both point to what cannot be attained by poem or poet. First, anything within a poem is, by definition, within the poem and cannot stand above it. To be sure, this tautology does not refute Weber so much as refuse to grant what he would have us grant. Yet the refusal is reasonable. What is in the poem is in the poem and not above it, and nothing in the poem stands above criticism. Similarly, what Fish argues about God's utterance would be true if it were truly the utterance of God. But it is not: it is the utterance of a fallen human being impersonating God. This poet may, or may not, be uttering God's speech through the grace of divine inspiration. Even if he is experiencing poetic rapture, that is no infallible indication of whether he is divinely inspired. Nor is the beauty of his poetry. Instead, we must weigh and judge. To examine critically God's first speech does not imply our self-justifying fallenness. Rather, it is precisely what the poet's fallenness demands of us. If God's speech is found wanting, the poet is wanting, not the living God.

Fish's defense of the speech takes up Irene Samuel's argument that God's voice is "toneless." This charge seems illuminated by Arnold Stein's remark, that its "language and cadence are as unsensuous as if Milton were writing a model for the Royal Society and attempting to speak purely to the understanding." The poet's use of "unsensuous" language and of theological abstractions is designed to give God a certain impersonality. For Samuel and Fish, God's "toneless" voice is the "omniscient voice of the omniscient moral law" that "speaks

3. Weber, *Construction of "Paradise Lost,"* 1–6; Fish, *Surprised by Sin,* 59–87.

simply what is."[4] These scholars have clearly seen the Bard's intention in his use of unsensuous language.

The speech, however, is not toneless because no speech can be. Even a seeming tonelessness proves a kind of tone. Furthermore, though the language may be unsensuous, the tone of God's utterance is clearly marked by its critics. Waldock comments that "the speech yields a perfect picture of an immaculate character on the defensive," one full of "nervousness, insecurity, and doubt." He continues his analysis: "The uneasy explanations, the hammering in of key words ('they themselves,' 'they themselves,' 'not I'), the anxiety to meet beforehand all possible lines of attack, the rhetorical pleading, the indignation before the event ('whose fault? Whose but his own? ingrate,' etc.): we could not counter such impressions even if we would; they are too strong for us to deny."[5] Harry Berger points to the thematic repetitions in the speech, for God keeps circling back "as if in morbid fascination, to the ignominy of the Fall and his own freedom from blame in the matter." John Peter observes that God's brooding on his lack of culpability gives to his theology an air of defensive rationalization, and his many verbal repetitions sound guilty.[6] As these critics reveal, tone comprises more than sensuous language and cadence. God doth protest too much. His insistence on his own impeccability is strident, and he sounds testy, querulous, and irascible.[7]

Alastair Fowler, like Stein, counters such criticism by finding it impertinent. He asserts that Waldock's insistence on the "human

4. Arnold Stein, *Answerable Style: Essays on "Paradise Lost"* (Seattle, 1967), 128; Irene Samuel, "The Dialogue in Heaven: A Reconsideration of *Paradise Lost* III, 1–417," *PMLA,* LXXII (1957), 601–11, esp. 603. Other analyses of the style of God's speeches include: Peter Berek, " 'Plain' and 'Ornate' Styles in the Structure of *Paradise Lost,*" *PMLA,* LXXXV (1970), 237–46; George Eric Miller, "Stylistic Rhetoric and the Language of God in *Paradise Lost,* Book III," *Language and Style,* VIII (1975), 111–26; and Michael Murrin, "The Language of Milton's Heaven," *Modern Philology,* LXXIV (1977), 350–65.

5. Waldock, *"Paradise Lost" and Its Critics,* 102–103. Gary D. Hamilton argues that God's seeming defensiveness comes from his taking an Arminian position in a controversy with the Calvinists. See "Milton's Defensive God: A Reappraisal," *Studies in Philology,* LXIX (1972), 87–100.

6. Berger, "Archaism, Vision, and Revision," 24–52, esp. 48; Peter, *Critique of "Paradise Lost,"* 11.

7. Michael Lieb agrees with these critics in "Milton's 'Dramatick Constitution': The Celestial Dialogue in *Paradise Lost,* Book III," *Milton Studies,* XXIII (1987), 215–40.

impression" left by God as a character is irrelevant. He argues that God "is not human, though he is personal; he is not a character, though he thinks and speaks."[8] Fowler is responding to the Bard's effort to set God above criticism, which we have also seen in Weber and Fish. But the same answer may be given: the Bard does not succeed with these principles, because he cannot. Any figure that appears in a poem proves one of its characters. Fowler's argument that because God is not human, he is not a character would make most of the characters of *Paradise Lost* no longer characters. Satan is not human either, and he is hardly beyond our judgment. Fowler's argument would possess force only if the voice of God in the poem were the voice of God in reality, which would occur only if the poet were divinely inspired in the way that Scripture is said to be. But this inspiration Fowler merely assumes when it needs to be argued.[9]

Many Miltonists defend the speech by ignoring its tone and concentrating on its doctrinal content.[10] Here Milton's defenders seem to hold the field, for his critics grant that its theology is both traditional and necessary to the poem.[11] Even on the score of doctrine, however, God's first speech may be faulted. Dennis Danielson finds that this first effort at theodicy in the poem presents the reader "with only a part of the truth, with only a limited view of reality." Milton's theodical technique characteristically raises a question and does not fully resolve it until later, when the poem has presented "a more complete view of reality, which serves at least in part to answer the question originally raised, and possibly to reevaluate the terms of that question." Even Danielson admits that God's first speech, considered by itself, "could conceivably be taken as evidence in support of Arthur Lovejoy's outrageous charge concerning 'the amazing superficiality of Milton's theodicy.' "[12]

8. Fowler, ed., *Paradise Lost,* 35. See Stein, *Answerable Style,* 127–28.

9. Anthony Low values God's stern and powerful voice in "Milton's God: Authority in *Paradise Lost,*" *Milton Studies,* IV (1972), 19–38. Sister Hilda Bonham reviews earlier considerations of the problem in "The Anthropomorphic God of *Paradise Lost,*" *Papers of the Michigan Academy of Science, Arts, and Letters,* LIII (1968), 329–35.

10. See Danielson, *Milton's Good God,* 104–107. Both Samuel and Fish explore the doctrinal content of the speech at some length. Their ideas have been challenged by Francis C. Blessington, "Autotheodicy: The Father as Orator in *Paradise Lost,*" *Cithara: Essays in the Judaeo-Christian Tradition,* XIV (1975), 49–60.

11. See Peter, *Critique of "Paradise Lost,"* 11.

12. Danielson, *Milton's Good God,* 107–108. He cites Arthur O. Lovejoy, *The Great Chain of Being: A Study in the History of Ideas* (Cambridge, Mass., 1936), 212.

This superficiality Berger locates in the distant abstraction of the divine overview. God uses the word *Man,* rather than *Adam* or *men,* and thereby fuses indiscriminately Adam's original sin and all the sins of fallen human beings. "God reads history as Adam's Fall writ large, or as a series of archaically determined repetitions of the first fatal act."[13] Moreover, God associates fallen humanity with the demons in a single category and for nearly thirty lines. "Sufficient to have stood, though free to fall" (III, 99) defines the moral position of "Man," then of "all th' Ethereal Powers" (100), and soon the fallen in both groups are called "they" indiscriminately. In fact, "they" seems at first to refer only to the already fallen angels: "Freely they stood who stood, and fell who fell" (102). At line 122, God slips from the past into the present tense ("They trespass"), and by line 130 we know that he has also been speaking about human beings, who have yet to fall in the poem ("The first sort by thir own suggestion fell, / Self-tempted, self-deprav'd: Man falls deceiv'd," 129–30). The poet is trying to represent God's eternal comprehension of time, "his prospect high, / Wherein past, present, future he beholds" (III, 77–78). But his effort falters. He represents the divine prospect as distant when, in Christian theology, God numbers the hairs on our heads and attends even to a sparrow's fall. He represents God's eternity as a consciousness in which time is relatively meaningless. In theology, however, eternity perfectly comprehends all temporal relations in intimate detail.

In sum, then, God's first speech in the poem fails in several respects. It has been defended with reason and not without weight, for its defenders have accurately perceived the Bard's designs in the speech, though they have taken them for his achievements. What he actually achieves, however, is best shown by his critics, who share my view in seeing God as a character in the poem and not beyond criticism. God's first speech is not toneless but reveals a character unamiable, at the least. His matter proves rather better than his manner, but even here his theodicy is superficial.[14] These conclusions point, not to Milton's achievement, but to his Bard's. Although the Bard

13. Berger, "Archaism, Vision, and Revision," 48.

14. For other criticism of God in Book III, see Douglas Bush, *English Literature in the Earlier Seventeenth Century, 1600–1660* (Oxford, 1945), 381, and Broadbent, *Some Graver Subject,* 144–48. For another defense of "Milton's God," see Georgia B. Christopher, *Milton and the Science of the Saints* (Princeton, 1982).

fails to impersonate God successfully, Milton has brilliantly impersonated the Bard's faltering attempt.

The Bard comes eventually to recognize this failure, for he recants this speech as best he can. He does not repudiate it, of course, for he is performing orally and he must sustain his performance. He cannot undo what he has said, for he is not a writer, so he cannot blot a line. But he can qualify, modify, and comment on his utterance so as to correct impressions subsequently felt to be mistaken. He recants God's first speech, then, at least in the etymological sense: he sings it again (*re-cantare*), later in the poem, in a different way. Moreover, he explicitly marks his resinging it.

The Fall has occurred, and we follow the angels' return to Heaven and their hastening "towards the Throne Supreme" (X, 28) perhaps with some trepidation. If God growls "ingrate" at "Man" (III, 97) with the Fall only in prospect and links all human beings with the demons, what will he say after the Fall has occurred in fact? The angels betray their anxiety at the encounter, as they "haste to make appear / With righteous plea, thir utmost vigilance" (X, 29–30) in guarding Adam and Eve. God speaks "from his secret Cloud, / Amidst in Thunder" (32–33), and yet he is all mildness. He does not scold the angels for their "unsuccessful charge" (35) but consoles them. He reminds them that their failure was inevitable, for he had "Foretold so lately" (38) the Fall of humankind "When first this Tempter cross'd the Gulf from Hell" (39). He elaborates this reference to his first speech by summarizing now what he said then:

> I told ye then he should prevail and speed
> On his bad Errand, Man should be seduc't
> And flatter'd out of all, believing lies
> Against his Maker; no Decree of mine
> Concurring to necessitate his Fall,
> Or touch with lightest moment of impulse
> His free Will, to her own inclining left
> In even scale. But fall'n he is, and now
> What rests, but that the mortal Sentence pass
> On his transgression. Death denounc't that day,
> Which he presumes already vain and void,
> Because not yet inflicted, as he fear'd,
> By some immediate stroke; but soon shall find

> Forbearance no acquittance ere day end.
> Justice shall not return as bounty scorn'd.
> (X, 40–54)

God then concludes by appointing to judge the fallen pair the Son, "Man's Friend, his Mediator, his design'd / Both Ransom and Redeemer voluntary" (60–61). In this way, God reveals that he intends "Mercy colleague with Justice" (59).

In the passage quoted above, God reviews what we are now to consider the essential points in his first speech: "Man" would be seduced by Satan's "lies" (*cf.* III, 91–95, 130–31) and fall of his own free choice, not compelled by any predestinating decree (*cf.* III, 96–130). For the purposes of argument, let us not quibble over the theology of the two speeches but grant God's insistence that it proves essentially the same in both. Even so, the two differ vastly in content and especially in tone.

In particular, the immediate referent and larger connections of the term *Man* change. In Book III, "Man" refers to us: we, too, are declared "faithless," for God transfers the epithet from Adam and Eve to their descendants. In Book X, "Man" refers solely to Adam and Eve. They have sinned, and they are to be judged and punished. Nor does God, in Book X, ever categorize fallen humankind with the demons. These two points, so offensive to readers in Book III and expounded at such length, God tactfully forgets in his summary recollection.

The tone of the later utterance also proves different, even where the content is similar. God's self-justification in Book X is simple, direct, and brief. Gone are the repetitions of words and themes that convey his guilty-sounding uneasiness in Book III. Gone, too, is the harshness of tone. God is consoling the angels with a simple statement of the facts and what he will do about them. The God of Book III might well have scoffed at humankind for thinking that "Forbearance" of punishment were "acquittance" (X, 53), but this God is simply explaining the situation. His manner is mild. He is kind to the angels and seems happy to name the Son as judge, because that will reveal divine mercy as well as justice. Although "Mercy" appears explicitly only at the end of this speech, as in the speech of Book III, here it does not sound like an afterthought. This God is not angry, and he is not insecure about the justice of his position. Mercy seems more like the fulfillment or natural outcome of this God's justice, rather than its opposite.

The Bard's resinging of God's first speech in these lines is all tact. God takes back nothing of what he said earlier. He purports merely to summarize the essential points, devoting only four lines to explaining that his foreknowledge did not necessitate the Fall. Yet, while repudiating nothing, God tactfully leaves out all that was offensive earlier. He recalls his first speech, as it were, to correct our memory of it. The Bard thereby sustains his epic performance, even as he modifies his portrayal of God.

The Bard effects this modification because his earlier experience in making God a palpable character has taught him to be wary of what he gives God to say. In the opening lines of Book X, the Bard speaks in his own voice, in the same tone he gave to God's voice in Book III:

> Meanwhile the heinous and despiteful act
> Of *Satan* done in Paradise, and how
> Hee in the Serpent had perverted *Eve,*
> Her Husband shee, to taste the fatal fruit,
> Was known in Heav'n; for what can scape the Eye
> Of God All-seeing, or deceive his Heart
> Omniscient, who in all things wise and just,
> Hinder'd not *Satan* to attempt the mind
> Of Man, with strength entire, and free will arm'd,
> Complete to have discover'd and repulst
> Whatever wiles of Foe or seeming Friend.
> For still they knew, and ought to have still remember'd
> The high Injunction not to taste that Fruit,
> Whoever tempted; which they not obeying,
> Incurr'd, what could they less, the penalty,
> And manifold in sin, deserv'd to fall.
>
> (X, 1–16)

The Bard proves more judicious here than in Book III. His own praise of God's wisdom and justice sounds better than would God's praise of himself. More important, because the Bard accuses the fallen Adam and Eve, God is relieved of the task. God thus appears a mild-mannered but firm parent who loves his children enough to discipline them. His defense of himself does not require him to vilify the faithlessness of Adam and Eve, for this the Bard has done already.

In addition, the Bard's accusing tones, though hard, are well measured, not excessive like God's in Book III. His words concern only Adam and Eve, not all their descendants. Yet the poetry is directed to all of us who know God's commandments and possess the free will to resist temptation. In Book III, God accuses all the "faithless progeny" of "Man" as "ingrate," and he justifies himself with obsessive repetition. In Book X, we begin to feel that there is more to God than we saw in Book III, precisely because now there is less of him in the poem.

These differences between God's first speech in the poem and his first speech after the Fall reflect the difference between the Bard's portrayal of God in Books III through VII and that in Books X and XI. The Bard has anticipated his critics. Lewis defines the poet's problem as "trying to make Heaven too like Olympus." He argues that "a God, theologically speaking, much worse than Milton's, would escape criticism if only he had been made sufficiently awful, mysterious, and vague." Waldock, too, argues that the God of *Paradise Lost* "is too obstinately there," for "human traits" are "too deeply etched" in his character. Hence, "the closer this God comes to the vanishing point the better he becomes."[15]

By Book X, the Bard has come to appreciate what these critics urge. In Book III, God is an epic character: a rhetorician at length, a vigorous interlocutor, a necessary agent in the plot. In Book X, however, he retires, as far as he may, from the action of the poem. He becomes less a character with a personality than the manager of the poem's divine machinery. The Bard effects this shift because he is now relying on the sequence of Scripture for his plot rather than on his own powers of invention. Hence, God in Books X and XI emerges more from the pages of Genesis than from the inspiration of classical epic. Few Miltonists have seen this change because they assume that "Milton's God" must be a consistent character. They attribute to the retiring God of Books X and XI the same characteristics they find in the active God of Books III through VI, but God's retiring from the action of the poem proves a significant change. Even if one does not admit a change in God's character, God surely appears less frequently

15. Lewis, *Preface to "Paradise Lost,"* 127, 126; Waldock, *"Paradise Lost" and Its Critics,* 100, 98.

and acts less vigorously in the later books of *Paradise Lost.* This change in the poem, I argue, reflects a change in the poet.

When the Bard is inventing his plot in Books I through VI, he often uses classical poetry for his narrative paradigms. Although the Bible implies the occurrence of councils in Heaven, for instance, none are narrated at any length; though it tells of a war in Heaven, it does not report the details. When the Bard needs a paradigm for writing his divine colloquy and angelic battles, therefore, he turns to the classical *concilium deorum* and to battle scenes from ancient epic. As a result, God often appears like an Olympian deity out of Homer or Vergil, as Lewis complained. In Book III, God responds irascibly to the "rage" that "transports" Satan (III, 80–81), and in Book VI he deputizes the Son to wage epic warfare in his stead. To be sure, God does not appear like a classical deity in every sentence or even in every speech, but he does so often enough to disturb Lewis. In Books X and XI, however, he makes but four speeches, and three of these emerge from plot points in Genesis: Adam and Eve must be judged (X, 34–62) and then expelled from the Garden (XI, 46–71, 84–125). Because the center of the action has shifted to Adam and Eve on earth, God appears less essential to the plot than he does in Books III, V, and VI. Hence, he seems to transcend the action as he cannot in the earlier books. When the Bard invents his epic in Heaven, God is embroiled in the plot. But when he follows the guidance of Scripture and sings a song "narrower bound" about human beings, God seems to be above the action because he is less involved in it. He directs more than he acts. He is more beneficent and less irascible, less classical and more Christian. This change in the poet's portrayal of God emerges as the poem shifts its balance from Christian *epic* to *Christian* epic.

If the Bard's use of narrative paradigms from classical poetry tends to skew his portrayal of God in Books III, V, and VI, making God too like an Olympian deity, the poet corrects this tendency in Books X and XI by taking the cue for God's speeches from Scripture. He makes this shift as tactfully as he can. God loses no epic dignity in these later books, as his words and deeds grow less directly informed by classical paradigms. Rather, he gains in stature as he comes to seem less like an Olympian deity, less swayed by what seem human passions. In Book VII, the Bard turns to the sequence of Scripture to guide his plot, and this turn gradually informs his portrayal of God, who comes to seem more Christian as he grows less classical. This reorientation occurs as the Bard shifts from inventing a plot for supernatural characters, in most of Books I through VI, to following the sequence of Scripture for a story about human beings, in Books VII through XII. Such a shift allows God to retire from the action, which now takes place on earth and which he thus seems to transcend as he cannot transcend the action in Heaven, where he proves a crucial agent.

To be sure, Christian and classical elements can be seen everywhere in the Bard's portrayal of God, as the genre of Christian epic implies. I am not suggesting that God is "more classical than Christian" in the earlier books, for his utterances there are rich in theological conception and biblical allusion. God appears more Christian in the later books, though, because he comes to seem less Olympian as he asserts himself less often, for the Bard has shifted his narrative from Heaven to Earth. Narrative necessity affects theological portrayal.

In this section, I propose to show how a classical paradigm underlies the Bard's presentation of the colloquy in Heaven and how it functions to skew his portrayal of God in the first speech. Although Miltonists have treated several allusions to pagan *concilia deorum* in Book III, the most important one has not yet been explored, the dialog between Venus and Jupiter in Book I of the *Aeneid.*[16] First, the term *paradigm* needs to be clarified, for the similar term *models* has been variously employed by Miltonists.

When Leland Ryken treats Milton's use of biblical models, he refers to "models of specific modes of discourse" and treats a range of phenomena, from stylistic traits through genres to intertextuality.[17] A

16. See Mason Hammond, "Concilia Deorum from Homer Through Virgil," *Studies in Philology,* XXX (1933), 1–16; O. H. Moore, "The Infernal Council," *Modern Philology,* XVI (1918), 169–93; and Joseph A. Wittreich, " 'All Angelic Natures Joined in One': Epic Convention and Prophetic Interiority in the Council Scenes of *Paradise Lost,*" *Milton Studies,* XVII (1983), 43–74. The biblical models are treated by Sister M. Christopher Pecheux, "The Council Scenes in *Paradise Lost,*" in *Milton and Scriptural Tradition,* ed. Sims and Ryken, 82–103. I have found no record of these allusions in Richard Bentley, H. J. Todd, or Thomas Newton, three of Milton's earliest and most learned editors.

17. Leland Ryken, Introduction to *Milton and Scriptural Tradition,* ed. Sims and Ryken, 3–30.

"classical *paradigm,*" however, refers to a model extensive enough to import classical conceptions into the Christian epic. Since Ryken is treating biblical models for a Christian poem, no conflict will arise between the two, and he can use the term broadly. But "classical paradigm" points to a model that skews the Christian elements in the poem, which should be primary and thus immune from interference. It may be possible to use a classical *model* that does not entail such distortion, but a classical *paradigm* always does, by definition. A classical paradigm, like a model, leaves its trace in the poem in various ways, but it also does something more: it proves a controlling conception, a master plan, that interferes with the Bard's Christian subject.

The Bard's classical paradigm for his colloquy in Heaven comes from Vergil's colloquy between Venus and Jupiter. It proves a paradigm because the Bard intends to overgo it thoroughly. He designs his divine colloquy to recall and surpass Vergil's in every important respect. He signals this overgoing program by alluding to the beginning and ending of Vergil's colloquy at the beginning and ending of his own. The structure and content of the Bard's colloquy in Heaven, thus, is governed by this overgoing program. There are, of course, other models for it, but its only paradigm is Vergil's, for the Bard intends to triumph over his great predecessor by displaying the superior scope and sweep of his Christian divine vision in a detailed overgoing.

To emphasize his achievement, the Bard frames his colloquy with echoes of Vergil's poem. The beginning and setting of both are analogous: Jupiter looks down from the sky on the world he rules, just as God regards his creation from the Empyreal Heaven. In the *Aeneid,* the scene follows Aeneas' speech to his men after their escape from the storm caused by Juno. Jupiter turns his gaze toward Libya and ponders the Trojans' plight:

> Et iam finis erat, cum Iuppiter aethere summo
> despiciens mare velivolum terrasque iacentis
> litoraque et latos populos, sic vertice caeli
> constitit et Libyae defixit lumina regnis.
> (*Aeneid,* I, 223–26)

And now there was an end [to the Trojans' eating and talking after Aeneas' speech] when Jupiter, from the sky's height gazing down on the sail-bearing sea and the low-lying lands and the shores and the

> widespread peoples, stood thus at the peak of heaven and fixed down his eyes on the kingdoms of Libya.

The Bard's allusions to this passage purport to exalt both his God and his poetic vision over Vergil's. God looks down from a greater height than Jupiter, from a spiritual Heaven rather than the physical sky:

> Now had th' Almighty Father from above,
> From the pure Empyrean where he sits
> High Thron'd above all highth, bent down his eye,
> His own works and their works at once to view.
> (III, 56–59)

Not only does the Bard exalt the spatial terms in Vergil, but he later redefines God's "prospect high" (77) as a comprehensive vision of all time as well as all space, "Wherein past, present, future he beholds" (78). From their prospects, both divine beings look down, Vergil's from the physical clarity of the sky's height, the Bard's from the spiritual purity of the Empyrean. Vergil's god, however, surveys the whole earth in a gaze moving from sea to lands to shores to peoples, in no special order, before he focuses his sight on Libya; the poet distinguishes these movements by shifting from a present participle ("despiciens," 224) to a verb in the perfect tense ("defixit lumina," 226). The Bard practically translates the latter in the single viewing action his God performs, "bent down his eye" (58). Yet the Christian God sits enthroned, at ease, whereas the pagan god stands ("constitit," 226) to peer down. Because the Christian God is both an eternal being and a creator, he can see, in a single action, "His own works and their works *at once*" (59, emphasis added). His gaze extends even beyond the universe, a far vaster vision than Jupiter's of the Earth. Although Jupiter is "the father of gods and men" ("hominum sator atque deorum," 254), he is not a creator, so his vision proves less powerful and his survey less orderly than that by the Christian God.

Jupiter's speech concludes dramatically, for Vergil's first readers, with reference to some recent events. He "prophesies" the glorious achievements of Caesar (*Aeneid*, I, 286–88) and his admission to the realm of the gods (289–90). Then a new Golden Age will come (291–93), war will be absent ("positis bellis," 291), and just rule will be divinely maintained (292–93). The "gates of war" on the temple of Janus "will be shut" ("claudentur Belli portae," 294), as indeed they were in 29 B.C. (and again four years later) for the first time since 235 B.C. Finally, Jupiter envisions "Furor impius" ("sinful Rage") bound and raging behind those closed doors, imprisoned, impotent at last (294–99).

Similarly, the Bard's God ends his final speech with a prophetic vision of demonic powers imprisoned and a new golden age:

> Then all thy Saints assembl'd, thou shalt judge
> Bad men and Angels, they arraign'd shall sink
> Beneath thy Sentence; Hell, her numbers full,
> Thenceforth shall be for ever shut. Meanwhile
> The World shall burn, and from her ashes spring
> New Heav'n and Earth, wherein the just shall dwell
> And after all thir tribulations long
> See golden days, fruitful of golden deeds,
> With Joy and Love triumphing, and fair Truth.
> (III, 330–38)

That Hell "shall be for ever shut" (333) clearly alludes to Vergil's "claudentur Belli portae," even as the Son's victory far exceeds Augustus'. All evil will be eliminated, not just war, and goodness will endure "for ever," whereas the Roman "gates of War" were later reopened. Likewise, the Bard assures us that the Son's "New Heav'n and Earth" will prove an enduring Golden Age for all the saved, rather than a symbol for benefits only Roman citizens received. In Vergil's prophecy, peculiarly Roman deities preserve justice in the new age: "cana Fides et Vesta, Remo cum fratre Quirinus / iura dabunt" ("white-haired Faithfulness and Vesta, Romulus with his brother Remus will give laws," 292–93). In the Bard's, there are no laws, only the triumph of universally human aspirations to Joy and Love and Truth.

In *Paradise Lost,* then, the Son's victory over all the powers of evil and his eternal rule both recall and exceed Jupiter's prophecies about the triumph of Rome and the Augustan Golden Age. Further, the Bard would have us understand that his Christian prophecy is true and a real prophecy, as compared to Vergil's. As W. H. Auden put it, Vergil's Roman history is "Hindsight as foresight": the Roman poet recasts a carefully chosen Roman past as a prophesied future for his characters.[18] The Christian poet is singing about events at the end of time. Moreover, the Bard knows that the movements of subsequent history have proven Jupiter's prophecy false: "Furor impius" did not remain imprisoned, and "Roma" was not "aeterna." The true savior is not Augustus but Christ.

In brief, the Bard's divine discourse offers us a Christian vision of history that purports to be true, where Vergil's is false, and more comprehensive, for it includes all humankind and all time, where Vergil's embraces only the "known world" up through the time of Augustus. This Christian transformation of Vergil is evident also in the Bard's reworking of Jupiter's famous lines on the Roman Empire: "his ego nec metas rerum nec tempora pono: / imperium sine fine dedi" ("I place no physical or temporal limits to their fortunes: I have granted them rule without end," 278–79). These words come immediately after the central line of Jupiter's speech, on Romulus' founding of Rome as a "city of Mars" ("Mavortia . . . moenia," 276–77). At the thematic and mathematical axis of Jupiter's speech, Vergil emphasizes the Romans' warlike qualities and their eternal rule.

The Christian poet knows the former to be true and the latter false. Here is his version of Vergil's lines:

> . . . because in thee
> Love hath abounded more than Glory abounds,
> Therefore thy Humiliation shall exalt
> With thee thy Manhood also to this Throne;
> Here shalt thou sit incarnate, here shalt Reign
> Both God and Man, Son both of God and Man,
> Anointed universal King; *all Power*
> *I give thee, reign for ever,* and assume
> Thy Merits; under thee as Head Supreme
> Thrones, Princedoms, Powers, Dominions I reduce:
> All knees to thee shall bow, of them that bide
> In Heaven, or Earth, or under Earth in Hell.
> (III, 311–22; emphasis added)

In the Bard's vision, the Christian God grants genuinely universal rule to the Son, an *imperium* truly *sine fine* since it comprehends all time

18. W. H. Auden, "Secondary Epic," *Collected Poems,* ed. Edward Mendelson, 455–56, l. 5.

and space.[19] Further, the Son's triumph comes from love and humility. These lead to true, that is, spiritual and eternal, glory, whereas the triumph of Vergil's Roman arms brings but a temporal glory that can only boast of itself as enduring. In the Christian vision, as opposed to Vergil's, Love triumphs over War.

The Son is the Bard's figure for that love, and he thus proves the counterpart to Vergil's Venus, goddess of a different kind of love. Where Venus speaks to Jupiter from a self-interested concern for her son Aeneas and for her future in Rome, the Son speaks to the Father in charity for "Man / *Thy* creature late so lov'd, *thy* youngest Son" (III, 150–51; emphasis added). The Christian Bard constructs his divine situation to mirror, yet countervail, Vergil's. In the *Aeneid,* Venus confronts Jupiter, her father, about the Trojans' continuing plight at the hands of Juno. In *Paradise Lost,* however, the "Almighty Father" (55) draws the Son's attention to Satan approaching the created world for his "desperate revenge" (85).[20] In both poems, the divine love and the divine father discourse about present danger to beloved human beings who are founding members of the race. In Vergil, on the one hand, Venus complains about Juno's injustices and implies that Jupiter, in failing to govern her, is reneging on his promise that the Romans "would hold sway over the sea and all its lands" (236). There is, thus, a certain irony in her addressing him as "You who govern the affairs of humans and gods with eternal decrees" (229–30). The Christian Bard, on the other hand, is anxious to portray the divine Father as truly almighty and supremely just. His Juno figure, Satan, has been expelled from Heaven, and there will be no compromise with evil, as in Vergil's pantheon. Christian readers have long noted inconsistencies in the portrayal of fate in the *Aeneid.* The Bard intends the providence asserted by his God to be theologically consistent, historically comprehensive, and morally just.

19. Davis P. Harding finds an allusion to this speech in Book XII, 371–72, where the opposition of Christ to Augustus is again emphasized. See *The Club of Hercules: Studies in the Classical Background of "Paradise Lost"* (Urbana, Ill., 1962), 38. Mario A. Di Cesare offers a counterargument in "*Paradise Lost* and the Epic Tradition," *Milton Studies,* I (1969), 31–50, esp. 32.

20. For Satan as a Juno figure, see Wolfgang E. H. Rudat, "Milton's Satan and Virgil's Juno: 'Perverseness' of Disobedience in *Paradise Lost,*" *Renaissance and Reformation,* n.s., III (1979), 77–82.

The tone of these divine colloquies also differs. Venus complains bitterly to her father and tries to manipulate him into acting against Juno. Jove sees this clearly, smiling with indulgent irony all the while ("Olli subridens," 254). When he begins his reply, he tells her not to fear and adds sarcastically that "the fate of your descendants is unchanged, by you" (257–58). The prevailing tone in the Christian Heaven, in contrast, purports to be more serene. The Son reminds his Father of his grace and justice (144–55) only after the Father has already declared that "Man therefore shall find grace" (131) and receive mercy as well as justice (132–34). The Bard would have us see concord reigning among his two gods, who are really one Godhead. The Son, unlike Venus, does change the fate of his descendants by volunteering to redeem humankind.

Clearly, the Bard bases his superiority over Vergil on the truth of Christianity. The Christian Heaven lacks an evil principal, because Satan is exiled, whereas Juno remains a powerful figure throughout the *Aeneid.* Hence, Juno's power presses closely upon Venus' awareness, for the latter's speech to Jove is filled with anger, resentment, and frustration. Such feelings prove comparatively absent from the Bard's divine discourse. He would have us feel that the Son merely amplifies what is implied in the Father's promise that "Man therefore shall find grace," just as the Father's last speech elaborates the Son's vision of future redemption. Their dialog purports to unfold without rancor and without manipulation: gracious, mutually complaisant, courtly, serene. Satan proves far away, physically and spiritually, from most of their discussion, which largely concerns the redemption of humankind. Juno, though physically absent, seems to brood over much of Venus' colloquy with Jove.

Thus the discord that rends Vergil's pantheon is absent from the Bard's Heaven, where concord reigns. Although Jupiter promises that Juno will eventually be reconciled to the Trojan future in Rome (279–82), her resentment has already destroyed many and will destroy more. The Bard's divine colloquy, in contrast, looks forward, not to reconciling the evil, but to vanquishing it. Satan proves ultimately impotent, whereas Juno remains a powerful figure to be feared and placated. Finally, Roman history, with all its conquests, does not appear in *Paradise Lost.* The Bard offers a far more sweeping vision of universal history as the spiritual triumph of the Redemption.

In setting forth this history, the Bard avoids the specific referents that abound in Vergil. The latter refers to many persons, places, and events in the Roman past. The text teems with names and details. The Bard, to the contrary, avoids mentioning all specifics of the Son's earthly life: no Jesus or Mary, no Pilate or Caiaphas, no Jerusalem or Calvary are named, though they might have been. This omission, striking when compared to Vergil's largesse of historical detail, underscores the generality of the Bard's divine discourse: it partakes of the height of the Christian divinity. The physical and temporal distance between God's "pure Empyrean" prior to time and Jupiter's "summus aether" seven years after the Trojan War proves analogous to the theological distance between the Bard's divine discourse and Vergil's. The Christian poet evokes that source to call attention to the differences between Vergil's theological poetry and his own.

The Bard even ventures so far as to overgo the implied allegorical significance of Vergil's divine characters. As Venus and Jupiter represent different parts of the soul, so the Son and God represent an allegory of the two testaments and thus of the universal history their dialogue considers. In Book I of the *Aeneid,* the female deities, Juno and Venus, clearly represent the passions, while the male gods, Neptune and Jupiter, stand for reason and order. Juno's storm of passion against the surviving Trojans leads directly to the tempest in which they come close to perishing, while Venus tries to manipulate Jupiter with her tears and special pleading. Neptune and Jupiter, in contrast, restore and reassert the order of nature and history. Divine order and reason control the divine passions in the *Aeneid,* though not without difficulty.

The Bard overgoes this allegory of the soul with a biblical allegory of the two testaments. God the Father represents justice and the Old Testament; the Son, mercy and the New. Where Vergil's divine allegory turns on conflict, the Bard's intends to unfold a harmony. Just as the structure of human history revealed in Scripture is greater than the structure of the soul, so would the Bard's allegory overgo Vergil's. His biblical and theological allegory would comprehend a truth greater than Vergil's classical and philosophical one.

Clearly, the Bard aims to transform *all* of his Vergilian source. He would leave out no central element. Rather, he reenvisions the whole at a Christian "height" that transforms Vergil's themes and ideas.

Venus' selfish love becomes the Son's selfless love; Roman history is replaced by Redemption history; Olympian discord turns into Empyreal concord; pagan error is transformed into Christian truth. It is a great and beautiful conception for an overgoing program, and the Bard executes it with learning and skill.

Unfortunately, the Bard's very success mars his achievement as a properly Christian poet. He believes that he can use the Vergilian paradigm without prejudice to his Christian subject. He thinks of the classical paradigm as a template or mold that he can simply fill with Christian substance. But he is wrong. He does not understand that a classical paradigm for his narrative entails classical conceptions of divinity, and these distort, in some respects, his representations of God and the Son. He fails to see how a classical paradigm for his narrative skews the Christian truth of his poem. Critics of God's first speech have pointed chiefly to its self-justifying tone and to its superficial theodicy. Both of these emerge, in large part, from the Bard's attempt to overgo Vergil.

The shallowness of God's theodicy has already been discussed, and those remarks need simply to be recalled in this context. The Bard's overgoing program requires his God to surpass Vergil's Jupiter in height of vision, for he believes that Christian Providence is superior to pagan Fate. Unfortunately, he can only portray the superior height of God's vision by making it more general, more abstract, than Jupiter's. As we saw, God uses "Man" to refer to Adam and Eve not only before but after the Fall, and the noun also embraces all subsequent human beings. God also collapses the fallen angels and fallen human beings into a single category for almost thirty lines. The Bard thereby achieves height of vision for God at the cost of his failure to make crucial distinctions.

Even if we grant the Bard's belief in the superiority of Christian Providence, nevertheless the poem shows us that his operative understanding of that superiority misrepresents it. Theologically, the height of Providence is not more general and abstract than Jupiter's Fate but more intimate, penetrating, and detailed. In the *Aeneid,* Jupiter knows the fates of whole peoples and of certain signal individuals, like Aeneas, upon whom the destiny of nations rests. Yet there seems to be no Fate for the common mortal: Vulcan tells Venus that "neither Jove nor the Fates forbade Troy to stand for another ten years" (*Aeneid,* VIII,

398–99). "Another ten years" would have made little difference to the ultimate destinies of Troy or of Aeneas, but it would have meant a great deal to innumerable Greeks and Trojans. According to Christian theology, however, every human being has an immortal destiny, and God knows not only the end of every person but the course he or she travels to it. Christian Providence embraces all individuals, even to the details of their daily acts, even to their motives, fluctuating as these are. Christian Providence proves superior to pagan Fate, not as higher or greater in the same order, but as *of a different order altogether.*

But the Bard's overgoing program commits him to portraying Providence as higher than Fate yet in the same order. The classical paradigm entails a classical conception of divinity. Hence, God appears merely as greater than Jupiter, when he should be presented as of another order altogether. The Bard's portrayal of God's superior height of vision takes its cue from Vergil, for he can only overgo Vergil's dialogue by accepting its terms and then outdoing them. This acceptance, however, necessarily betrays his rendering of Christian Providence.

It may be objected that the intimate and detailed vision of Providence cannot be rendered literarily. The God who numbers the hairs on our heads and notices the fall even of a sparrow cannot be given a speech that adequately represents the plenitude of his knowledge, and this is true. Therefore, a judicious Christian poet will not attempt to represent God's Providence in God's own voice. The Bard's attempt is doomed to misrepresentation. It may succeed poetically, but it must fail theologically.

If a judicious Christian poet wishes to represent the Providential order, he will do what the Bard does in Books XI and XII: give the part to a speaker other than God. In these books, Michael treats the Providential order of history as God enlightens him to do so (XI, 115). He meets Adam "Not in his shape Celestial, but as Man / Clad to meet Man" (XI, 239–40), and he unfolds, not a divine vision, but a biblical exposition. The sweep of universal Redemption history is exposed and explained in a manner suited to fallen human beings. The aspiration to divine vision, so prominent in Book III, is left behind. The Bard no longer attempts to render what simply cannot be rendered, God's own Providence in God's own voice.

In short, the Bard's problem with God's first speech is neither lack of learning nor want of skill but, rather, a failure of judgment. He attempts to do what cannot be done. His ambition to sing "Things unattempted yet in Prose or Rhyme" leads him to put God's Providential vision in God's own mouth and to do so in a Vergilian paradigm. His epic ambition leads him to misrepresent Christian truth.

Critics of God's first speech have pointed not only to its theodical superficiality but to its self-justifying tone, which also emerges from the program to overgo Vergil. God represents justice in the Bard's allegory of the two testaments, and the poet's overgoing program commits him to giving God a substantial speech. The Bard's God cannot overgo Jupiter by being silent or laconic. He must assert himself at some length, and being a figure of divine justice, he must assert his own justice. This he does, not only from a height superior to Jupiter's, but at a length that is supposed to evince his superior vision in a more extensive rhetoric. As critics have pointed out, however, this program entails unfortunate consequences. The longer God asserts his own justice, the weaker his rhetoric comes to seem. Self-justification becomes a defense that grows increasingly defensive. The longer he speaks, the more unsteady his own position appears. The rhetorical technique of repeating key points might be effective were he a lawyer defending someone else, but when God defends his own justice, the rhetorical strength of the method instead points up the seeming weakness of his case.

Here, saying less would suggest more, as the Bard understands when he resings this speech in Book X, where God spends just four lines on the justice of his own position. He is simply explaining the facts, not justifying himself. God thereby appears confident of his own freedom from blame, as he does not in Book III, when he insists repeatedly on it. The Vergilian paradigm in Book III dictates a long speech, because a short one, in the overgoing Bard's eyes, would make God look weaker than Jupiter. In Book X, however, he is no longer working with a classical paradigm, and he resings the earlier speech with consummate tact.

The Bard manages this tact because he has freed himself from his overgoing ambition. He has learned that he can overgo his predecessors only if he first accepts their classical terms, and he understands that these distort the Christian truths he would sing. Also, he has finally plumbed the innate superiority of his Christian subject to the classical epics. He does not need to overgo the ancients; he merely needs a style answerable to his "higher Argument." Like the Christian God, Christian virtue is not higher than pagan in the same order but of another order altogether. "The better fortitude / Of Patience and Heroic Martyrdom" is unsung in pagan epic because it cannot be imagined without belief in the Redemption.

The Redemption is itself sung in Book III and sung beautifully. God, in his justice, has pronounced that "Man" must die, so "Die hee or Justice must" (210), and he looks for a volunteer to redeem "Man's mortal crime" (215). "Dwells in all Heaven charity so dear?" (216), he asks, and all is silence. Then the Son speaks, and after a brief *exordium* on grace, he offers himself for us in these lines:

> Behold mee then, mee for him, life for life
> I offer, on mee let thine anger fall;
> Account mee man; I for his sake will leave
> Thy bosom, and this glory next to thee
> Freely put off, and for him lastly die
> Well pleas'd, on me let Death wreak all his rage;
> Under his gloomy power I shall not long
> Lie vanquisht; thou hast giv'n me to possess
> Life in myself for ever, by thee I live,
> Though now to Death I yield, and am his due
> All that of me can die, yet that debt paid,
> Thou wilt not leave me in the loathsome grave
> His prey, nor suffer my unspotted Soul
> For ever with corruption there to dwell;
> *But I shall rise Victorious,* and subdue
> My vanquisher, spoil'd of his vaunted spoil;
> Death his death's wound shall then receive, and stoop
> Inglorious, of his mortal sting disarm'd.
> I through the ample Air in Triumph high
> Shall lead Hell Captive maugre Hell, and show
> The powers of darkness bound. Thou at the sight
> Pleas'd, out of Heaven shalt look down and smile,
> While by thee rais'd I ruin all my Foes,
> Death last, and with his Carcass glut the Grave:
> Then with the multitude of my redeem'd
> Shall enter Heav'n long absent, and return,
> Father, to see thy face, wherein no cloud

Of anger shall remain, but peace assur'd,
And reconcilement; wrath shall be no more
Thenceforth, but in thy presence Joy entire.
(236–65; emphasis added)

The Son's speech is moving and beautiful. It rings with biblical echoes, and its second half is suffused with images of *Christus victor* from homily, commentary, and art. The structure of the thirty lines quoted above is modeled on Paul's kenosis hymn in Philippians 2:6–11, which narrates the descent of the Savior in its first half and his exaltation in its second. Similarly, "But I shall rise Victorious" (250) occurs in the fifteenth of thirty lines. Thoroughly Christian in structure and texture, this speech identifies the Redemption with Christ's victory in the Resurrection, followed by his triumphal return to Heaven.

Still, for all its glories, the speech fails theologically in two signal respects. It purports to represent the virtue of humility and the truth of the Redemption. In fact, though, it misrepresents them both. Attempting to overgo classical epic commits the Bard to an exalted style and a triumphal vision that misrepresent Christ's humility and Redemption.

Evidence for this misrepresentation may be found in the Bard's resinging of the passage in Book XII. Michael is explaining the Redemption to Adam, who has asked about the battle between the Serpent and the Son: "say where and when / Thir fight, what stroke shall bruise the Victor's heel" (XII, 384–85). The angel tells him that their fight will not be "As of a Duel" (387), for the Savior redeems "Not by destroying *Satan,* but his works" (394) in human beings. With the epic imagery of warfare set aside as misleading, Michael explains how the Son shall pay the penalty for Adam:

The Law of God exact he shall fulfil
Both by obedience and by love, though love
Alone fulfil the Law; thy punishment
He shall endure by coming in the Flesh
To a reproachful life and cursed death,
Proclaiming Life to all who shall believe
In his redemption, and that his obedience
Imputed becomes theirs by Faith, his merits
To save them, not thir own, though legal works.
For this he shall live hated, be blasphem'd,

Seiz'd on by force, judg'd, and to death condemn'd
A shameful and accurst, nail'd to the Cross
By his own Nation, slain for bringing Life;
But to the Cross he nails thy Enemies,
The Law that is against thee, and the sins
Of all mankind, with him there crucifi'd,
Never to hurt them more who rightly trust
In this his satisfaction; so he dies,
But soon revives, Death over him no power
Shall long usurp; ere the third dawning light
Return, the Stars of Morn shall see him rise
Out of his grave, fresh as the dawning light,
Thy ransom paid, which Man from death redeems,
His death for Man, as many as offer'd Life
Neglect not, and the benefit embrace
By Faith not void of works; *this God-like act*
Annuls thy doom, the death thou shouldst have di'd,
In sin for ever lost from life; *this act*
Shall bruise the head of Satan, crush his strength
Defeating Sin and Death, his two main arms,
And fix far deeper in his head thir stings
Than temporal death shall bruise the Victor's heel.
(XII, 402–33; emphasis added)

These two accounts of the Redemption customarily move Miltonists to explore their consistency.[21] Implied in their assumption is that "Milton" sings the poem, that every part of *Paradise Lost* represents the historical Milton's view. To be sure, these two passages contain many similarities. Nevertheless, the theology of the Redemption in Book XII corrects that in Book III, and this correction reveals a change in Milton's narrator, the Bard.

21. Recent studies of the Son include Randel Helms, " 'His Dearest Mediation': The Dialogue in Heaven in Book III of *Paradise Lost*," *Milton Quarterly,* III (1971), 52–57; Marilyn Arnold, "Milton's Accessible God: The Role of the Son in *Paradise Lost*," *Milton Quarterly,* VII (1973), 65–72; Peter A. Fiore, " 'Account Mee Man': The Incarnation in *Paradise Lost*," *Huntington Library Quarterly,* XXXIX (1975), 51–56; William J. Rewak, "Book III of *Paradise Lost:* Milton's Satisfaction Theory of the Redemption," *Milton Quarterly,* XI (1977), 97–102; and Robert J. Wickenheiser, "Milton's 'Pattern of a Christian Hero': The Son in *Paradise Lost*," *Milton Quarterly,* XII (1978), 1–9.

The doctrinal difference proves the most significant and is thus the most clearly marked. In Book III, the Son's victory lies in his Resurrection ("But I shall rise Victorious," 250). In Book XII, however, the "God-like act" (427) is the Son's "death for Man" (425), a "ransom paid, which Man from death redeems" (424). Not by rising, but by suffering and dying does he nail to the cross the enemies of humankind (XII, 415–19). Moreover, in Book III, Death is the enemy, the Son's enemy (III, 240–53); in Book XII the enemies are ours, the Law and our own sins. Where Book III celebrates Christ as epic victor over his enemy, Book XII sets forth Christ as redemptive victim, saving us from our enemies. Christ's obedience unto death, not his Resurrection, defeats Sin and Death and crushes Satan's strength (XII, 429–32). In Book XII, Christ proves victor because he is victim, and the Resurrection stands merely as the sign of that victory, as his triumphal Ascension (451–55) simply celebrates it.

These two theological views cannot, strictly speaking, be reconciled, and the later proves superior in several respects. Most obviously, it articulates the traditional doctrine of the Redemption as found in Scripture. Although Paul celebrates the Resurrection in passages of memorable force, he explains the Redemption through the metaphors of sacrifice and ransom, both of which emphasize Christ's death as the saving act. The Resurrection proves, rather, the evidential sign that salvation has been brought to us. Moreover, the theology of Book XII embraces and comprehends that of Book III, though the reverse does not obtain. Book III presents the Son's death as the regretable prelude to his resurrective victory, with little positive value in his dying, except that expressed in the half-line "yet that debt paid" (246). Book XII, in contrast, treats that death as the victory itself, because it is the signal act of love and obedience. Book XII thereby exalts the Son's descent to humanity more highly than does Book III, because it dwells on what his love for us really cost him. At the same time, the later book does celebrate the Resurrection as the sign of the Son's victory on the cross. In this way, the Redemption theology of Book XII comprehends, as well as corrects, that of Book III. Finally, it proves superior simply by being the poet's last word on this crucial subject, and as such, it remains the final and true word on any issue of controversy about the Redemption theology of the poem. The sequential principle implies as much. Where the poem contradicts itself on any crucial point, the later utterance proves decisive.

The Bard's theological misknowing in Book III is engendered by his Vergilian paradigm and his overgoing program. As Vergil's divine colloquy culminates in the triumph of Roman arms and empire in "universal" peace, the Bard intends to overgo him by celebrating the truly universal peace wrought by the Son's victory. But he can hardly overgo Vergil's history of triumph by emphasizing the "reproachful life and cursed death" (XII, 406) whereby the Son redeems humankind. Suffering and dying are not themes for celebration in the high style of epic. The Bard's classical paradigm thus leads him to an epic theology of the Redemption; full of military images, it emphasizes Resurrection, victory, and triumph. He can overgo Vergil only by accepting the terms implied in the classical paradigm of epic achievement. Hence, he must emphasize Christ as victor and must scant or avoid Christ as victim. Significantly, the Son's speech does not even mention the Cross. The Bard avoids the supreme Christian symbol because it does not fit into his overgoing program. In Book XII, however, he corrects this misrepresentation. All the struggle and suffering excluded from Book III find their rightful place, for by that point, the Bard has fully understood the better Christian fortitude unsung in ancient epic. A classical paradigm of epic narrative cannot be reconciled with "Patience and Heroic Martyrdom." The high style of epic is designed to celebrate heroic self-assertion, not suffering and humble obedience unto death.

Hence, the passage from Book III, though modeled on Paul's kenosis hymn, also fails to represent adequately Christ's humility. The Bard's Vergilian paradigm compels him to sing in the high style of epic, but humility in a high style proves a contradiction in terms. The Bard, following Paul, wants to glorify the Son's descent to humanity and his redeeming death. His epic paradigm, however, leads him to images that Paul avoids. The paradigm dictates that the Son slight his death and celebrate his victory over death in military images. As Berger puts it, the way the Son offers himself "reveals that he expects at most to be mildly and temporarily inconvenienced by his sacrifice."[22] The Son's descent to death purports to enact a humility without any humiliation: the Bard sings an epic humility.

22. Berger, "Archaism, Vision, and Revision," 49.

Humility is not an epic virtue. The high style cannot rightly glorify that which shuns human glory. To be sure, the Bard manages to reconcile these irreconcilables rather impressively, for the Son's speech is beautiful and moving. Nevertheless, he implicitly admits his failure to represent Christ's humility in Book III when he resings the Redemption in Book XII. There he employs a lower style, closer to the *sermo humilis* of Scripture, and he pointedly exposes Christ's humiliation (*cf.* XII, 405–406, 411–14). This he now shows to be the victory itself. By the time he sings Book XII, the Bard has abandoned his overgoing ambitions and classical paradigms for his narrative. With Scripture as his paradigm in style and substance, he can resing Christ's humility and thus correct its misrepresentation in Book III.

Now, it may be objected that the differences between these accounts of the Redemption effect a balance in *Paradise Lost* created by "Milton." In this view, Books III and XII both represent the historical Milton's views, and their differences reflect the balance enacted over the poem as a whole. Book III articulates his heavenly vision of the Redemption, whereas Book XII presents an earthly and fallen one, appropriate for the fallen Adam to hear. This view holds to the ambiguity of "Milton" as simultaneously author and narrator. It therefore insists on reconciling differences between different parts of the poem into his total vision.[23]

One can hardly object to many aspects of this view. Scholars have long interpreted correspondences between different parts of the poem and will rightly continue to do so. Moreover, the poem as a whole clearly embraces the heavenly and the earthly, the unfallen and the fallen, the divine and the human, in its total design. I want only to insist on the unfolding of the poem as the process of the Bard's composition. Where Miltonists have sought the total design of the work, I emphasize the Bard's *act* of balancing the later books against the earlier ones. Furthermore, he often balances in the sense of "righting the balance," because something needs correcting. True, express contradictions on crucial issues in the poem are rare. Nevertheless, even on issues of style, where there can be no contradiction, we should attend to the poet's *act of completing* the total design. The lower style of Michael's

23. Carrithers and Hardy, *Milton and the Hermeneutic Journey,* emphasize movement and dynamism in *Paradise Lost* yet still consider Milton to be both author and narrator.

discourse, then, proves the Bard's counterbalancing the higher flights in Books I through VI, because these books, by themselves, would make a Christian epic out of balance. This much, at least, is implied by the metaphors of balance and total design when they are applied to *Paradise Lost,* not as a static entity, but as a work of literature unfolding in time. The later books balance the earlier ones because the Bard is righting the balance of his poem as he completes its total design.

Nevertheless, though direct contradictions in the poem are rare, the Redemption theology of Book XII does correct and supersede that of Book III, implying that the latter cannot have been Milton's heavenly vision. The account in Book XII presents the traditional doctrine, as the earlier one does not. Furthermore, we have seen how the Christian representations in Book III are deformed by the Bard's Vergilian paradigm. In this regard, the book articulates less a heavenly than an epic vision of the Redemption. When Book XII counters and corrects it, that epic vision is shown to be myopic.

This argument does not assert that Book III lacks all heavenly vision, nor does it imply that divine inspiration and epic ambition need be strictly opposed. Yet Miltonists should not assume that their poet receives the divine inspiration for which he prays, for the case needs to be argued passage by passage, since divine inspiration and human response prove a delicate affair. On the crucial point of the theology of the Redemption, Book XII shows Book III to be limited and partial. When the earthly account supersedes the heavenly vision, the vision cannot be considered divinely inspired. To be sure, the Bard's Vergilian paradigm in Book III does not vitiate all his Christian representations, but this one it does, despite its Pauline model and biblical echoes. That it vitiates the central truth of salvation, the Redemption, should give us pause.

In short, the fallen Bard's epic ambition leads him to misrepresent the central truth of salvation in Book III, so he recants this Redemption theology in Book XII, resinging it correctively. He also recants his earlier treatment of Christ's humility, emphasizing the "reproachful life and cursed death" (XII, 406) ignored earlier. From the perspective of Book XII, the "heavenly vision" of humility in Book III appears more like a fallen fantasy, for it proves a humility with little cost and immense rewards. In Book III, the Son's "descent" does not touch on Christ's human struggle, rejection, or suffering, and it envisions his death as a regrettable fact, not as the Passion. The only humiliation that excites the Son in these fourteen lines (III, 236–50) is found, not in life, but after it: the corruption of the grave, which, though treated in four lines (246–49), he shall not feel. After this brief vision of difficulty comes triumph upon triumph: the Son's vision of his Resurrection and victory (III, 250–65), the Father's paean of praise for his redeeming love (274–343), and the angels' casting of their crowns at his feet and singing of the praises of Father and Son (344–415). The poetry is glorious, and the celebration, moving. It lacks only the reality of humility, which it purports, in part, to represent. It ignores what love and obedience really cost the Son and cost those who take up their crosses to follow him. Hence, the Bard resings the Son's humility in Book XII, for Book III represents a humility without humiliation, with little difficulty and with immediate glory. This is no heavenly vision, but a fallen fantasy of Christian humility. Book XII presents it more starkly and truly.

These differences between Books III and XII reveal a change in the poet of *Paradise Lost,* not a mere variation, but his progress in understanding what his Christian epic truly requires. The crucial realization is registered in the fourth proem. There the Bard finally understands that he does not need to overgo pagan epic, because the Christian subject given to him has already surpassed it. His "higher Argument" is "sufficient of itself to raise" the name of epic, and all he needs is an "answerable style." Christian truth is higher than classical achievement, not in the same order, but in a different order altogether. Christian fortitude is better than classical bravery, not because it rages more valiantly on the field of battle, but because it imitates Christ's obedient suffering unto death. Hence, a Christian poet cannot use a classical paradigm for his narrative and prove true to the Christian substance he would present, because a classical paradigm entails classical conceptions of virtue and divinity. In Book III, the Bard does not yet understand this, for he is intent on overgoing the ancient epic poets. By the time he sings Book XII, however, he does understand it, for he has abandoned his overgoing ambitions.

In sum, at certain crucial points in Book III, the Bard falters as a Christian poet, not from lack of piety or lack of talent or lack of learning or lack of skill, but from a failure of judgment that emerges from his epic ambition. He believes that he can employ a classical paradigm for his narrative without prejudice to his Christian subject, and he designs a magnificent program to overgo Vergil. Although his program largely succeeds, its very success mars his presentation of Christian truth. The Bard cannot make God greater than Jupiter without making him too like Jupiter. He cannot make the triumph of the Redemption overgo that of Rome and preserve Christ's humiliation and Passion. He cannot do these things, not because he lacks the ability, for no poet has greater ability, but simply because they cannot be done. The tension between Christian truth and epic representation proves too great. His Vergilian paradigm and overgoing ambition deform his Christian subjects so crucially in certain respects that later in the poem he resings them correctively.

FOUR

Raphael, Michael, and the Bard

Miltonists have often compared the conclusions of both halves of *Paradise Lost.* The differences between Raphael and Michael as narrators have often been found to balance and complete one another in Milton's design for the poem.[1] In this understanding, the Son's victory over Satan in Heaven in Book VI proves the type of his victory on earth in Book XII. This typological parallel confirms the consistency of Milton's authorial intentions.[2] Michael's narrative is held to balance and support Raphael's in Milton's plan for *Paradise Lost* as a whole.

The present argument relies on this body of critical perceptions but organizes them in a different way. It acknowledges the parallel differences between the discourses of Raphael and Michael as part of

1. The fullest treatment of Raphael and Michael in the poem is by Swaim, *Before and After the Fall.* See ix–xii, 1–25, and the notes on 239–45 for a summary of her views and for bibliography on the issue. See also Riggs, *Christian Poet in "Paradise Lost,"* 102–42.

2. See, among others, William Madsen, *From Shadowy Types to Truth: Studies in Milton's Symbolism* (New Haven, 1968), 85–113; Jon S. Lawry, *The Shadow of Heaven: Matter and Stance in Milton's Poetry* (Ithaca, 1968), 199–202; Austin C. Dobbins, *Milton and the Book of Revelation* (University, Ala., 1975), 26–27; William B. Hunter, Jr., "Milton on the Exaltation of the Son: The War in Heaven in *Paradise Lost,*" *English Literary History,* XXXVI (1969), 215–31; and John Knott, *Milton's Pastoral Vision* (Chicago, 1971), 71–74.

Milton's design for the whole poem, but it views that design as a movement, as the Bard's progress from Raphael to Michael. In my view, Michael's discourse does not merely balance Raphael's but counters it, completing and correcting it. Within *Paradise Lost,* we have two versions of Christian epic. Raphael's version presents a Christian subject through classical paradigms of narrative, whereas Michael's is a biblical epic, which alludes to classical epic only to criticize it. Michael's proves the ultimate version of Christian epic within the poem, the last and therefore final version but also the definitive one because it corrects the excesses of Raphael's. To be sure, Raphael's war in Heaven is not wholly vitiated by its classical paradigms, but the Bard is troubled enough by certain of its aspects to resing them correctively in Michael's biblical epic.

In short, the movement of *Paradise Lost* from Raphael's epic to Michael's represents the Bard's growth as a Christian poet because it reveals his changed sense of his vocation to Christian epic. As in Book III, the Bard's theological representations in Book VI are deformed, not by lack of piety or lack of poetic skill, but by his epic ambition. In Books XI and XII, he corrects these misrepresentations through a fuller submission to Scripture for the subjects of his poem as well as for its narrative sequence, its paradigms, and its humbler, didactic style. The parallel differences between Raphael's and Michael's epics evince Milton's design for the Bard's story in *Paradise Lost.*

The present chapter unfolds this argument in three sections. The first treats the theological misrepresentations entailed in the Bard's classical paradigms in Book VI and their avoidance or corrective resinging in Books XI and XII. The second examines the two versions of epic as didactic narratives with two audiences, one inside the poem and another outside it. Both sections argue that Raphael's war in Heaven falters as a didactic Christian poem because the Bard uses classical paradigms for his narrative in order to overgo his epic predecessors. Similarly, both argue that Michael's discourse succeeds because it takes Scripture as its paradigm. The history of critical debate on these parts of the poem supplies most of the material for my argument. Although telling the Bard's story in *Paradise Lost* often compels me to take a particular side, distinguishing Milton from his Bard sheds new light on these debates. The final section of the chapter also draws on familiar materials, as it points to the Bard's self-critical gestures within Books VII through XII—gestures that illuminate his progress from Raphael's version of epic to Michael's.

Critics of the war in Heaven have long understood that its incongruities emerge from the poet's use of classical epic to sing of a war between spirits. Samuel Johnson found the whole narration pervaded with "the confusion of spirit and matter," filling it "with incongruity." Thomas Newton found so many allusions to Homer and so many instances of the Homeric manner as to frustrate detailed commentary, and he thought Milton led to "excess, in great measure, by his love and admiration of Homer."[3] Modern critics of the war have developed these insights in detail.[4] All of them understand the war to be Milton's in propria persona, so they find its incongruities to be his culpable inadvertencies or failures of judgment. On the other side, a modern group of critic-defenders has also emerged. Arnold Stein finds the incongruities so conspicuous as to be Milton's deliberate acts in a poetry, not heroic, but mock-heroic, and William Riggs concurs, modifying the genre to mock*ed* heroic.[5] All of these, critics and critic-defenders alike, find the appearances of Book VI often awkward, incongruous, even laughable.

Yet the war in Heaven has its defenders *tout court*. They are defending Milton's honor as a Christian poet by justifying the representations in Book VI. To be sure, they feel the problem of its appearances, too, but they tend to justify these by pointing to a deeper or further meaning. Although some, such as Stella Revard and Leland Ryken, point to poetic traditions that seem to validate the representations in and of themselves, sooner or later all of them resort to

3. Samuel Johnson, "Life of Milton," *Selected Poetry and Prose,* 439–40; Newton's observations may be found in Riggs, *Christian Poet in "Paradise Lost,"* 126 (which cites Newton's note to VI, 239), and 116 (which cites his note to VI, 568, from which the quotation is taken). Riggs is using the 1749 edition of *"Paradise Lost": A Poem in Twelve Books,* ed. Thomas Newton (London, 1749).

4. See especially Waldock, *"Paradise Lost" and Its Critics,* 106–18, and Peter, *Critique of "Paradise Lost,"* 77–79. See also Wayne Shumaker, *Unpremeditated Verse: Feeling and Perception in "Paradise Lost"* (Princeton, 1967), 119–29.

5. Stein, *Answerable Style,* 17–37, and Riggs, *Christian Poet in "Paradise Lost,"* 117–21. James G. Mengert makes an argument similar to Riggs's in "Styling the Strife of Glory: The War in Heaven," *Milton Studies,* XIV (1980), 95–115.

hermeneutic traditions on accommodation, allegory, and typology to elucidate the meanings of Book VI.[6]

In short, both critics and defenders consider Book VI to be Milton's in propria persona, and both find the appearances of the war in Heaven in some sense inappropriate. To be sure, the poet himself features the problem of appearance and reality when Raphael speaks on the difficulty of accommodation (V, 563–76). Milton's defenders simply find the accommodation adequate, while his critics and critic-defenders do not. Significantly, no problem of accommodation arises in Michael's discourse. When we distinguish Milton from his Bard, we find the Bard progressing from a highly problematic mode of Christian epic in Book VI to one significantly less so in Books XI and XII. Milton designed the conspicuous incongruities in Book VI to reveal the ambitious Bard's difficulties in using classical paradigms for a Christian song.

In general, then, critics of the war prove the best guides to the Bard's actual achievement in Book VI, for they treat the appearances of the poetry and so explore his faltering attempt to be a Christian poet. The defenders of the war prove the best guides to the Bard's aims and hopes in the narrative because they dwell on the realities to which his appearances would point. Furthermore, their treatment of typology, of figure and fulfillment within the poem, reveals how the Bard rescues what he can from Book VI even as he resings it correctively in Books XI and XII. Finally, when the war is considered as an isolated narrative, the critic-defenders offer the soundest treatment of Milton's relation to it. Yet they are mistaken in thinking the Bard is attempting comedy or mock-epic: he is everywhere trying to overgo all

6. Stella Purce Revard treats the Renaissance poetic tradition on the war in Heaven in *The War in Heaven: "Paradise Lost" and the Tradition of Satan's Rebellion* (Ithaca, 1980); Leland Ryken emphasizes Milton's use of the Book of Revelation in *The Apocalyptic Vision in "Paradise Lost"* (Ithaca, 1970). Allegorical interpretations of Book VI include Helen Gardner, *A Reading of "Paradise Lost"* (Oxford, 1965), 67–68, who finds the war an allegory on tragic human history; Fish, *Surprised by Sin,* 176–208, who interprets it as a parable of Christian heroism; and Madsen, *From Shadowy Types to Truth,* 83–113, who finds it a parable of Christian patience. See also Jason P. Rosenblatt, "Structural Unity and Temporal Concordance: The War in Heaven in *Paradise Lost,*" *PMLA,* LXXXVII (1972), 31–41, for the allegory implied in Exodus allusions, and Walter R. Davis, "The Languages of Accommodation and the Styles of *Paradise Lost,*" *Milton Studies,* XVIII (1983), 103–28, esp. 109–24, for a typological interpretation.

previous martial epics with his war in Heaven. That is why we do not laugh at his incongruities, which emerge from his attempt to accomplish what cannot be accomplished.

When Revard treats the Renaissance tradition of poetry on the angelic rebellion, she reveals the Bard's overgoing program in Book VI. Previous poets feature a single day of fighting, climaxed by the rebels' defeat after a duel between Michael and Satan. The Bard plans to overgo this with three days of battle, placing the duel between Michael and Satan at the climax of an inconclusive first day.[7] After this day of Homeric combat, the second day features modern warfare in the rebels' cannon, followed by the hurling of hills in Heaven. In this way, the Bard intends to overgo Ludovico Ariosto's cannon and the *gigantomachia* of Hesiod and of Claudian. These two inconclusive days of battle set the stage for the victory of Messiah, who single-handedly vanquishes the entire rebel host.

The Bard's understanding of poetic superiority in this program is implied in the technique of overgoing. The superior poet imagines more greatly, more powerfully. Because the Bard's characters have powers superior to those of any mortal or giant, he can overgo Homeric and Hesiodic warfare by imagining his characters in Homeric and Hesiodic battles. The Bard intends to overgo the great ancient poets of martial epic while he overgoes the cannon and the angelic rebellions of his Renaissance predecessors. He justifies this overgoing program, theologically, by its climax in the Son's glorious victory. His plan is fully epic, and its telos, fully Christian. The Bard's poetic triumph over his predecessors is intended, ultimately, to exalt the Son's glory. His whole design purports to enact the full resolution of classical epic and Christian truth.

The Bard's plan seems both good and sound, but it contains tensions that cannot be fully resolved, not even by a poet of his skill. Its first victim, theologically, is God. As John Peter observes, God "hoodwinks" the loyal angels.[8] The Bard portrays God this way, not because he believes in a deceiving God, but because the success of his narrative plan compels him to do so. Uniquely in the tradition, Milton's war in

7. Revard, *War in Heaven*, 182–90.

8. Peter, *Critique of "Paradise Lost,"* 77–79. For a positive treatment of God in Book VI, see Kitty Cohen, "Milton's God in Council and War," *Milton Studies,* III (1971), 159–84, in addition to the works cited earlier.

Heaven denies victory to the loyal angels. The reader familiar with this tradition expects the loyal angels to win, and they are sent into battle confident of victory. God calls them "Invincible" (VI, 47) and commands them to drive the rebels out of Heaven. Raphael calls them "irresistible" (63) and "the Victor Host" (590), and both Abdiel (114–26) and Michael (256–60) seem confident of early victory. On the one hand, the loyal angels enjoy the advantages of faithfulness. They are "unobnoxious to be pain'd" when wounded (404), and Michael, at least, has a special sword (320–23). The rebels, on the other hand, do suffer pain. Although they are routed by the loyal angels on the first day, yet they are not defeated by them. And though the loyal angels enjoy a singular advantage the second day in the hill-hurling, because the rebels, "now gross by sinning grown" (661), suffer both pain and constriction as the good angels seem not to, the battle ends unresolved. Or rather, the Bard conspicuously closes it off, cutting it short with the end of the day, because the advantages enjoyed by the good angels must not result in victory or his narrative plan fails.

There is, then, this tension between the Bard's theology and his narrative. The faithful angels must enjoy the advantages of faithfulness or the Bard's moral theology fails. The advantages cannot prove decisive, however, or his narrative plan fails. The good angels must thus prove better than the rebels, but not that much better.

At the same time, the Bard must also preserve God's omnipotence while involving us in the first two days of battle. He does this by having God tell the Son, at the beginning of the third day, that he has allowed the loyal angels to fight entirely on their own, without any help from him (689–92). God has thereby suspended the doom of the rebels so that his might can be fully revealed to them in the Son's victory. He originally sent the angels into battle, commanding them to assault the enemy fearlessly and so "drive them out from God and bliss, / Into thir place of punishment" (52–53), and the reader joins their expectation that they will succeed. After all, since they are fighting on God's side, they expect him to be fighting on theirs, and they and we look forward to the victory to which God urges them. But God is not fighting on their side. He commands them to expel the rebels from Heaven, knowing all the while that he has arranged matters to prevent it.

This is why Peter finds that God hoodwinks the loyal angels, a piece of bad theology, yet one necessitated by the Bard's overgoing program. Victory is reserved for Messiah on the third day. Hence, the loyal angels must battle for two days inconclusively, yet they and we must look forward to their victory or the narrative fails dramatically. At the same time, the Bard must preserve our sense of God's power. Hence, God must not lend his force to the loyal angels but only to Messiah on the third day, when it proves overwhelming. Narrative necessity affects theological portrayal. The Bard's overgoing program for three days of fighting necessitates God's misleading the loyal angels.

Peter's interpretation has hardly found favor with Miltonists, who defend "Milton"'s piety by arguing that God intends the angels to learn a lesson in Christian patience.[9] Revard elaborates this view, insisting that God "dispatches his saints to learn a humbling lesson." They will not win glory or renown or conventional honors, and "it is highly significant that Milton's God promises them none of these." She argues that "the loyal angels must learn how vain is their trust in material arms and the glory of material warfare."[10]

This view cannot be defended. The loyal angels do not trust in material arms and glory. That is the rebels' view, and their view alone. The loyal angels trust in God, for that is precisely what makes them loyal, and they do, or attempt to do, precisely what he commands of them. They do not seek glory or renown or honors: they only obey. They do not know that God has arranged matters to frustrate them. It is not at all clear that the loyal angels need a lesson in patience. Neither God nor the Son ever reinforces such a lesson by his words, though the Son does praise their faithfulness (803–806), which has never been in doubt. Clearly, Miltonists want the loyal angels to need a lesson in patience, for they wish to save the appearances of God's misleading them. But this inference, intended to honor Milton's piety, does not answer to the representations in the poetry.

In sum, the tensions in the Bard's overgoing program can be resolved only at the cost of God's sincerity with the loyal angels. If God

9. See Dick Taylor, Jr., "The Battle in Heaven in *Paradise Lost*," *Tulane Studies in English,* III (1952), 69–92; Summers, *Muse's Method,* 126–36; Fish, *Surprised by Sin,* 190–96; Madsen, *From Shadowy Types to Truth,* 83–113; and Lewalski, *"Paradise Lost" and the Rhetoric of Literary Forms,* 145–46.

10. Revard, *War in Heaven,* 170, 190.

does not mislead them and us, the three-day narrative fails. The Bard could have preserved God's sincerity by continuing the tradition of one day of battle. He could even have made an innovation by giving the Son a leading role in the angels' victory, though it would hardly prove as exalted as that in Book VI. Either of these, however, would have cost him part of his overgoing program. In the tension between Christianity and epic, between theological truth and poetic superiority, the Bard favors his own epic superiority.

His plan to exalt the Son justifies this effort, yet precisely here comes his most disturbing theological misrepresentation, the one he later works most carefully to correct. It occurs where his Christian epic, in Books I through VI, achieves its highest point, where Christian truth and the epic genre seem fully resolved in the Son's glorious victory over evil. To be sure, this argument labors directly against the main currents of Milton studies, for even critics of Book VI have praised the poet's achievement in the third day of battle. Although Wayne Shumaker, for instance, devotes several pages to incongruities in the war, he finds the poet transformed when narrating the third day, when the earlier "failures of vision are overwhelmed by authentic elevation and a breathtaking rush." One can hardly disagree with him, for the Son's victory is told with a sustained magnificence that "makes us helpless by its brilliance and energy."[11] This very success, however, proves its greatest danger, as the Bard subsequently sees. For in presenting Christ as hero so magnificently, he utterly misrepresents Christian heroism.

Evidently, Messiah's epic victory does not enact "the better fortitude / Of Patience and Heroic Martyrdom" (IX, 31–32). Hence, when Miltonists interpret it, they turn away from its epic appearances to the theological realities it symbolizes. The dissonance between Messiah's epic acts and the Christian virtues celebrated elsewhere in the poem requires his victory to be treated as a parable or allegory. Only in this way can scholars make sense of "Milton"'s achievement in Book VI, and this method is confirmed by the conclusion of the poem. Clearly, Messiah's victory in Book VI proves the type that is fulfilled in Christ's Resurrection and Second Coming, sung in Book XII (450–65, 539–51). With these well-established interpretations, one can only agree.

11. Shumaker, *Unpremeditated Verse,* 129, 130. He treats the third day of battle on 129–32.

These interpretations explore Milton's meaning in the whole poem viewed as a static entity, whereas I am treating the story of his Bard. Hence, the typological interpretation of Messiah's victory is not merely implied by the end of the poem but created by the way the Bard ends the poem. It is not an interpretation merely offered by the work but one created by the poet. Without the Bard's singing of Christ's Resurrection and Second Coming in Book XII, there would be no typological fulfillment within *Paradise Lost* for Messiah's victory in Book VI. That fulfillment is created by the Bard's act.

Moreover, the Bard fulfills Messiah's victory even as he resings and corrects it, and he marks this correction rather carefully. After Michael reveals Messiah's birth from a Virgin Mother (XII, 358–71), Adam finally understands "Why our great expectation should be call'd / The seed of Woman" (378–79), and he looks forward eagerly to Messiah's revenge on the Serpent: "say where and when / Thir fight, what stroke shall bruise the Victor's heel" (384–85). Adam remembers the climax of Raphael's war in Heaven, and he expects Messiah's future victory over Satan to occur in much the same way. Michael corrects this misapprehension carefully and at some length, and the correction proves all the more pointed coming from the greatest angelic warrior:

> *Dream not of thir fight,*
> *As of a Duel, or the local wounds*
> *Of head or heel: not therefore joins the Son*
> *Manhood to Godhead, with more strength to foil*
> *Thy enemy;* nor so is overcome
> *Satan,* whose fall from Heav'n, a deadlier bruise,
> Disabl'd not to give thee thy death's wound:
> Which *hee, who comes thy Saviour, shall recure,*
> *Not by destroying Satan, but his works*
> *In thee and in thy Seed:* nor can this be,
> But by fulfilling that which thou didst want,
> Obedience to the Law of God, impos'd
> On penalty of death, and suffering death,
> The penalty to thy transgression due,
> And due to theirs which out of thine shall grow:
> So only can high Justice rest appaid.
> (XII, 386–401;
> emphasis added except to "Satan")

Then follows Michael's treatment of the Redemption, quoted in the previous chapter. It dwells on Messiah's loving obedience to God and his humiliation in a "reproachful life and cursed death" (406). Even after Michael moves from the Crucifixion to the Resurrection (415–23), he returns to Messiah's death to emphasize that *here* is the victory:

> *His death for Man,* as many as offer'd Life
> Neglect not, and the benefit embrace
> By Faith not void of works: *this God-like act*
> *Annuls thy doom,* the death thou shouldst have di'd,
> In sin for ever lost from life; *this act*
> *Shall bruise the head of Satan, crush his strength*
> *Defeating Sin and Death, his two main arms.*
> (XII, 425–31; emphasis added except to "Satan")

Christ's victory over Satan comes, not by an act of epic self-assertion, as in Book VI, but by humble obedience unto death. Christ proves victor by his willingness to be victim.

The Bard's corrective resinging of Messiah's victory does not necessarily undermine it as an accommodated vision of the war in Heaven, only as a representation of the Redemption and of Christian heroism. If we wish, or if we judge it right, we are free to consider Book VI as the Bard's heavenly vision of what really occurred in that warfare before the creation. Or we may follow those critics who find its incongruities a failed or faltering vision. Or we may find some of both in Book VI, as does Shumaker. But the Bard does reveal unambiguously in Book XII that Messiah's appearances in Book VI need correcting, for he wants to avoid the kind of misunderstanding evinced in Adam's eager appeal to Michael. *Messiah's victory over Satan occurs in the Redemption, in his death on the cross.* His victory in Book VI reveals not the Redemption but, as scholars have seen, its aftermath in the Resurrection and Second Coming, which Michael also sings. In Book XII, then, the Bard not only fulfills Messiah's victory in Book VI typologically, but he also corrects any misunderstanding that might have arisen from its appearances.

This corrective resinging discloses that the tension between Christianity and epic remains unsuccessfully resolved even in Messiah's victory. Ironically, the Bard's very success in singing it makes it dangerous theologically, for, as Shumaker observes, it "makes us helpless by its brilliance and energy."[12] Its poetic power sweeps us away, and, we are meant to understand, the oral Bard is also swept aloft as he composes "Above the flight of *Pegasean* wing" (VII, 4). The power of the poetry might compel one to see, in its depiction of Christ as hero, a valid form of Christian heroism and a valid representation of the Redemption. However, the Bard later comes to see that it quite misrepresents "the better fortitude / Of Patience and Heroic Martyrdom," and he then sings the Redemption explicitly so as to distinguish it from Messiah's epic heroism in Book VI. Epic heroism and Christian heroism prove antithetical: self-assertion in battle is the opposite of Christ's humble obedience unto death. The Bard's epic aspiration in Book VI leads him to misrepresent the truth of Christ.

We must understand that the Bard *has chosen* to tell the fall of the angels as an epic, for he might have done otherwise. There were several versions of that fall in Christian tradition.[13] The unfolding of *Paradise Lost* simply requires Raphael to tell the story in a way didactically appropriate to Adam and Eve. One such way is offered by Dante's version. At their creation, all the angels are given the choice of turning obediently to God and acknowledging that their goodness comes from him or refusing. In their pride, Satan and the rebels refuse, and they fall immediately, while the others are raised to everlasting bliss.[14] This version emphasizes the lesson Raphael purports to teach: happiness comes from adhering to God in obedience, and disobedience brings misery swift and sure (V, 520–43). Didactically appropriate though the lesson may be, the Bard rejects it, for he does not want to teach a moral lesson so much as he wants to overgo his epic predecessors. Instructing Adam and Eve in obedience matters less, at this point in his singing, than his epic ambition.

Having chosen the epic genre, the Bard could have kept Christ out of the battle, as did his Renaissance predecessors. For the genre dictates that superior force equals superiority; the rebels lose because they prove physically weaker than their opponents. Traditionally, the faithfulness of the loyal angels gives them decisive advantages: their

12. *Ibid.,* 130.

13. For a brief summary of these, see Peter, *Critique of "Paradise Lost,"* 63–65, and Revard, *War in Heaven,* 28–47, 67–78.

14. See Dante, *Par.* XXIX, 49–66.

physical superiority emerges from their moral superiority. But classical paradigms of narrative entail classical conceptions of virtue. Hence, what the loyal angels gain by Christian faithfulness must be manifested in epic fortitude and prowess in battle, not in humility and suffering. Moreover, once Christ enters the battle, he must display epic virtues or suffer epic defeat. (That the poet might have Christ slay the wicked with the breath of his lips [*cf.* Isaiah 11:4;2 Thessalonians 2:8] hardly bears consideration.) The Bard, however, does not keep Christ out of the battle, because his overgoing program must climax with Messiah's victory on the third day. Hence, Christ must appear as an epic, not as a properly Christian, hero.

A reason for this is given by the Son: he must prove his superior force against the rebels "since by strength / They measure all, of other excellence / Not emulous, nor care who them excels" (VI, 820–23). Within the Bard's fiction, this reason is true, but since the Bard has chosen the epic genre and chosen to feature the Son as a martial hero, these lines reflect ominously on him. For the Bard is measuring his poetic excellence by poetic "strength," by his ability to overgo his epic predecessors. He has conceived his overgoing program, not simply to exalt the Son, but to exalt himself. The Son's epic prowess in warfare displays the Bard's epic prowess in poetry. In his singing of the Son's victory, the Bard adopts Harold Bloom's poetics of strength and accepts Satan's measure of superiority. He has chosen the epic genre because by strength he is measuring his own excellence. To be sure, he proves a superbly strong poet. In the event, however, he necessarily misrepresents his Redeemer.

It is hard to say when he begins to recognize this, but he clearly understands by the fourth proem, where he distinguishes, for the first time, the Christian subject he receives from the style in which he sings it and declares himself the poet of "the better fortitude." He corrects the misrepresentation at some length in Michael's discourse. Only after Adam's final words in the poem is the Bard content that he has sung truly of his Redeemer:

> Henceforth I learn, that to obey is best,
> And love with fear the only God, to walk
> As in his presence, ever to observe
> His providence, and on him sole depend,
> Merciful over all his works, with good

Still overcoming evil, and by small
Accomplishing great things, by things deem'd weak
Subverting worldly strong, and worldly wise
By simply meek; that suffering for Truth's sake
Is fortitude to highest victory,
And to the faithful Death the Gate of Life;
Taught this by his example whom I now
Acknowledge my Redeemer ever blest.
(XII, 561–73; emphasis added)

These final words of Adam declare his correct understanding of the true Christian heroism of Messiah, and they mark the Bard's recognition that he has conveyed his corrective resinging of Messiah's victory in Book VI adequately to his audience. It occupies, all told, over a hundred lines.

Although the Bard explicitly corrects his misrepresentation of Christ, he changes his portrayal of God only by implication, in the way already treated in the previous chapter. In Raphael's war, God is an agent in the action, speaking at length, sending the loyal angels and then the Son into battle. He thus often appears like an Olympian deity, as active in Raphael's war as Zeus in Homer's. In Michael's discourse, however, God transcends the action because he does not appear directly in it. He thereby seems more Christian because he is less classical a deity. In Book VI, God's Providence and the Bard's invention prove indistinguishable. God must mislead the loyal angels in order to effect the Bard's overgoing program for a three-day narrative. In Books XI and XII, the Bard labors, not as a poetic inventor, but as a biblical exegete, selecting from Scripture the points he will treat in Michael's epic. God's Providence thereby emerges from the story as a whole and bears the authority of its source in Scripture. The classical paradigm in Raphael's war deforms its representations of God and the Son; the biblical paradigm in Michael's discourse enables the Bard to resing Book VI correctively.

Both Raphael's epic and Michael's present themselves as didactic narratives, and both have two audiences: Adam and Eve within the fiction, and ourselves outside it. I shall argue that Raphael's war proves inappropriate for both audiences and therefore falters didactically; Michael's discourse, in contrast, succeeds because it proves didactically appropriate. To be sure, Raphael's narrative must fail to confirm Adam and Eve in obedience because the story requires them to fall. But the fact of success or failure may be distinguished from the methods employed, and these occupy the center of my treatment. Raphael's war falters didactically because it uses classical paradigms for a Christian subject, and these create inevitable dissonance between its epic appearances and its Christian truths. Michael's discourse succeeds precisely because it avoids this difficulty, using a biblical paradigm for biblical teaching throughout.

Raphael's narrative proves didactically inappropriate in several ways. Most obvious, it is unsuited to its audience within the poem. Adam and Eve, of course, have no experience of warfare; they have not even seen animals fighting and will not until after the Fall. Much of Raphael's epic must be all but meaningless to them, ignorant as they are of even the paraphernalia of warfare. Although it might be called a gesture of accommodation when Raphael likens the angels on a flying-march to all the "Birds in orderly array on wing" (VI, 74) when they came to receive their names from Adam, it will not help him understand a battle formation. The gap between unfallen and fallen experience cannot be bridged by a martial epic as a moral tale for characters who do not know what death is (IV, 425).

Miltonists have defended "Milton"'s artistic integrity on this obvious point in two ways. First, they have appealed to traditions on Adam's unfallen capacity for knowledge, evident in *Paradise Lost* in the intelligence and poise of Adam and Eve. Second, they have pointed to the fact that Raphael is sent to them precisely to extend their experience (V, 224–45), and his discourse proves part of the process whereby Adam and Eve grow toward greater perfection. Moreover, Raphael makes various efforts to accommodate his epic to them, and he features this very problem at the beginning to warn them of certain difficulties in interpreting his narrative. Adam and Eve, it is argued, are able students, and Raphael does what he can to accommodate the war in Heaven to their understanding.[15]

These observations are true, but are they adequate? Miltonists defending the war as properly "Milton"'s must find them so. In my view,

15. See Lewalski, *"Paradise Lost" and the Rhetoric of Literary Forms,* 39–50, 205–19, and notes.

these passages represent the Bard's attempt to bridge unbridgeable gaps in Raphael's narration, between unfallen and fallen experience and between the appearances of classical epic and underlying Christian truths. Raphael's narrative contains too many incongruities in itself, and between itself and its fictional audience, to be smoothed over by what Miltonists have said in defense of the war, true as their observations are.

For not only does Raphael present a plethora of novelties to Adam and Eve, but he also treats them as though they were ancient Greeks or Romans, able to understand epic warfare but as astounded at the cannon as were the loyal angels. His references to the implements of war on the first day of battle are given without explanation, though they stand outside of Adam's experience and come thick and fast in the telling. One would think that among the heavenly host in its pre-rebellion harmonies no armor or weapons need have existed. Yet Raphael treats the implements of war as though they had always been part of angelic life, and he narrates the first day of battle as though Adam and Eve could have little trouble understanding it. Then he presents the cannon as an object both strange and horrible, as a "dev'lish machination" (VI, 504) utterly unheard of before. He thereby treats his innocent listeners as though epic warfare were readily familiar to them but modern warfare were not. This pretense is absurd.

Such inconsistencies are part of the incongruity that Samuel Johnson criticized and that Miltonists have labored to defend. Revard mounts the most learned defense in her treatment of the Renaissance poems on the angelic rebellion. She answers Johnson's criticism of spirits bearing material arms by pointing to the tradition. "Had Dr. Johnson read any of the celestial epics of the sixteenth and seventeenth centuries, he would hardly have been surprised at the ease with which Milton's angels adopt material arms."[16] Revard assumes that this tradition provides sufficient warrant for angelic weaponry in Book VI. Hence, that spirits bear material arms may be incongruous, but the incongruity does not signify. Perhaps "Milton" did not notice it as such; perhaps the tradition rendered it nugatory. Whatever the explanation, Johnson's criticism of incongruity in the poem cannot be adequately answered by a tradition filled with such incongruities. He

16. Revard, *War in Heaven,* 175. See Samuel Johnson, "Life of Milton," *Selected Poetry and Prose,* 439.

has indicated a fault in the poetry, and his point cannot be deflected by appealing to a faulty tradition.

In fact, Revard's careful scholarship reveals the limitations of her argument, for Book VI rather features its incongruities. The Renaissance epics she examines contain angelic armor, weaponry, and warfare, but not one represents horses and chariots in Heaven, as does Book VI (388–91). Flying angels do not need them, yet they appear in Raphael's narrative because they appear in Homer. Moreover, Revard does not find in the tradition such a minute attention to the physiology of the rebel angels as Book VI reveals on two occasions (327–53, 655–61). Only Erasmo di Valvasone shows the rebel angels writhing in pain, though others explain that sin weakens their resolve in battle. Milton's Bard alone presents detailed explanations of angelic physiology.[17] This display of incongruous novelties needs to be explained, but it is hard to do so and defend "Milton"'s decorum.

In my view, these incongruities belong to the Bard's attempt to overgo his epic predecessors. Homer has horses and chariots, so the Bard includes them. He treats angelic physiology because he feels compelled to explain why the rebels suffer pain and constriction. Furthermore, his overgoing ambition aims to out-imagine the ancients. Hence, where Homer's immortals have ichor in their veins, the Bard's angels must have something similar but of superior power. So, where Paieon heals Ares, wounded by Diomedes' spear, at the end of Book V of the *Iliad,* the rebel angels enjoy the power to heal themselves. These overgoing novelties are rarely happy, and they have been singled out by Milton's critics. But they are not Milton's in propria persona. They emerge from his Bard's attempt to surpass Homer.

So, too, does the incongruity between Raphael's narrative and his fictional audience. The Bard has set himself to overgo the *Iliad,* so he must deploy a Homeric paradigm of battle-narrative. Hence, he must pretend that Adam and Eve are familiar with ancient warfare, because to explain its details would spoil his narration. The manifest incongruity between their unfallen experience and the Bard's epic warfare he must largely ignore if he is to overgo Homer's battle scenes, and he does. There are other traditions on the angelic fall more didactically appropriate to Adam and Eve, but since they have little epic potential, the

17. Revard, *War in Heaven,* 183.

Bard chooses not to use them. He resolves the tension between didactic decorum in his fiction and his own epic superiority in favor of the latter.

These incongruities prove but the symptoms of a deeper dissonance affecting even fallen readers. When God commissions Raphael, he asserts that Adam will never fall "By violence, no, for that shall be withstood, / But by deceit and lies," and he commands the angel, "this let him know" (V, 242–43). The fallen, too, are led into sin by the deceits of temptation, not by violence, so Raphael's mission to Adam and Eve ought to instruct us, as well as them. In this regard, his story of Abdiel succeeds admirably. As Miltonists have often observed, Abdiel proves a fit model of heroism for Adam and Eve and for us.[18] His solitary defiance, maintaining "Against revolted multitudes the Cause / Of Truth" (VI, 31–32), is approved as "The better fight" (VI, 30). Moreover, Abdiel's way of treating temptation is exemplary. He does not fence with Satan, as Eve does in Book IX, but defies him forthrightly and simply refuses to be taken in. He "stands" by holding firmly to the truth he knows.

The didactic appropriateness of the Abdiel story, however, simply highlights the inappropriateness of the war in Heaven. Although Satan will not overcome Adam by violence, Book VI presents him as formidable because of his tremendous physical force. His single combat with Michael, we are told, bids fair to dwarf the dissolution of the cosmic order (VI, 296–315). The epic paradigm for battle-narrative, of course, puts a premium on physical force. Having chosen the epic genre to tell the fall of the angels, the Bard must portray Satan as physically powerful, not as a deceiver. While Book V shows us something of Satan's wiles in seducing his followers, Book VI abandons the theme entirely. The bulk of Raphael's epic portrays Satan in a way didactically inappropriate for Adam and Eve and for us. Here, the Bard aims less to edify his audiences than to overgo his epic predecessors.

This didactic failure emerges from the dissonance between the Bard's epic genre and the Christian moral he purports to convey. His model is the tradition of interpreting classical literature allegorically. Beginning in the twelfth century, Christians sought to justify their reading of the *Metamorphoses* by finding moral lessons in its stories.

18. See, among many instances, Lewalski, *"Paradise Lost" and the Rhetoric of Literary Forms,* 43–44, 158–60.

These were set forth briefly, often in poetry, so a long and complex Ovidian tale was thus reduced to a maxim. That *sententia* was sometimes closely related to the story as we understand it: the Narcissus tale, for example, proves an exemplum against "pride," or self-love. Sometimes, however, the moral seems less closely connected to the tale as we read it. Actaeon's being devoured by his hounds was taken to warn against keeping large hunting establishments, which devour one's patrimony. This tradition enjoyed a long life. It can be seen in Arthur Golding's dedicatory epistle to his 1567 translation of the *Metamorphoses,* from which these interpretations are taken. The simple Christian moral for Raphael's Homeric epic imitates this tradition.[19]

The Bard knows this tradition, and he imitates it consciously. Once he chooses epic paradigms to convey Christian truth, he must imitate it. A complex pagan tale can be assimilated to Christianity only if it is understood to convey a moral that ignores much of the narrative. Pagan literature did not adapt itself easily to the *sententiae* Christianity demanded. Similarly, Raphael's epic contains many representations that we must ignore when we find Christian meanings in the story. We are not meant to find a moral application in the fact that bad angels tell bad puns when they think they have the upper hand or that Satan is big and strong but Messiah is stronger. Miltonists have long recognized this in their allegories on Book VI.

The war in Heaven thus possesses an unruly surplus of meanings. Miltonists have not drawn on this surplus because, seeking for Milton's meanings, they act as Christian readers. They know what meanings are permissible, and they find only those that Christian tradition and *Paradise Lost* as a whole authorize. None has ever suggested that bad angels whine when defeated, though the narrative, by itself, warrants this as true. But its bad taste makes it silly. In short, Miltonists have moralized Book VI in precisely the way that Christian readers moralized Ovid and other pagan writers. When a fully elaborated classical genre is said to have Christian meanings, they cannot do otherwise. They must ignore many of its representations because the classical paradigms generate an unruly surplus of meanings for a Christian interpreter.

19. See Arthur Golding, *Shakespeare's Ovid: Being Arthur Golding's Translation of the "Metamorphoses,"* ed. W. H. D. Rouse (1567; rpr. Carbondale, Ill., 1961), 3.

Michael's discourse, however, works on different principles and so obviates this difficulty.[20] In the first place, his narrative paradigm is biblical, not classical, so he can employ it directly in order to edify the fallen Adam and the fallen reader. The Bard thereby creates a consonance between the biblical appearances of his poetry and the truths to which they point. Moreover, it is not a sustained narrative, like Raphael's, but a coordinated series of instructions in which Michael tests Adam's responses and corrects them. Through commentary, he directs Adam's understanding of what he shows. Although Adam often makes erroneous inferences, the angel is ready to set him right. Most important, Michael's discourse is directly governed by the moral lessons he is teaching. These he declares at the beginning: "True patience, and to temper joy with fear / And pious sorrow, equally inur'd / By moderation either state to bear, / Prosperous or adverse" (XI, 361–64). Michael directs the ensuing visions, discourse, and dialog to inculcate precisely these virtues. His success is evident in Adam's final words in the poem: their substance and tone reveal that he has assimilated his master's lessons very well indeed.[21]

Yet though we, like Adam, are fallen and in need of Michael's teaching, we stand in a different relation to it. What is unknown to Adam is already known by us in Scripture. The Bard's two audiences present him with a formidable artistic problem, yet he handles it

20. For Adam's education by Michael, see F. T. Prince, "On the Last Two Books of *Paradise Lost,*" *Essays and Studies by Members of the English Association,* XI (1958), 36–52; George Williamson, "The Education of Adam," *Modern Philology,* LXI (1963), 96–109; Mary Ann Radzinowicz, "Man as a Probationer of Immortality: *Paradise Lost* XI–XII," in *Approaches to "Paradise Lost": The York Centenary Lectures,* ed. C. A. Patrides (Toronto, 1968), 31–51; and Jason P. Rosenblatt, "Adam's Pisgah Vision: *Paradise Lost,* Books XI and XII," *English Literary History,* XXXIX (1972), 66–86. See also the discussions by Fish, *Surprised by Sin,* 300–11, and Lewalski, *"Paradise Lost" and the Rhetoric of Literary Forms,* 259–66. Fish studies changing opinion on the literary value of Books XI–XII in "Transmuting the Lump," 33–56.

21. The mix of genres in Michael's discourse has often been explored. Studies include Lawrence A. Sasek, "The Drama of *Paradise Lost,* Books XI and XII," in *Studies in English Renaissance Literature,* ed. Waldo F. McNeir (Baton Rouge, 1962), 181–96; Balachandra Rajan, "*Paradise Lost:* The Hill of History," *Huntington Library Quarterly,* XXXI (1967), 43–63; Michael Cavanagh, "A Meeting of Epic and History: Books XI and XII of *Paradise Lost,*" *English Literary History,* XXXVIII (1971), 206–22; and Thomas Amorose, "Milton the Apocalyptic Historian: Competing Genres in *Paradise Lost,* Books XI and XII," *Milton Studies,* XVII (1983), 141–62.

beautifully. The visions in Book XI unfold mysteriously for Adam and for us, though we are able "to solve the mystery" of the vision and so understand more. In Book XII, the frequent prolepses help Adam to understand the prophecy about "the woman's seed," while they enable us to interpret the narrative in its typological richness.[22] If we are well versed in Scripture, we may find absorbing the way the Bard tells the history of salvation, what he says, at what length, and what he excludes. In fewer than eleven hundred lines, he renders a comprehensive account of salvation history while portraying Adam's moral formation. He must abridge certain passages of time, yet he must also render an instructive account for his two audiences. He must achieve a complete treatment that is not overhasty, and he must dilate on certain figures without impeding the flow of the whole. Although he has Scripture to guide him, the artistic problems are daunting. Nonetheless, the Bard manages to speak to two audiences purportedly thousands of years apart.

The war in Heaven, on the contrary, is really meant not for Adam and Eve but for us, and not so much for us as Christians but for us as readers of ancient epic. It lacks the carefully directed moral instruction of Michael's discourse, where each vision and every passage prove telling to both audiences. The war in Heaven proves didactically inappropriate for its two audiences simply because Christian instruction is but one of the Bard's aims and that not central. In this regard, Raphael's epic and Michael's are clearly opposed. The Bard's singing in Book VI proves less didactic because he uses classical paradigms in order to overgo the ancients. His singing in Books XI and XII, however, proves more didactic and more fully Christian because he has rejected classical paradigms and embraced Scripture as his narrative model.

As Miltonists well understand, Michael also sings a story of epic sweep and of spiritual warfare: its subject is "supernal Grace *contending* / With sinfulness of Men (XI, 359–60; emphasis added). Like Raphael, he tells of "great things and full of wonder," for Adam and for us, particularly when he treats the Redemption and the Second Coming. Both epics present spiritual conflict yet in very different

22. For typology in Michael's discourse, see Barbara Kiefer Lewalski, "Structure and the Symbolism of Vision in Michael's Prophecy, *Paradise Lost,* Books XI and XII," *Philological Quarterly,* XLII (1963), 25–35, and William Walker, "Typology and *Paradise Lost,* Books XI and XII," *Milton Studies,* XXV (1989), 245–64.

terms: Raphael's epic projects an ultimate division between good and evil into Heaven before time, whereas Michael's instruction harrows the ground of human moral choice on earth and in time. Miltonists have also long recognized the differences between Raphael's classical and Michael's biblical styles. They have pointed to the absence of epic similes in Michael's narrative and to its relative lack of classical allusions, especially compared to the classical texture of Raphael's war.[23] They have shown how the two stylistic models represent two different traditions of poetics in the Renaissance, one envisioning the poet as an inventor and allegorist, the other proposing "instead a direct recourse to the Bible as repository of truth."[24] William Riggs even argues that "the style of Books XI and XII constitutes Milton's final comment on the poetics of *Paradise Lost*."[25]

Yet though Miltonists understand the Protestant poetics of Books XI and XII and recognize Milton as a great Protestant poet, because they consider the war in Heaven to be "Milton"'s, they have not seen how Michael's epic corrects Raphael's in the Bard's progress through his song. For by the time the Bard sings Books XI and XII, he has a different understanding of his vocation to Christian epic than he did in Book VI.

In sum, though Michael's epic is related to Raphael's in all the ways that Miltonists understand, the relations are principally corrective. The Bard's submission to Scripture for the substance and style of Books XI and XII opposes the epic ambitions of Books V and VI. The lower style of Michael's narrative counters the high style of Raphael's. The artistic and didactic coherence of Michael's epic points up the incongruities and didactic inappropriateness of Raphael's. Michael's portrayal of Messiah both corrects and completes Raphael's, revealing precisely wherein the Savior's victory over Satan lies. Although Raphael's narrative may please more, it teaches less, and its treatment of spiritual warfare is revealed by Michael to be an epic fantasy, neither close nor true to the experience of moral struggle we fallen human beings know. Hence, the Bard's progress in *Paradise Lost* enacts

23. See Riggs, *Christian Poet in "Paradise Lost,"* 137.

24. Barbara Kiefer Lewalski, *Protestant Poetics and the Seventeenth Century Lyric* (Princeton, 1979), 4. Swaim provides a thoughtful discussion of these issues, with extensive bibliography, in *Before and After the Fall*, 159–214.

25. Riggs, *Christian Poet in "Paradise Lost,"* 134.

a Christian paradox: Michael's lower subject and style actually prove higher than Raphael's, for Michael's epic possesses more artistic coherence, moral integrity, and theological truth. In nearly every important way, Michael's biblical epic corrects Raphael's classical epic, and this correction represents the Bard's growth as a Christian poet.

The preceding argument runs counter to the taste of the ages and may therefore be criticized as counterintuitive. Not only does it imply that some of the most Miltonic passages of the poem are not properly Milton's, but it also insists on the superiority of what readers have long considered the flattest parts of *Paradise Lost.* It is natural to enjoy both the Son's triumph in Book VI and his epic self-offering in Book III. To prefer Michael's treatment of the Redemption in Book XII simply because it proves the poet's last word on a crucial issue perhaps seems a grim expedient or even perverse. Complaints against the style of Michael's discourse have been heard for centuries, joined with admiration for the earlier books. Addison praised Milton's "great Pregnancy of Invention, and Strength of Imagination" in Book VI, finding that the poet "rises, if possible, above himself," while he complained that in Books XI and XII "the Author has been so attentive to his Divinity that he has neglected his poetry."[26] His criticism of Michael's discourse has often been echoed, and only in the past three decades have some Miltonists begun to find signal poetic virtues in the speech.[27] Milton has consistently drawn readers by what Johnson called his "gigantic loftiness" and "his peculiar power to astonish," little of which may be found in Books XI and XII.[28]

These points are well taken. Although certain aspects of Books III and VI are sung correctively in Book XII, it must be admitted that the earlier poetry is more enjoyable. In my experience, close study improves Michael's epic while discovering Raphael's to be frequently absurd, yet Book VI retains poetic splendors to which the great and wondrous events in Book XII do not even aspire. Our natural enjoy-

26. Revard quotes the remarks on Book VI in *War in Heaven,* 17, 15. Addison's remark on Books XI and XII may be found in *Spectator,* No. 369, *Works of Addison.*

27. Fish explores this shift in critical opinion in "Transmuting the Lump." Lewis criticized Books XI and XII as "an untransmuted lump of futurity," in *Preface to "Paradise Lost,"* 125. Ricks agrees with Addison and Lewis in *Milton's Grand Style,* 17.

28. Samuel Johnson, "Life of Milton," *Selected Poetry and Prose,* 435.

ment of these splendors and our lack of immediate pleasure in Michael's discourse make my argument counterintuitive.

In my view, Milton anticipated these responses. He deliberately counterposed Raphael's entertainment with Michael's instruction, high spectacle in Heaven with low teaching on Earth. The final books in each half of the poem thereby weigh pleasure and truth-content differently: Raphael offers the pleasures of spectacle veiling a few allegorical truths, whereas Michael offers close and careful instruction that, by its nature, proves low in style and somewhat flat in the reading. The delights of epic in the high, classical style with a few Christian truths are counterposed by many Christian truths set forth, some explicitly and some typologically, in a lower style imitating that of Scripture. Milton weighted the conclusions to both halves of *Paradise Lost* in precisely this way, as Miltonists have long recognized. Readers, over the centuries, have favored the earlier over the later narrative, preferring poetic pleasure to Christian truth. And while some contemporary Miltonists have worked to rehabilitate our taste for Michael's epic, they have insisted on the balance of Milton's total design and so have found Michael's epic merely different from Raphael's, not better.[29]

This was not Milton's view, I have argued, for Michael's epic correctively resings Raphael's in certain crucial ways. Milton designed not simply a balance but a movement: a balance completed by the poet's act of correcting a previous imbalance. Moreover, since the poem enacts a movement and since its climax resolves the poem as a whole, its final corrective gestures are definitive. The Bard's story in *Paradise Lost* enacts his progress from one understanding of Christian epic to another one, different because differently balanced. The climax of Raphael's epic represents the height of his achievement according to his earlier understanding, and the climax of Michael's correctively resings it according to the Bard's final understanding. The self-presentation of the poem as the unfolding of the Bard's oral song underscores as it enables this movement in *Paradise Lost* as a whole. Although this movement might suggest a reevaluation of the late Milton's Christian humanism, it only reasserts what we know he thought: simple Christian truth possesses greater ultimate value than

29. Fish tells the story of this rehabilitation in "Transmuting the Lump."

the most splendid ancient achievements. Michael's discourse merely implies what Jesus asserts in *Paradise Regained* when he repudiates Satan's offer of pagan wisdom. Milton's position on this issue remains constant in his two epics. The illusion of "Milton"'s different positions arises from considering all the earlier parts of *Paradise Lost* as properly Milton's. When the movement of the poem is given its due as the story of the Bard's progress, however, we can see that the late Milton wrote both epics from a single, consistent understanding of the right relation between Christianity and pagan culture.

What Milton gained by designing the Bard's story in *Paradise Lost* will be considered in the next chapter. Here I want simply to acknowledge certain justifiable criticisms of my argument and to locate them in some traditional assumptions about and responses to the poem. Our traditional taste for certain parts of the poem hinders the acceptance of my argument. Yet Milton anticipated this, for he used the Bard's progress from Raphael to Michael in an effort to lead us from one kind of taste to another. As the Bard moves from a relish for high epic splendors to the humble yet steady inculcation of Christian truths, we are meant to follow him so that we, too, come to prefer Michael's epic to Raphael's. To be sure, the reception history of the poem proves that Milton's effort failed. Nevertheless, the Bard moves gradually from Book VI to Book XII, and Miltonists have pointed to the self-critical gestures in Books VII through XI that make his movement intelligible. Since the Bard registers the crucial shift in the fourth proem, I shall begin with these gestures in Books VII and VIII, for they lead to his explicit critique of pagan epic in Book IX.

The first self-limiting gesture comes at the very beginning of Book VII, when the Bard determines to keep the second half of his song "narrower bound / Within the visible Diurnal Sphere" (VII, 21–22). He recognizes a danger in the exalted singing of Book VI, and he explicitly characterizes it as theological presumption. He determines to sing the rest of his poem "Standing on Earth, not rapt above the Pole" so that he will be "More safe" (23–24), for a "mortal voice" dares too dangerously when it sings of Empyreal events at length, even with the Muse's guidance. He does not declare his reasons for believing that he has been presumptuous, and perhaps he does not yet know what they are, but he does declare his determination to limit the bounds of his singing more narrowly. When Adam asks Raphael for the story of creation ("Deign to descend now lower and relate / What may no less perhaps avail us known" [VII, 84–85]), the Bard is echoing his invocation ("Descend from Heav'n, *Urania*" [VII, 1]). The poet has firmly set a downward course, and he will hold it over the second half of his song.

As Riggs shows, the poet's self-limiting gestures reflect his concern with the proper limits of human knowledge.[30] Adam carefully qualifies his request for the story of creation: "if unforbid thou mayst unfold / What wee, not to explore the secrets ask / Of his Eternal Empire, but the more / To magnify his works, the more we know" (94–97). Riggs insists that the crucial issue involves the motives and ends for seeking knowledge and, hence, the manner of its pursuit. Its unchecked pursuit is not a good, for the desire for knowledge in itself proves mere *curiositas,* a vanity. The danger of pursuing "matters hid" lies less in the subjects themselves than in the manner of pursuit, for "apt the Mind or Fancy is to rove / Uncheckt, and of her roving is no end" (VIII, 188–89). Adam asserts the proper end of knowledge: "To magnify [God's] works, the more we know." Or, as Raphael asserts later, God wisely concealed "His secrets," for they are not "to be scann'd by them who ought / Rather admire" (VIII, 74–75). The proper end of knowledge is wonder and worship.

Riggs argues that this vein of remarks in Books VII and VIII reveals the Bard's self-critical reflection on his visionary adventure in Book VI.[31] The Bard has clearly explored—or attempted to explore—the secrets of God's eternal empire (*cf.* VII, 95–96), but his aim was not simply "the more / To magnify his works, the more we know." His overgoing program aimed to exalt not only the Son but himself. Moreover, when we compare Adam's request in Book VII to that in Book V (544–60), we find that his asking for the higher story lacks the qualification marking his request for the lower. This reverses what we would expect. In Book V, Adam asks eagerly for "The full relation" (556) of the angelic rebellion "if thou consent" (555), whereas he modifies his request in Book VII with "if unforbid thou mayst unfold" it. In other words, the Bard marks his story of creation, drawn from Scripture and the hexameral tradition, with Adam's concern that it

30. See Riggs, *Christian Poet in "Paradise Lost,"* 56–62.

31. *Ibid.,* 57–58.

might be forbidden, but his overgoing inventions for the war in Heaven are marked by no such concern. Adam's qualified request in Book VII thereby reveals the Bard's sense that his visionary adventure in Books V and VI may have been, wholly or partly, a forbidden attempt. In Book V, Raphael wonders whether it is perhaps lawful for him to reveal "The secrets of another World" (569), but his hesitation is brief. Books VII and VIII, in contrast, return again and again to the proper limits and ends of human knowledge, a theme well understood by Miltonists.

To be sure, Books VII and VIII reflect on Books V and VI only indirectly. The oral Bard, composing in the present, sustains his performance as well as he can. He never repudiates what he has sung, however much he may qualify or question it. When he feels it necessary to recant, he resings correctively; he modifies yet does not reject. Hence, these exhortations by Raphael indirectly question the inventions of Book VI rather severely yet refuse to undermine them completely:

> . . . such Commission from above
> I have receiv'd, to answer thy desire
> Of knowledge within bounds; beyond abstain
> To ask, *nor let thine own inventions hope*
> *Things not reveal'd, which th' invisible King,*
> *Only Omniscient, hath supprest in Night,*
> To none communicable in Earth or Heaven:
> Anough is left besides to search and know.
> (VII, 118–25; emphasis added)

> *Heav'n is for thee too high*
> *To know what passes there;* be lowly wise:
> Think only what concerns thee and thy being;
> *Dream not of other Worlds, what Creatures there*
> *Live, in what state, condition or degree,*
> Contented that thus far hath been reveal'd
> Not of Earth only but of highest Heav'n.
> (VIII, 172–78; emphasis added)

The dialogue between Raphael and Adam in these books reflects a dialectic within the Bard. He is reconsidering his earlier aspiration to heavenly knowledge, his own motives and ends. How much of true good lies in the "revelations" of Books I through VI? How much did he aspire to glorify God, and how much to magnify himself? How much has he served his Christian audience, and how much his own poetic superiority? When we consider only poetic effect, these pairs need not be strictly opposed. The pious Bard can glorify God and serve his audience while displaying his superiority over all his epic predecessors, and he may have accomplished all these in Book VI at acceptably high levels. Nevertheless, when he scrutinizes his motives, the play of forces in his soul proves paradoxical. He aspired to reveal God's truth to human beings, yet he cannot now be sure whether he was primarily moved by the ambition to reveal, by the Divine truth he would reveal, or by the need of human beings to hear the revelation. Raphael's dialogue with Adam emphasizes the limits of human knowledge and the right motive for it: the worship of the Creator in his works. Yet the Bard cannot be sure that this was his primary motive in Books V and VI, partly because he attempted to exceed the limits of human knowledge.

The Bard answers his self-questioning about his motives by turning away from the visionary adventures of Books I through VI. Never again does he aspire to revelatory visions or soar to the Empyrean for any length of time. He does not repudiate his previous heavenly visions; he merely resings them correctively where necessary. Although he prays for revelations in Book III, he can never be sure to what extent his prayer is granted. He cannot say that his supra-Pegasean rapture led him unambiguously to revelations of what were heretofore "The secrets of another World" (V, 569), but then he cannot say unambiguously that it did not. He simply cannot know. Nor can he see clearly into his motives for his visionary aspirations because, like all fallen human beings, he is capable of self-deception, and he knows it. But he does come to recognize that his song in Book VI was theologically dangerous. He explores that danger indirectly in Books VII and VIII and never risks it again.

In this general process of self-questioning, one point in particular reflects on the Bard's overgoing program in Book VI. Adam has asked about the disposition of the heavenly bodies. He wonders why "So many nobler Bodies" (VIII, 28) seem to exist "merely to officiate light / Round this opacous Earth, this punctual spot" (22–23). The earth's small size and lack of luminosity make it, for Adam, far less noble than the stars. Raphael's answer, when it comes, directly counters these assumptions. He asserts "that Great / Or Bright infers not

Excellence" (90–91) and that the earth, though small and dark, "may of solid good contain / More plenty than the Sun that barren shines" (93–94). Moreover, the angel insists that the heavens do not exist to bring light to the earth but to Adam, "Earth's habitant" (99). He thereby implies that human beings contain much more of solid good than do the large and luminous stars.

These remarks reflect critically on the poetics of Book VI. There, "Great" and "Bright" were held to confer excellence. The Bard's implied claim to overgo Homer lay in his imagining the angelic warriors and Messiah with powers vastly superior to those of Homer's greatest heroes. In the single combat climaxing the first day, Michael and Satan carry shields as large and bright as suns (VI, 305–306), and the force of their commotion is said to be greater than "Two Planets rushing from aspect malign / Of fiercest opposition in mid Sky" (313–14) to confound the cosmos. Raphael's remarks in Book VIII, however, signal the Bard's turning away from overgoing programs. For if "Great / Or Bright infers not Excellence," neither do more spectacular imaginations necessarily confer poetic superiority. In short, poetic power is not the measure of Christian poetic excellence. In fact, it is Satan's measure, for he measures all "by strength" and is "of other excellence / Not emulous" (VI, 820–22). The Bard's overgoing of Homer's battle narrative does not necessarily make him a superior poet. Raphael's remarks point to a different measure of excellence, simultaneously poetic and moral. "More of solid good" makes one work or poet better than another, not the power and splendor of the imagination. Such an idea proves a revolutionary notion in the unfolding of *Paradise Lost.*

This principle is made explicit in the Bard's fourth proem when he distinguishes, for the first time, the Christian subject he receives from the song he is composing. In the previous proems, he has claimed that *his song* soars above the achievements of the ancients. Now he insists only that *his argument* proves higher, and he seeks merely an answerable style. He judges the arguments of the great ancient epics to be less heroic than his own (IX, 13–20), and he criticizes the "long and tedious havoc" of warfare in poetry (28–41). What "justly gives Heroic name / To Person or to Poem" (40–41) is not heroism in battle but "the better fortitude / Of Patience and Heroic Martyrdom" (31–32), virtues unimaginable in pagan epic but revealed in Christ's life and Passion in the New Testament.

To put this in Raphael's language: The New Testament has historically proven less compelling as literature than Homer and Vergil, for it lacks the color, verve, rhetorical splendor, and imaginative energy of the ancient epics. Nevertheless, it contains more of solid good because it reveals the truth of God's incarnate Word. The Bard has discovered that his higher argument itself deserves the name of epic (IX, 41–44). It does not need to be exalted by his soaring song, for it is already more exalted than any poet can make it. It contains more of solid good than the splendors of ancient epic because it contains God's truth. What this higher argument requires of the Bard is simply fidelity to that truth, a style answerable to it. Not until Books IX through XII does he achieve that fidelity in any sustained way, for not until Book IX does he seek it. In Books I through VI, he was seeking something different: to soar above the ancient epic poets in the greatest epic ever composed.

The poet's self-questioning in Books VII and VIII is enabled, in part, by Satan's sustained exclusion from the poem for the first time. These books thereby function as a kind of interlude, a period of cultivated leisure, the classical *schole* or *otium,* suited to the pleasures of contemplation and the examination of oneself.[32] Curiously, in Books I through VI the Bard cannot seem to get rid of Satan, though he tries. He turns away from demonic subjects for the first time only in Book III, and he so reduces his fascination with Satan that the latter, in Book IV, emerges as unheroic and unattractive. At the end of that book, Satan flees from single combat with Gabriel, and he appears to be expelled from the poem for a time, keeping away from the Garden for a week (IX, 53–69). Nevertheless, he is back in the poem in fewer than fifty lines, in Eve's dream in Book V. If this proves but a brief episode (V, 26–135), Raphael's story of the angelic rebellion soon returns Satan to prominence. The Bard, having begun his narrative with Satan, cannot seem to be rid of him for longer than a few hundred lines. He depends on Satan for every significant turn of his plot in Books I through VI. Even the Redemption is poetically motivated by Satan. Not until Messiah's victory in Book VI is Satan finally

32. See Lewalski, *"Paradise Lost" and the Rhetoric of Literary Forms,* 210–19, and Anna K. Nardo, "Academic Interludes in *Paradise Lost,*" *Milton Studies,* XXVII (1991), 209–41.

expelled from the poem, and from the poet's consciousness, for any sustained length of time.

His absence from Books VII and VIII occurs as the Bard makes a new beginning in his song. He takes up the narrative sequence of Scripture as the guide to his composing. Hence, he does not feel the pressure to envision and invent that so urges the extrabiblical plot of Books I through VI. He relies on Scripture and tradition to provide the substance and structure for his singing, and he does not need to exercise his powers of invention and disposition so strenuously as he did everywhere in Books I through VI. The song of the creation suspends the dialog between Raphael and Adam on the proper limits and ends of human knowledge, but these themes are renewed in the first part of Book VIII and, with them, the Bard's self-examination. He comes to the crucial realization that "Great / Or Bright infers not Excellence" (VIII, 90–91) partly because he has not aspired to overgoing greatness since the beginning of Book VII. Significantly, the sustained exclusion of Satan from the poem occurs as the Bard takes up Scripture for his narrative paradigm and begins to question the overgoing poetics in Books I through VI.

When Satan returns to the poem in Book IX, he has a different status. When the Bard first began his poem, he was relying on his own powers of invention to create the sequence of his plot, and he went directly to Satan in Hell to begin it. Now that the Bard has taken up the sequence of Scripture as the guide for his composing, however, Satan returns to a poem established on a different basis and thus has a new status in it. True, the Bard still needs Satan for the next turn in his plot, but that turn is recorded in Scripture, so the poet need only elaborate it in an answerable style. He now uses his powers of invention primarily for the narrative exegesis of the Bible, not to overgo the ancients. He takes Satan brilliantly through Eve's temptation and soon dispatches him. Satan is no longer necessary to the movement of the poem, as he was recurrently in Books I through VI. When the Bard returns to Satan and Sin and Death in Book X, he is simply rounding out a subplot begun in Book II and so fulfilling the exigencies of his storytelling. His final reduction of Satan and the demons proves their definitive exclusion from a poem that no longer needs them. For the poet has now envisioned the problem of sin and evil in a different way, one rooted in human, rather than demonic, agency.

The human agency of evil is evident everywhere in Michael's discourse, whose subject is "supernal Grace contending / With sinfulness of Men" (XI, 359–60). But the Bard devotes pointed attention to the human agency of evil in Michael's fourth vision and commentary, which form the most severe critique of classical epic in *Paradise Lost.* Miltonists have seen how the fourth proem reflects indirectly on the heroic apparatus of Books I and II and V and VI, and they have often treated Michael's condemnation of conquest as Milton's.[33] Michael attacks the heroic ethos for glamorizing the *libido dominandi* of human beings. That ethos admires only "Might" yet calls it "Valor and Heroic Virtue" (XI, 689–90). To "bring home spoils with infinite / Man-slaughter" is considered "the highest pitch / Of human Glory," and for this, "great Conquerors" are styled "Patrons of Mankind, Gods, and Sons of Gods" when they should more rightly be called "Destroyers" and "Plagues of men" (693–97). When "Might" is clothed in the robes of "Heroic Virtue" and awarded "human Glory" and "fame," then "what most merits fame" is "in silence hid" (699). The virtues celebrated by martial epic are not true virtues. What is worse, their glamor eclipses the true heroism that "most merits fame."

Michael's critique of martial values argues against the epic genre celebrating those values. This argument proves all the more pointed because, as is well known, the fourth vision alludes extensively to Homer's shield of Achilles (*Iliad,* XVIII).[34] The center of the shield contrasts the city of peace and the city at war, opposing the peaceful resolution of a dispute to a violent one. The shield as a whole pictures the works of peace largely excluded from the *Iliad:* ploughing, reaping, wine-making, cattle-herding, dancing at a festival. When the Bard alludes to this passage in Michael's fourth vision, the few works of peace only underscore the violence overwhelming them. He juxtaposes different kinds of violence, rather than peace and war. Where Homer

33. Riggs treats the fourth proem as an indirect critique of the heroic poetry in *Paradise Lost* (*Christian Poet in "Paradise Lost,"* 116–17, 131–34). For Michael's critique of warfare, see, among many, Revard, *War in Heaven,* 289–93; James A. Freeman, *Milton and the Martial Muse: "Paradise Lost" and European Traditions of War* (Princeton, 1980); and Swaim, *Before and After the Fall,* 154–55.

34. See the discussion by A. S. P. Woodhouse, *The Heavenly Muse: A Preface to Milton,* ed. Hugh MacCallum (Toronto, 1972), 203–205. Martindale, *Milton and the Transformation of Ancient Epic,* 94–95, remarks briefly on the allusion.

dwells on the peaceful resolution of a dispute, the Bard shows Enoch's failure to resolve one through transcendent principles of equity. Enoch's effort to make peace only succeeds in uniting all the disputants violently against him. In short, the poet's evoking of the *Iliad* underscores his critique of martial values as a critique of martial epic. When these values hold sway in poetry as in society, he is arguing, the true virtues of Enoch lie hidden in silence, though they most merit fame. What a poet does not celebrate remains unrecognized as virtue, and when the virtue appears, it is not only not praised but even attacked.

In sum, these passages from Books VII through XI mark an intelligible movement for the Bard. He begins with self-limiting gestures in the third proem, and these grow self-questioning as he considers the proper limits, motives, and ends of human knowledge. In Raphael's dialog with Adam, he is reconsidering his motives in having attempted to sing the secret things of Heaven. Moreover, when Raphael demonstrates that Adam, though small and physically "opacous," possesses more of solid good than the sun for all its size and luminosity, the Bard is reevaluating the overgoing poetics of Book VI. Adam has more of solid good because he is made in the image and likeness of God, an inner splendor revealed by Scripture and not apparent to sense. The principle of true greatness, then, is not physical but spiritual: it lies, not in size and luminosity, but in truth and goodness, as these are revealed in Scripture. To be sure, the Christian Bard has always known this, in some sense, yet he has not fully appreciated it. In his fourth proem, however, he argues that the fortitude of Christian suffering proves higher than that of epic self-assertion, an understanding not apparent in Book VI because the paradigm of classical epic does not allow its representation. His quiet critique of classical epic in the fourth proem becomes a denunciation in Book XI. As the Bard moves further away from Raphael's classical epic in the course of his ongoing song, he distances himself further from the epic values implied in its representations. Finally, near the end of the poem, he sings the true Christian heroism of his Redeemer. He has come far enough from the climax of Book VI, in time and in mind, to resing it correctively.

Miltonists have not clearly recognized this movement because they have assumed that the Bard's utterances are properly Milton's. Hence, they have sought for "Milton"'s consistent position on certain issues, and they have made valuable discoveries. For instance, they have often pointed to Milton's hatred of war, arguing that which is explicit in Michael's discourse is implied in Book VI and in the demonic panoply of epic glory in Books I and II.[35] Milton's hatred of war is well known, and since this interpretation seems to strike directly against my thesis, it needs to be met.

Here, a distinction between war and the poetry of war is in order. Doubtless, the Bard hates war from the beginning of his song, but he also loves the splendor of martial epic, and he relishes the opportunity to sing it as gloriously as he can. Granted, when a Christian poet gives martial displays to demons, he is implying a critique of martial displays. Nevertheless, the Bard of Books I and II elaborates the matter and manner of classical epic with all the verve he possesses, and that is considerable. Readers have often found Satan heroic in these books because the Bard's ebullient display of epic prowess often casts its aura around the leader of the demons. Moreover, though the senseless havoc of the war in Heaven is occasionally remarked and rightly laid against Satan, far more prevalent is the Bard's energetic performance as a poet of martial epic. His criticism of war all but disappears in the epic brilliance of his song, especially in the triumph of the Son. In short, the Bard's hatred of war is commingled with his love of martial epic. His desire to overgo the ancient epic poets leads him to slight his criticism of war while he features his prowess as a martial poet.

In the second half of his song, however, the Bard comes to understand the conflict between his Christian hatred of war and his love of classical epic. In Books VII and VIII, he questions the poetics of Book VI. In his fourth proem, he criticizes the matter and manner of classical epic. Finally, in Michael's discourse, he denounces the heroic ethos celebrated in martial epic. He has realized that his war in Heaven, notwithstanding its criticism of warfare, nevertheless celebrated the heroic ethos. Once he chose the paradigm of martial epic to relate the fall of the angels and embarked on an overgoing program to exalt Messiah as victor, he was committed to portraying the Son of God as a martial hero, as a super-Achilles. When Michael remarks that

35. See Revard's fine discussion, *War in Heaven,* 291–97; see Freeman, *Milton and the Martial Muse,* for an extensive treatment of Milton's critique of war. For the war in Heaven epitomizing war in general, see James Holly Hanford, "Milton and the Art of War," *Studies in Philology,* XVIII (1921), 232–66.

in the heroic ethos martial victors are styled "Gods, and Sons of Gods" (XI, 696), the Bard is reflecting critically on himself for styling the Son of God a martial victor. The Bard's hatred of war, evident earlier though outshone by his overgoing display of poetic prowess, now receives its full and severe articulation. It does so simply because the Bard has examined himself and abandoned his overgoing aspirations.

In short, the Bard shares Milton's hatred of war from the beginning of *Paradise Lost,* but he does not arrive at a full realization of that hatred until Michael's discourse. When Miltonists seek for "Milton"'s consistent positions in the poem, they illuminate the historical Milton's concerns, but they ignore the *movement* of the poem and of its poet on these issues. In my view, the Bard shares Milton's concerns from the beginning of his song, but he does not always evince a right understanding of them or a right balance among them.

The Bard's growth as a Christian poet in *Paradise Lost* brings him to Milton's understanding of poetic vocation and Christian epic, thus enacting a Christian paradox: the humble are exalted. From the perspective achieved in Books IX through XII, the soaring poetry of Books I through VI often falters as a properly Christian song. True, the Bible suggests the poet's subjects and often provides models for treating them. As we have seen, though, the overgoing Bard often takes his narrative paradigms from classical epic, and these paradigms gild the demons and deform, in certain respects, his representations of God and the Son. In Book VII, however, the Bard takes the sequence of Scripture as the guide for his plot: he makes a new beginning with the biblical story of the beginning. The rest of the poem unfolds, with some interpolations, according to the sequence of Scripture. Where in Books I through VI the Bard's inventions emerge from classical paradigms as he aspires to reveal the secret things of Hell and of God's eternal empire, in Books VII through XII he takes Scripture as his narrative paradigm and works largely as an exegete. His inventions now serve principally to elaborate the Bible, to fill in its narrative gaps, or to abridge it for the sweep of Michael's epic. In Book XII, the matter and manner of Scripture inform the verse with a sustained density unmatched elsewhere, for the Bard comprehends almost the whole sweep of the Bible in brief compass while imitating its humble style. Near the close of Michael's discourse, he correctively resings his earlier representations of the Savior's victory. This scriptural density and corrective resinging climax the Bard's descending song. Michael's epic is the lowest part of the poem stylistically, yet it proves the highest in its treatment of Christian truth. The most densely biblical part of the poem and the most attentive to edifying its fallen audience, it contains more of solid good than all the poetic splendors of Raphael's epic.

The Bard's growth in understanding proves a growth in self-understanding. From the beginning of his song, he knows that Christian epic must give primacy to Christianity over epic, but he does not fully understand wherein that primacy lies. Moreover, though his first proem reveals his desire to instruct his audience, his attempts to overgo the ancients often distract his didactic aim. But as he abandons his overgoing ambitions in Books VII through XII, he comes to a clearer understanding of these issues, and he sings a poetry more truly Christian and more fully didactic.

We are meant to follow the Bard on this journey of understanding. His movement in the poem is designed to move us along with him. After we follow his soaring flights, we are meant to join in his descent, to follow his self-questioning in Books VII and VIII and its emergence into the explicit critique of classical epic in Books IX and XI. As Christian readers, we are meant to find "the better fortitude" actually better, to approve of Michael's treatment of the Redemption as right and proper, and to see how it corrects the representation of Messiah in Book VI. We are meant to follow sympathetically the intelligible course of the Bard's descending song so that we, too, come to prefer Michael's epic to Raphael's.

FIVE

Milton and the Bard's Story

For the most part, Miltonists have treated Christian epic as though it were an unproblematic genre. Like the Bard in Books I through VI, they have assumed that Christian subjects can be sung in the manner of classical epic without any inherent conflict or tension. Renaissance poems on the war in Heaven, not to speak of *Gierusalemme Liberata,* could be adduced as evidence. In this view, a Christian subject makes for a Christian poem, regardless of the manner in which it is sung. The high classical style proves merely a style for the exalted portrayal of Christian subjects, a form to be filled with Christian substance. A Christian subject and an epic style together make for a Christian epic.

I have argued that Milton did not hold this view of Christian epic, though its practice animates the first half of *Paradise Lost.* When the poem is considered as a whole and understood as a movement, we see the Bard indirectly criticizing the classical manner and matter of the first six books. At the beginning of Book VII, he sets a descending course for his song, and though he soars stylistically often in Books IX and X, especially for fallen beings, his style gradually descends until it reaches its lowest pitch in Book XII. This stylistic *askesis* emerges because he expressly turns away from the visionary adventure of Book VI and its theological dangers. He begins to question and then to criticize Book VI's epic poetics, always indirectly and yet with increasing clarity and force. He comes to understand that the better fortitude of Christian heroism cannot be properly represented on the paradigm of classical epic. The poet's use of these paradigms in Books III and VI deform his representations of God and the Son in certain crucial respects, and these he resings correctively in the final books of the poem. He resings the Redemption not only in substance but in style, for these prove more closely connected than he suspected in Book III.

Two related principles have emerged often in this analysis. First, a classical paradigm of narrative entails, by definition, classical conceptions of virtue and divinity, and these deform the poet's Christian representations. Second, narrative necessity affects theological portrayal. Once the Bard decides to overgo Vergil's divine colloquy in Book III, he will be subject to C. S. Lewis' criticism that his Heaven is too like Olympus. As long as God is a crucial agent in the plot, he can never seem wholly to transcend the action. As long as the Bard is singing in the high style, he cannot represent the Redeemer's humiliation and death as a victory. Similarly, once the poet chooses to treat the angelic fall in the epic genre with the Son as hero, he must glorify the Son, not with "the better fortitude" revealed in Christ, but with the lesser fortitude of epic strength. The Bard's epic ambition leads him to make these narrative and theological decisions in Books I through VI, but he makes different decisions in these regards in Books IX through XII—decisions that both correct and indirectly criticize the epic and visionary poetry of Books III through VI.

Correction, I have insisted, is not repudiation. Much of the correcting proves indirect, as much in style as of substance. Even when the Bard articulates his final treatment of the Redemption, he does not reject his portrayals of the Son as glorious victor in Books III and VI, for these are not wrong, only overemphasized and thus possibly misleading. They are filled with allusions to Scripture and ring with the Bard's piety. They are not likely to harm a devout Christian reader. Neither are they likely to instruct one, for they misrepresent true Christian heroism. The Bard corrects without rejecting, as he labors to instruct and edify an audience he had earlier attempted to dazzle.

In the Bard's critical reflection on his earlier singing, we can see that Milton understood Christian epic as a problematical genre, containing inherent tensions. To be sure, this was not the Renaissance view, for the Italian poets labored to recover the full range of ancient, martial epic for their Christian subjects. This was the older Christian view, however, and it can be found in Augustine.

Early in the *Confessions,* Augustine reflects on the love for Vergil's poetry he felt as a boy (*Conf.,* I, 13). He loved to indulge himself in poetry of high tension and pathos: Dido's passion, the Trojan horse, the burning of Troy, the ghost of Creusa. The mature Augustine criticizes the vanity of these spectacles and of his involvement in them, for he wept at Dido's death and learned by heart all of Aeneas' wanderings (*errores*), yet he did not weep at his own dying to God in his sins and paid no attention to his own *errores.* This chapter forms only one critique of classical literature in the *Confessions,* but it remains the most famous. The *Aeneid* was a school book, studied not only for its beauty but for its noble morality. Aeneas was held up as a model of *pietas,* valor, devotion to duty, and moral fortitude, as he struggles against irrational passion in the gods, in others, and in himself. Yet Augustine criticizes the poem for its deleterious moral influence on himself as a boy: it offered nothing but poetic fictions about the gods and even about its hero, and the very beauty of the poetry seduced him away from self-knowledge by its "most sweet spectacle of vanity." Augustine clearly implies that Scripture would have made far better study, for it contains, not *poetica figmenta,* but God's truth about God himself, which alone enables one to know the truth about oneself.

Outside of this chapter, Augustine makes only a few direct allusions to the *Aeneid* in the *Confessions.* Nevertheless, as Andrew Fichter brilliantly shows, the *Aeneid* proves a persistent subtext in the work, for Augustine persistently counters it in oblique and subtle ways.[1] Vergil treats of Aeneas' physical wanderings; Augustine, of his own spiritual wanderings. Both protagonists move from North Africa to Italy. Aeneas struggles to establish the race that will eventually rise to Roman greatness, whereas the young Augustine travels first to Rome and then to Milan, the new imperial capital (the center of empire has been moved since Vergil's day, and by the time Augustine is writing, the pagan empire has become officially Christian). Augustine's story counters Aeneas' as it reflects these changes. Furthermore, Vergil praises the "universal" scope of the Roman empire: in Jupiter's famous words, "I have given them empire without end" in time or

1. See Andrew Fichter, *Poets Historical: Dynastic Epic in the Renaissance* (New Haven, 1982), 40–69.

space (*Aen.*, I, 279). But Augustine sees how limited Roman rule actually is. He praises instead the universal scope of the Church, which began with the creation of Adam and will not end even with the end of time, since the Mystical Body of Christ will rejoice throughout eternity. Throughout the *Confessions,* as Fichter shows, the heavenly Jerusalem implicitly counters the earthly Rome.

In short, the *Confessions* proves a Christian *Aeneid.* For Augustine, though, a Christian *Aeneid* is necessarily a counter-*Aeneid* or an anti-*Aeneid.* The young Augustine may be its protagonist, but its hero is God, who leads the young man to conversion and finally impels him toward it in a terrible moment of self-knowledge. The self-assertion of an epic hero proves tantamount, in a Christian, to pride and sin, and the young Augustine becomes true to himself only when he humbly submits himself to God in his conversion. The loving and wise God of the Christian work opposes the self-centered and passionate gods of the pagan, for Augustine's volume is based on Scripture, as Vergil's poem is based on Homer. Even the genre of Augustine's work is designed to counter Vergil's: his truthful prayer in prose as he scrutinizes himself in God's light opposes the *poetica figmenta* of Vergil, who sang of legends he knew to be false and of gods in whom he did not believe.

Augustine acutely understood and dramatized the conflict between Christian truth and ancient epic, for it proved a central issue in the cultural struggles of the late empire. Yet even when those struggles were long over, his understanding of the tension between Christianity and epic remained normative for writers in the Middle Ages. They avoided the genre of martial epic for religious narrative, using either the quest-romance or, as in Dante, the Augustinian model of spiritual autobiography.[2] On the whole, the model of classical epic, which is martial epic, does not enter Christian poetry until the Renaissance.

Scholars have long recognized Milton's critical view of martial values—a view that opposes him to the general Renaissance writer of epic. They have pointed to the radical reassessment of epic heroism made explicit in Books IX and XI, and some have found *Paradise Lost*

2. John Freccero has explored the Augustinian model for Dante's *Commedia* in several essays. See his *Dante: The Poetics of Conversion,* ed. Rachel Jacoff (Cambridge, Mass., 1986), esp. "Medusa: The Letter and the Spirit," 119–35, and "The Significance of *Terza Rima,*" 258–71.

to be revising or even refuting epic in a Christian anti-epic.[3] This understanding of Milton's poem is well established. I wish to add merely an insistence on the movement of the poem as a whole and on the poet's critical reflection on his earlier practices. For the first six books of *Paradise Lost* would not prove so clearly antimartial and anti-epic if we did not have the last four. The spectrum of scholarly debate on Book VI shows how much we need Books IX and XI to reveal the Bard's critical attitude toward classical epic and its heroic ethos.

Wide reading in the scholarship on the war in Heaven tempts one to say that everything ever written about it is true. It proves to be both Renaissance martial epic and mock or mocked heroic poetry; it is glorious and ridiculous, richly Homeric and deeply Christian, epic and anti-epic, noble and ludicrous, and almost everything in between, somewhere or other. Yet while Miltonists disagree wildly about the war in Heaven, they agree widely about Milton's critical view of warfare. This agreement is made possible because the proem of Book IX and Michael's fourth vision and commentary criticize and denounce the heroic ethos. That criticism enables scholars to highlight the few moments in Book VI where war is criticized and then to attribute these to "Milton." Without Books IX and XI, though, these few moments in Book VI would be even more eclipsed than they are already by the poet's celebration of classical heroism in the loyal angels and the Son. If *Paradise Lost* ended with Book VI, scholars would be debating "Milton"'s attitude toward warfare as variously and vigorously as they debate the character and quality of Book VI.

In my view, *Paradise Lost* proves anti-epic because it becomes an anti-epic over the course of its second half. No book in the poem proves more expressly anti-epic than Book XI because it contains Michael's denunciation of the heroic ethos. No book proves more anti-epic in style than Book XII, which contains the Bard's fullest presentation of true Christian heroism in his singing the Redemption.

3. For Milton's reassessment of epic heroism, see especially two books by Steadman, *Milton and the Renaissance Hero* and *Milton's Epic Characters.* For *Paradise Lost* as anti-epic, see T. J. B. Spencer, "*Paradise Lost:* The Anti-Epic," in *Approaches to "Paradise Lost,"* ed. Patrides, 81–98; J. A. Kates, "The Revaluation of the Classical Hero in Tasso and Milton," *Comparative Literature,* XXVI (1974), 299–317; Joan Webber, *Milton and His Epic Tradition* (Seattle, 1979); and Leland Ryken, "*Paradise Lost* and Its Biblical Epic Models," in *Milton and Scriptural Tradition,* ed. Sims and Ryken, 43–81.

Miltonists have rightly considered these to represent Milton's critical attitude toward classical heroism and its ethos. But they have wrongly considered this attitude to be fully present in Books I through VI, because they have assumed these books to be Milton's in propria persona. I contend that this attitude is but imperfectly present in Books I through VI and that its full emergence in Books IX through XII should be understood as an achievement of self-understanding by the oral Bard. Milton's Bard eventually comes to have Milton's own understanding of these issues, but in Books I through VI his understanding proves very imperfect. There he tries to sing of the Christian God on the basis of classical paradigms, not realizing that these inevitably deform his representations because they entail classical conceptions of divinity. He does not yet understand that Christian epic must necessarily be anti-epic. The evidence for anti-epic in the early books emerges largely from scholars' assumption that these books are "Milton"'s, so they thereby project the Bard's later, mature understandings into them. In part, the evidence is latently there, implied in the tension between the Bard's Christianity and his epic paradigms.

This view of the poem has consequences for scholarship at once serious and slight. On the one hand, it clearly rejects many things that have been written about Milton with regard to the early books of *Paradise Lost.* On the other, it preserves them for both the poem and the Bard. These consequences flow directly from the two principles governing my analysis: (1) the distinction between Milton and his Bard, and (2) the sequential principle, a proper emphasis on the movement of the poem as a whole. I should like to illustrate these consequences by considering briefly the vein of scholarship on Milton as a visionary poet in *Paradise Lost.*

This line of interpretation is, of course, fully traditional and continues to be maintained with learning and skill. Its contemporary expositors include Leland Ryken, William Kerrigan, Joseph Wittreich, and Michael Lieb.[4] Different as the critics' views on various issues are, a "visionary Milton" in *Paradise Lost* necessarily emphasizes the first half of the poem, especially the first proem and Books III through VI.

4. See Ryken, *Apocalyptic Vision;* Kerrigan, *Prophetic Milton;* Wittreich, *Visionary Poetics;* and Michael Lieb, *Poetics of the Holy: A Reading of "Paradise Lost"* (Chapel Hill, N.C., 1981).

It is thereby committed to the ambiguity of "Milton" as simultaneously the author of the whole and the narrator of every part. It must ignore the sequential principle, and it tends to scant the various ways that subsequent remarks in the poem reflect critically on these visionary books.

In my view, the mature Milton did not present himself as a visionary poet in *Paradise Lost.* For one thing, he presented himself not directly at all but only indirectly, through his Bard. True, all of the Bard's concerns are Milton's concerns, but in the early books the Bard does not yet have Milton's mature understanding on many points. Although Milton did not present himself as a visionary poet, I would argue, he did present his Bard attempting to be one. The Bard prays that he "may see and tell / Of things invisible to mortal sight" (III, 54–55), and in Books III through VI he attempts to envision and reveal the things of Heaven before time and the creation of the world. In Book VII, however, he begins to question these visionary adventures, and he never embarks on one again. Hence, insofar as *Paradise Lost* as a whole represents the mature Milton's understanding of himself and his poetry, Milton appears, not as a visionary poet, but as a poet who calls visionary poets into question. Miltonists can continue to regard Milton as a visionary poet in *Paradise Lost* only by holding to the ambiguity of "Milton" and by denying the movement of the poem as a whole.

My view merely qualifies the interpretations of the scholars mentioned above; it does not reject them. What is true in their remarks about the poem remains true. What they assert about a "visionary Milton" can be readily adapted to the aspirations of a visionary Bard. Nor do I dispute the visionary impulse in the historical Milton, for the evidence outside the poem and within it proves more than ample. Nevertheless, the mature Milton did not present himself as a visionary poet in *Paradise Lost,* because its second half reveals the poet chastening his ambitions and not only questioning his visions but correcting them where necessary. Milton recognized the visionary impulse in himself and understood its spiritual dangers. Hence, he did not present the visionary attempts in Books I through VI in propria persona, and he designed them to falter because they are based on classical paradigms. If we wish to see Milton behind the Bard in these visionary books, we should see him composing, not from the Bard's aspirations in them, but from the critical perspective represented in Books IX through XII. In this regard, Milton was simultaneously indulging his love of epic and his aspiration to vision, exercising the splendor of his talents and chastening his delight in all of these. For Milton was the author of all of *Paradise Lost,* and if we would speculate on what he was doing behind the Bard in the early books, we should think from the perspective achieved by the Bard at the end of the poem.

All this perhaps seems overly complicated, but it proves much less so, in fact, than the variety of positions about "Milton"'s views in *Paradise Lost.* Scholarly debate confounds in "Milton" the historical author of the poem as a whole and its narrative voice at every part. Since everything that voice asserts is considered " Milton"'s, different Miltons emerge from the different emphases that scholars give to these assertions. Granted, my understanding makes it more difficult to write about Milton's views in the poem, but that may be considered one of its virtues. If we would distinguish Milton from his Bard and adhere to the sequential principle, we would more often come to the kind of agreement we share on Milton's view of warfare, for instance, than the kind of disagreement we have on "Milton"'s war in Heaven. In short, my understanding of the poem makes Milton's views in it not more complicated but more readily discernible. It clarifies a muddled critical debate and opens new problems for exploration.

A crucial question remains to be treated, deliberately postponed until after the Bard's story and its implications could be adequately set forth. The question is simple: what did Milton gain by composing *Paradise Lost* in this way? The Bard's story in the poem may be plausible, but it cannot prove fully persuasive without our considering its artistic advantages for Milton. Since readers have long enjoyed the epic as "Milton"'s, what does this view of the poem add to their appreciation?

First, and most obvious, Milton's having created a Bard who changes in the course of his singing proves a brilliant innovation in the epic tradition. Its brilliance lies in its originality, for it draws on the sources of that tradition and channels them in a new way. Homer was an oral poet, and in deference to him later epic poets presented themselves as "singers." Milton transformed what was a mere convention into a poetic resource. With it he created a new level of meaning.

He not only told a story but also implied a story about his storyteller. Just as there are two poets of *Paradise Lost,* so are there two stories: the story being told and the implied story of the teller. Milton's Bardic fiction is not merely an original contribution to the epic tradition but one that transforms its fundamental convention into a poetic resource. It thereby proves an innovation of genius.

Second, with this innovation Milton acquired a protagonist for a poem that seems to lack one. The debate about "the hero of *Paradise Lost*" is old, and I do not intend to rehearse it. Nor am I suggesting that the Bard is Milton's real hero. But the Bard is his protagonist, the only figure consistently before us, if we care to look. Milton knew that his poem lacked a central character, though his hero was doubtless the Son. The lack of a central character is commonly considered a failing in an epic poem, and Milton countered this potential failing with his Bardic narrator. The Bard may be less than a hero, but he certainly proves more than merely a mask for Milton. As a narrator who audibly wrestles with his material and responds to what he is singing in the course of his song, he emerges as Milton's protagonist, one that changes over the course of his poem.

We have also seen that the Bard's progress implies a Christian moral: those who exalt themselves are humbled, and those who humble themselves are exalted. In Books I through VI, the Bard aims to overgo all his epic predecessors by composing the greatest Christian epic ever, and indeed he sings much wonderful poetry. But he comes to understand that his epic ambitions have led him to falter in presenting Christian truth, and he turns away from his epic and visionary aspirations. In so doing, he submits himself increasingly to the guidance of Scripture, and in the stylistically low song of Books XI and XII he achieves his most profoundly Christian poetry. It may be neither great nor bright like Books III and VI, but these qualities do not confer excellence. It does contain that "more of solid good" found in Scripture. Being less classical, the poetry proves more deeply biblical. Hence, though it proves lower in style, we are meant to understand it as more truly exalted.

Furthermore, the Bard's progress imitates human experience, both in the small and in the large. In the large, an epic aims to embrace reality as fully as possible. The plot of the *Divine Comedy,* like that of the *Aeneid,* reaches to the depths of the underworld and the heights of the divine as it attempts to encompass the range of humanly significant experience. *Paradise Lost* clearly enjoys the same ambition—an ambition it realizes not only in the settings and plot of the story it tells but also in the way the Bard tells the story.

For the story mimes the movement of culture, as Milton understood it, from the classical world to the Christian. The first half of *Paradise Lost* draws largely on classical models to develop its settings and episodes; its second half draws increasingly on the Bible, nowhere more than in Book XII. To be sure, Christianity governs the aims of Books I through VI, and the poetry there is filled with biblical allusions. I am not suggesting that Milton plotted a strict imitation of the *translatio studii* from pagan to Christian culture in the two halves of his poem. Given the inclusive aims of epic, however, there is warrant for seeing a general movement of this sort over the whole poem.

In the small, Harry Berger, Jr., finds that this movement illustrates the experience of a person's moral development, which "proceeds through a dialectic of self-expansion and self-limitation." In Books I through VI, Milton's Bard exercises himself in vast, epic gestures, exploring the limits of his visionary powers. In Book VII, he criticizes these ambitions and confines himself to the earth, which he nevertheless gradually expands "by making it the new moral center of the universe." The expansive, spatial journeying of vision in the first six books is eventually replaced by the temporal exploration of moral conflict, the Bard's true subject. Arriving at it marks his growth in understanding his true vocation as a Christian epic poet, but he must undertake the visionary adventures of Books I through VI in order to achieve this understanding. "The moral gesture of self-limitation cannot take place until the mind has first probed its expansive powers, has tried to fulfill its wishes by making the whole universe its place."[5] In Blake's proverb, "You never know what is enough until you know what is more than enough."[6] For Berger, the dialectic of self-expansion and self-limitation underlies the moral development of every human being, and the experience of Milton's Bard proves an instance of this universal truth. In short, Milton's poem is not simply *about* the experience represented in the story; because he created a changing Bard to

5. See Berger, "*Paradise Lost* Evolving," 489.

6. William Blake, "The Marriage of Heaven and Hell," *The Poetry and Prose of William Blake,* ed. David V. Erdman (Rev. ed.; Garden City, N.Y., 1970), 36.

tell it, the poem *enacts* the human experience of its narrator. Because of the Bard's story, *Paradise Lost* proves even more inclusive of significant human experience than we have hitherto thought.

In this regard, Milton anticipated Samuel Johnson's criticism that "the want of human interest is always felt" in *Paradise Lost,* because its plan "comprises neither human actions nor human manners." Here, Johnson was thinking of the supernatural beings and unfallen characters who occupy almost two-thirds of the poem. He assumed that the voice of the poem was Milton's, and he did not hear that voice responding to its own creations, like Louis Martz does, or setting interpretive traps, like Stanley Fish contends. This kind of involvement Johnson did not feel in the poem, intent as he was on the story and on what he saw as its "characteristic quality," sublimity.[7] Milton himself recognized this inherent defect in a poem that achieved its sublimities by singing about supernatural beings. The "want of human interest" had to be countered, and Milton did so by placing the Bard's human consciousness as the medium of vision and narration. For Johnson, that consciousness did not exist as part of the poem, but it does exist for any reader as attentive as Martz and Fish to the subtle movement of the poet's voice in the verse. These critics feel no want of human interest in the unfolding of the poem. That interest is intensified when we appreciate the Bard's story in *Paradise Lost:* a fallen poet struggling to achieve unfallen visions as he employs a variety of materials to sustain his performance. We are not meant to see him as "Milton," a poet-prophet who enjoys divine vision and reports it for us. We are meant to see the Bard's struggle, to weigh his visionary success, to appreciate the human story of the singer in *Paradise Lost* outside of the proems, as well as within them.

Furthermore, the Bard's story enabled Milton to treat the danger of visionary poetry without risking it in his own voice. Such poetry has frequently been ascribed to Milton and to Dante. They have often been compared as poet-theologians, and Milton has been understood to have accomplished in *Paradise Lost* something equivalent to what Dante achieved in the *Divine Comedy.* This comparison, however, has rarely distinguished either the various Dantes—Dante the maker,

7. Samuel Johnson, "Life of Milton," *Selected Poetry and Prose,* 439, 437–38, 435; Fish, *Surprised by Sin,* 1–35; Martz, *The Paradise Within,* 109–10.

Dante the pilgrim, and Dante the poet of the pilgrimage made—or Milton and the Bard. The *Divine Comedy* presents itself as the true record of a real pilgrimage: the poet records what he saw as a pilgrim. But we know that Dante the maker made it all up. His fiction is so obviously fictional that his divine visions have no inherent religious authority. The very extravagance of the fiction denies its literal truth, no matter how persistently the fiction maintains that truth. What Dante the poet-once-pilgrim insists he saw, Dante the maker made up, and everyone knows it.

Paradise Lost does not blazon its fictionality in this way. Quite the opposite, in fact. So readers have traditionally understood Milton to present himself as achieving divine inspiration in what he sings—an understanding that has been shared by Milton's defenders and critics alike, though the latter have mocked it. In this regard, the work of Berger and William Riggs proves a valuable departure, for whereas Berger attends to the Bard's experience of singing Books I through VI, Riggs rightly insists that the poet never claims to achieve the height of inspiration he earlier prays for. Milton's Bardic fiction, then, distanced him from the visionary adventures of the first six books: from the Bard's fitful satanism in Books I and II and from any claim to divine revelation in Books III through VI. The *Bard* aspires to the height of Mosaic inspiration in his first proem, but whether or where or to what extent he is granted it, he does not say. What may be said about the historical Milton on this score is open to speculation. He founded no sect on the basis of any divine revelation he may have received, nor did he preach a sermon or write a tract on one. In sum, in *Paradise Lost* Milton was not like Dante in presenting himself as a poet of divine visions. Rather, he was like Dante in having adroitly distanced himself from such a self-presentation, with its implied claim to religious authority.

With Berger and Riggs, then, we can see that Milton used his Bardic fiction to raise questions about how the poet represents supernatural and unfallen realities. It may be objected that this is merely a modern projection onto a seventeenth-century work, that Milton was not possessed by our contemporary mania for the problematic. But it was, in truth, simply good common sense for Milton not to claim the authority of a prophet, in propria persona, during the Restoration. His Bardic fiction provided him with a ready defense on that score, should he need one. Moreover, this fiction invites readers to reflect on the representations made by the poet, to judge whether and where and to what extent he has been divinely inspired. Readers who accept this invitation become at once more deeply involved in thinking through the poem as they become critical of its modes, especially when comparing them to Scripture. For the reader who recognizes Milton's Bardic fiction and accepts its invitation, even its most spellbinding passages can become occasions for instruction and insight. Modern Miltonists have put these occasions to good use, even when they have not recognized the Bard's existence.

Finally, Milton's Bardic fiction enabled him to write an epic in twelve books. This assertion should surprise us less than it does, for the declared subject of the poem is told completely in Books IX through XII: from "Man's First Disobedience" to the restoring acts of "one greater / Man." In this regard, *Paradise Lost* rather features its excess: it does not need twelve books to convey the story promised in its first proem. Obviously, though, Milton wanted to write a full-length epic, and without Books I through VIII much of the epic's splendor and meaning would be lost. He accomplished this end by a Bardic fiction that distended the "cause" of the Fall into eight books of poetry.

This distention of Milton's epic is remarkable, especially given the classical precedents evoked in the first proem. Its opening lines allusively bid us compare it to the epics of Homer and Vergil. After the proem, the poet goes on to explore the "cause" (I, 28) of the promised action, as Homer and Vergil had. The *Iliad* devotes less than 50 lines to the cause of the *menis* of Achilles, and the *Aeneid* rather less to the cause of Juno's *ira,* before they embark on their promised stories. The Bard spends over three books and 2,600 lines of poetry simply to bring his Satanic "cause" within sight of Adam and Eve, and he sings eight full books before he reaches the subject declared in his opening line. Given the classical precedents evoked in the first proem, this is an odd disposition of material, to say the least.

Such an unconventional disposition has never been felt as remarkable, I think, because it has always been accepted as "Milton"'s. In my view, Milton wanted us to notice this distention in his epic and to reflect on it as an anomaly. He used it to indicate his Bardic narrator. He tried to alert us to the Bard's story by appealing to epic precedent in the first proem, then immediately contravening it with excessive exposition of the "cause." Readers have not noticed this excess, not because they lacked classical learning, but because Books I through VIII contain the most extraordinary poetry. Milton's greatness as a poet would not be so evident without them, and he surely designed the Bard's story in the first six books as a way to display his talents. Nevertheless, *Paradise Lost* as a whole testifies that its promised story does not comprise an epic in twelve books, for that story is completely told in Books IX through XII. Books I through VIII are not necessary to the narration of "Man's First Disobedience." They are necessary, however, to the story of the Bard's progress in *Paradise Lost.*

Milton's Bardic fiction, then, gave him some signal artistic advantages. It enabled him to counter the potential want of human interest in his supernatural characters through the human consciousness of his narrator. The Bard's experience, enacted in his narrating, gave even greater scope to Milton's aspiration to include all humanly significant experience in his epic, for the Bard's story adds a new level of meaning to the poem. Moreover, it provided him with a means for exploring the tensions implied in Christian epic. In this way, he offered a critique of those Italian poets who sought to fuse uncritically Christian truths with martial epic. At the same time, Milton could indulge his love of the high style yet distance himself from its classical allure. He could enjoy his display of epic prowess as a poet, even as he remained critical of the epic ambition it implied. He could overgo his predecessors yet show his Bard learning to abandon his overgoing ambitions. Scholars have rightly insisted that Milton embraced all the elements of his epic: classical and biblical, unfallen and fallen, Platonist and Protestant, and so on. I have simply insisted on the movement of the poem and its Bardic fiction. Milton embraced the whole poem, but the whole is achieved by the Bard's movement, and the whole is balanced because the Bard corrects its earlier imbalances.

In this way, the Bard's story enabled Milton both to have his overgoing flights and to criticize them. He displayed not only the power and splendor of his imagination but also his understanding that true poetic excellence lies elsewhere. He thereby acknowledged his love of the classics and his poetic ambition while he subjected both to Christian criticism and correction. Perhaps, as Berger suggests, the Bard in Books I through VI represents Milton's "late autumnal portrait of his youthful spirit."[8] The expansive gestures and ebullient ambition in these books savor of youthful vitality, and where they falter as properly Christian poetry, they may be excused by the excess that often accompanies youthful high spirits. Whatever the merits of Berger's suggestion, Milton's Bardic fiction was an innovation of genius in the epic tradition, for it enabled him to embrace and explore the range of experience in a new way because it gave his poem a level of meaning unrealized in any previous epic.

8. Berger, "Archaism, Vision, and Revision," 52.

SIX

Song "Above Heroic": Milton's Bard and *Paradise Regained*

Paradise Lost proves but the first work in the Bard's oeuvre. Subsequently, he goes on to sing a second Christian epic, and he begins it by recalling his first: "I who erewhile the happy Garden sung, / By one man's disobedience lost, now sing / Recover'd Paradise to all mankind" (I, 1–3). As is well known, this imitates the traditional opening of the *Aeneid,* usually omitted from modern editions:

> Ille ego, qui quondam gracili modulatus avena
> carmen, et egressus silvis vicina coegi
> ut quamvis avido parerent arva colono,
> gratum opus agricolis, at nunc horrentia Martis
> arma virumque cano. . . .
>
> (*Aeneid,* note to I, 1)

> I am he who once tuned my song on a slender pipe, and then leaving the woods made the neighboring fields obey the husbandman however greedy, a work to win favor with farmers, but now I sing of the bristling arms of Mars and the man. . . .

Arnold Stein interprets the allusion as "a literary joke of unprecedented dimensions," for it means that "*Paradise Regained* is the real epic, not *Paradise Lost*!" The earlier work is treated as an "entertaining poem" on " 'the happy Garden'—a felicitous expression to describe his 'early pastoral,' the Virgilian apprentice-work he is about to graduate from."[1] Stein acutely recognizes the challenge that Milton threw down in this allusion, and he comes to grips with it admirably. But since he considers *Paradise Lost* to be Milton's in propria persona throughout, he does not understand how *Paradise Regained* completes the Bard's story and reflects on his achievement in the earlier poem.

The present chapter completes my account of the Bard's story by considering his final work as Milton's true Christian epic. Miltonists understand the implications of its opening allusion, but because they have failed to see the Bard's growth as a Christian poet in *Paradise Lost,* they find the implications surprising. They have assumed that *Paradise Lost* is properly Milton's throughout, and they have generally preferred its splendid passages to the sterner poetry of Michael's epic and *Paradise Regained.*[2] When the movement of *Paradise Lost* is understood to reveal the progress of its Bard, however, *Paradise Regained* becomes intelligible as Milton's true Christian epic.

Previous chapters have set forth the principles underlying that claim, but it would be well to review them briefly. First, in poetry as in the world, "Great / Or Bright infers not Excellence" but "solid good" does (*cf. PL,* VIII, 90–96). The New Testament lacks the splendors of Homer's poetry, but it proves not only the superior work because it reveals the highest divine truths but also the more heroic one because it sets forth "the better fortitude" of Christ. Similarly, Michael's epic and *Paradise Regained* are superior to the spectacular poetry of Books I through VI of *Paradise Lost,* for they set forth Christian truth and its better fortitude more truly because they eschew classical paradigms of narrative and embrace biblical ones.

Second, *Paradise Lost* often falters as a Christian poem in its first half because the Bard does not have an adequate understanding of what his Christian epic truly requires. Filled with epic ambition and Christian piety mingled together, he intends to surpass the epics of his predecessors by his overgoing flights, which will prove the superiority of Christian truth to classical achievements. But no proof is needed. Not until Book IX does he fully realize that the Christian

1. See Arnold Stein, *Heroic Knowledge,* 6–7. Barbara Kiefer Lewalski agrees with his interpretation in *Milton's Brief Epic: The Genre, Meaning, and Art of "Paradise Regained"* (Providence, R.I., 1966), 6.

2. Mary Wilson Carpenter explores the relations between the two in "Milton's Secret Garden: Structural Correspondences Between Michael's Prophecy and *Paradise Regained,*" *Milton Studies,* XIV (1980), 153–82.

truth he receives from Scripture and proclaims in his song has already surpassed the mighty works of antiquity, and all he needs is an answerable style. The Bard begins *Paradise Regained,* however, with the right understanding of these issues. Where *Paradise Lost* often proves a falteringly Christian poem in its first half, *Paradise Regained* is a truly Christian epic from beginning to end. Moreover, because the Bard has achieved a mature understanding of his vocation, *Paradise Regained* is more firmly organized and enjoys greater artistic coherence and integrity. Its later books do not reflect critically on its earlier ones, because there is nothing wrong with those earlier books. In addition, it takes the Bard eight books in *Paradise Lost* to arrive at the subject announced in its opening line. No such dispositional distention afflicts *Paradise Regained.*

Because Miltonists have not recognized the Bard's story in *Paradise Lost,* they have not seen these reasons for the superiority of *Paradise Regained,* but they have seen others, all of them important. Stein admits that the theme of *Paradise Regained* is "higher, formally," and he recognizes that "this 'brief' epic on a biblical model ought to be more exalted than the epic on a classical model." The later work's claim to superiority lies in Jesus' "deeds / Above Heroic" (I, 14–15). Stein explores this higher heroism in light of the traditional *contemptus mundi* as a "dying to the world," whereas Barbara Lewalski treats it typologically, arguing that Jesus' rejection of the temptations illustrates his offices as prophet, priest, and king. Burton Jasper Weber, from a third perspective, finds its superiority in its sublime resolution of the epic and tragic genres.[3] Scholarly debate on the poem has largely revolved around the structure and meaning of the temptations in light of Jesus' heroism and the structure and genre of the work as a whole.[4] Important as these debates are, they prove but obliquely

3. Stein, *Heroic Knowledge,* 7, 112–34; Lewalski, *Milton's Brief Epic,* 133–321; and Burton Jasper Weber, *Wedges and Wings: The Patterning of "Paradise Regained"* (Carbondale, Ill., 1975), 1–3, 108–10.

4. See Walter MacKellar, Introduction, *A Variorum Commentary on the Poems of John Milton,* Volume IV, *Paradise Regained* (New York, 1975), and John Carey, Introduction to Milton's *Paradise Regained,* ed. John Carey, in *The Poems of John Milton,* ed. John Carey and Alastair Fowler (London, 1968). On the issue of structure, see, more recently, John T. Shawcross, *"Paradise Regained": Worthy T' Have Not Remain'd So Long Unsung* (Pittsburgh, 1988), 45–58; William B. Hunter, Jr., "The Double Set of Temptations in *Paradise Regained," Milton Studies,* XIV (1980), 183–94; and Weber, *Wedges and Wings,* 3–14.

related to the Bard's story as it culminates in *Paradise Regained*. I draw on them freely here but only as they inform my argument.

This chapter unfolds in two sections. The first explores, through the genre of the work and its use of classical materials, Milton's understanding of the right relations between Christianity and classical culture as they are embodied in *Paradise Regained*. Milton and the Bard have precisely the same views on this important issue in the poem, for the Bard arrived at Milton's view at least by the time he sang Michael's discourse and probably by the proem to Book IX. In this regard, *Paradise Regained* is Milton's true Christian epic, for it proves the Bard's only truly Christian epic from beginning to end. In my view, the radically biblical preference in the late Milton's Christian humanism has not received sufficient emphasis, largely because scholars have assumed that Books I through VI of *Paradise Lost* are "Milton"'s, and they want to harmonize or balance *Paradise Regained* with them. The later epic, however, simply reveals what has been Milton's mature understanding of truly Christian humanism since the Bard began singing *Paradise Lost*. It is more radically biblical than many Miltonists have so far appreciated.

The second section explores the Bard's indirect reflection in *Paradise Regained* on his poetic practices in the first half of *Paradise Lost*. These occur largely during the second day of Satan's temptations, when Jesus is offered "the world" in various forms. Here the Bard is indirectly reflecting on the overgoing poetics of *Paradise Lost,* Books I through VI, or on what may be called "the poetics of strength." The temptations of worldly fame, power, magnificence, and eloquence that Satan offers Jesus also represent a kind of poetic achievement for which the Bard had once striven. Jesus repudiates these in various ways, but all his refusals hinge on his humble obedience to God's will. I argue that this conflict reflects the Bard's rejection of the overgoing poetics of strength, along with the ambition that animates it and the classical paradigms it entails. The conflict culminates in Jesus' rejecting the wisdom and eloquence of Athens—a rejection that simply makes explicit what the Bard's poetic conduct in *Paradise Regained* has already implied.

Scholarly debate over the genre of *Paradise Regained* has a long history. Lewalski's ground-breaking research has made the discussion better informed but has not brought it to a conclusion. E. M. W. Tillyard denies that *Paradise Regained* is an epic, taking his standards for the genre from Homer, Vergil, Tasso, and Milton himself, whereas Louis Martz, dwelling on the didactic character of the poem, finds it similar in form and style to Vergil's *Georgics*.[5] Lewalski, on the other side, affirms its epic character, taking as her standard the Book of Job, which a long tradition has considered "a brief model" of the "epic form." She traces that tradition from patristic times through the seventeenth century, and she locates *Paradise Regained* in it.[6] Most scholars accept this rubric, yet they continue to ponder what it means, for they find in the poem something more than epic alone. The battle of speeches between Satan and Jesus is longer than normal for epic and fundamentally dramatic. John T. Shawcross argues that Milton originally shaped his material as a drama, and he discusses both its dramatic and epic qualities.[7] Weber finds that Milton subordinated epic to drama and thereby achieved a superb resolution of the genres.[8]

Lewalski's scholarship points the way toward a resolution of this problem, but neither she nor her successors have taken it, because they have not fully appreciated Milton's radical preference for Scripture. Like the church fathers and their followers over the centuries, they have taken the classical genres as primary and applied them to Scripture. The Book of Job thus becomes a "brief biblical epic," an eccentric or defective version of a classical genre. Lewalski shows that the tradition found the heroic action of the book in Job's combat with Satan, located in what modern exegetes consider the frame tale.[9] This view of the Book of Job as epic necessarily slights the speeches of Job and his interlocutors, which make up the bulk of the book. Milton's epic on the Jobean model, to the contrary, clearly emphasizes the dramatic exchange between Jesus and Satan. Because Miltonists have

5. See E. M. W. Tillyard, *Milton* (London, 1966), 316, and Louis L. Martz, *Poet of Exile: A Study of Milton's Poetry* (New Haven, 1980), 241–71.

6. The phrases in quotation marks come from Milton's *The Reason of Church Government,* in Milton, *Complete Poems and Major Prose,* ed. Hughes, 668. See Lewalski, *Milton's Brief Epic,* 3–129, for an extensive treatment of the tradition on the Book of Job as a brief biblical epic.

7. See Shawcross, "*Paradise Regained,*" 9–28, on Milton's plan to write a drama on the temptation of Christ, and 29–44, on the dramatic and epic qualities of the poem. See also his treatment of the genre of the poem, 92–101.

8. Weber, *Wedges and Wings,* 108–10.

9. See Lewalski, *Milton's Brief Epic,* 17–28.

conducted the debate about genre by giving primacy to the classical terms, their debate remains unresolved. It can be resolved only when we recognize that Milton gave primacy to the biblical genre embodied in the Book of Job, not to classical ones, for the latter are foreign to Scripture and prove inadequate to describing it.

In short, we are not to measure either the Book of Job or *Paradise Regained* against the standard of classical epic. Rather, we are to judge classical epic as a defective version of what is achieved in *Paradise Regained.* Milton's brief epic is not an eccentric version of "heroick song." Since it sings of Jesus' "deeds / Above Heroic," it proves a song above heroic, and classical epic should be measured against *its* standard. In other words, Milton has revolutionized the terms of discussion. Since "brief epic," by its very formulation, grants primacy to the classical genre, we might call *Paradise Regained* a "supra-epic," because it sings of "deeds / Above Heroic." Ugly as the neologism is, this name for the genre will help us to explore its character.

With the Book of Job and *Paradise Regained* as our instances of supra-epic, we can induce its two chief characteristics. First, and most important, its subject is spiritual warfare. That the action is warfare makes it heroic, and the genre, epic; that the warfare is spiritual makes it "Above Heroic," and the genre, supra-epic. As the soul is superior to the body because it informs the body and governs its acts, so is spiritual warfare superior to physical combat and supra-epic to epic. The consequences of physical combat prove no more than temporal, whereas those of spiritual warfare may well be eternal. Second, the nature of spiritual warfare makes supra-epic necessarily less narrative and more dramatic than classical epic. We cannot see souls in conflict, but we can hear them. In both the Book of Job and *Paradise Regained,* therefore, much of the action takes place as controversy in the conflict of spiritual attitudes and understandings, in what Blake called "Mental Fight." Milton embraced the Jobean model for *Paradise Regained,* not because it was a brief biblical version of classical epic, but because its depiction of spiritual warfare made it a work above heroic, beyond what the ancients had achieved.

Supra-epic should be distinguished from super-epic. In the first half of *Paradise Lost,* the Bard repeatedly attempts to sing a super-epic: he overgoes the imaginations of the ancient epic poets by using their paradigms to sing of supernatural beings. In Book VI, he tries to sing of spiritual warfare in this super-epic manner, and the very attempt reduces spiritual conflict to the measure of physical strength. In the second half of *Paradise Lost,* however, the poet abandons his super-epic aspirations, and in *Paradise Regained* he sings of spiritual combat between the Son of God and Satan in an entirely different way than he did in Raphael's war. The principles of supra-epic cannot be drawn from classical epic, because spiritual warfare proves utterly different from physical combat. Milton took the model for *Paradise Regained* from the "Mental Fight" he found in the Bible: in the Old Testament, from the Book of Job, and in the New Testament, both from the temptation story in Luke and from Jesus' controversies with various opponents. For the height of literary achievement is not defined by the ancient classics, however brilliant they are, but by the "solid good" of spiritual truth revealed by Scripture.

Now *supra-epic* is a polemical term, and it, too, draws as much on classical terminology as does *brief biblical epic.* After all, we have few proper names for the biblical genres as their authors understood them, so we must use the classical. But *supra-epic* serves its turn insofar as it reminds us of the primacy of Scripture for Milton and its superiority over the works of the ancients. That superiority, in Milton's view, proved as much literary as spiritual, for the two cannot actually be separated, though the merely stylistic and the spiritual can. Calling the Book of Job and *Paradise Regained* "supra-epic" simply acknowledges that superiority as Milton understood it. From the perspective of classical epic, which is to say, from the taste of Milton's readers over the centuries, that superiority can hardly be granted, for it proves well-nigh incomprehensible. Yet though an argument will not change one's literary tastes, it will perhaps render intelligible Milton's claim for the superiority of his last epic over *Paradise Lost.*

Less polemically and more descriptively, the spiritual combat between Jesus and Satan could be called a biblical *controversia* and distinguished from philosophical dialog. The genre of the *controversia* has been well explored in *Paradise Regained,* so little need be said about it here.[10] In the ancient world, a *controversia* was a debate on a

10. See Thomas O. Sloane, *Donne, Milton, and the End of Humanist Rhetoric* (Berkeley, 1985), 249–78, and James M. Pearce, "The Theology of Representation: The Meta-Argument of *Paradise Regained,*" *Milton Studies,* XXIV (1988), 277–96. On the Socratic dialogue with respect to the poem, see Elaine B. Safer, "The Socratic Dialogue and 'Knowledge in the Making' in *Paradise Regained,*" *Milton Studies,* VI (1974), 215–26. For the war of words in the poem, see Leonard Mustazza, "Language as Weapon in Milton's *Paradise Regained,*" *Milton Studies,* XVIII (1983), 195–216.

given subject, whether in a court case or simply as a school exercise. It becomes a literary genre in Latin poetry; perhaps the most famous instance is the contest for Achilles' armor between Ajax and Ulysses in Book XIII of Ovid's *Metamorphoses.* Satan's temptations and Jesus' refusals, especially on the second day, unfold as a series of *controversiae* on the value of regal magnificence, wealth, fame, and so on.

Jesus' responses in these encounters often draw on works of ancient philosophy, and his debate with Satan could be regarded as philosophical, rather than biblical. I term it "biblical" for two reasons. First, and most obvious, the characters come from Scripture and Christian tradition. Even where Jesus reproduces classical arguments, they thereby come to have a biblical tenor that they lack in the works of Plato or Aristotle. Second, that tenor emerges from the ground of Jesus' response: his loving obedience to his Father's will. Obedience to God's will is not a factor in ancient ethics, though it is central to the morality of Scripture. Ultimately, Jesus refuses Satan's offers, not because wealth or fame or power are necessarily bad in themselves, but because his Father does not will them for him now. This principle of obedience guides the whole series of *controversiae,* making them biblical, not philosophical.

But a *controversia* on such subjects proves an alien literary form from the classical perspective. It is a rhetorical, not a philosophical, genre. Plato firmly established the dialogue as the premier literary genre for philosophy, for a dialogue has neither winners nor losers because there is no contest. When conflict breaks out in a Platonic dialogue, it emerges from Socrates' interlocutors, usually young sophists like Callicles in the *Gorgias* or Thrasymachus in the *Republic,* and Socrates uses all the resources of his tact to keep them a part of the discussion. Later writers like Cicero, Augustine, and Macrobius bring conflict into a philosophical dialogue only to resolve it socially at least, if not intellectually. The philosophical dialogue is fundamentally an antitragic genre.[11]

The biblical *controversia,* to the contrary, has no use for the distinction between tragedy and comedy because it stands beyond them. In Jesus' *controversiae* with the Pharisees and the Sadducees, his opponents are confronted with the ultimate decision for people of the

11. See Martha C. Nussbaum, *The Fragility of Goodness: Luck and Ethics in Greek Tragedy and Philosophy* (Cambridge, Eng., 1986), 122–35.

New Testament: offense or faith. They can be offended by Jesus or believe in him.[12] To be sure, the Gospels present this choice as being offered to everyone, but the *controversia* is always begun by Jesus' opponents. The genre itself is neither tragic nor comic, for its outcome depends on a decision by Jesus' interlocutors. That decision stands outside the genre, and the Gospels rarely report it as being made definitively, once and for all, in the encounter with Jesus. Moreover, for Milton, the importance of that outcome exceeded all the horror or joy that ancient tragedy or comedy could imagine. For the ancients had no concept of eternal life in the presence of God or eternal death apart from it.

In short, the biblical *controversia,* like the biblical supra-epic, transgresses and transcends the generic distinctions of ancient literature. The classical terms and conventions for the genres will therefore always prove inadequate to assessing what the Bible achieves. Moreover, from Milton's perspective, these biblical genres demonstrably surpass their classical analogs, simply because the Bible presents ultimate truths. We are not to measure Scripture by classical standards. We are to measure classical achievements against Scripture.

This argument simply asserts the traditional position of the Fathers, as all Miltonists understand. Augustine tells Christians to study the works of the pagans without qualms of conscience because wherever they find truth, it is their Lord's.[13] The standard of truth is to be found in Scripture, and the achievements of the pagans may be judged according to it. Nevertheless, Milton's giving the Bible a *literary* primacy in the consideration of genres extended patristic principles beyond the Fathers' scope. *Paradise Regained* claims superiority over the ancient epics because it embraces Scripture as the standard for its genre as for its truth. Its biblical supra-epic presents a spiritual warfare, so it necessarily proves a biblical *controversia.* This biblical supra-epic/*controversia* enacts a spiritual warfare on the ultimate questions of human life, where obedience to God's will means eternal life, and disobedience, eternal death. That warfare takes place within "nature's bounds" (I, 13), but its consequences extend beyond time and the cosmos. In Milton's view, these supracosmic consequences exist

12. For the relation between offense and faith in the gospels, see David McCracken, *The Scandal of the Gospels: Jesus, Story, and Offense* (Oxford, 1994).

13. Augustine, *On Christian Doctrine,* II, 18, 28.

not only for his hero but for his readers. No ancient epic envisions a struggle of such magnitude. How could it? For Milton, only the Christian revelation displayed the essence and ultimacies of spiritual warfare.

This argument perhaps seems an extreme, and therefore unbalanced, version of the traditional understanding of right relations between Christian and classical culture. After all, Jesus' speeches in *Paradise Regained* are filled with the echoes of ancient philosophy. He rejects the temptations of wealth, glory, and power with arguments drawn from Plato, Aristotle, Seneca, and others. Miltonists have therefore seen the poem as the work of a Christian humanist, and they have often argued that Jesus proves a hero of Platonic or Aristotelian inspiration.[14] Milton's Christianity here achieves a humanist flowering, as the poet draws richly on ancient philosophy to present a Christian humanist hero in Jesus.

But this view of *Paradise Regained* misses how Milton has transformed his ancient sources, sometimes in local context, yet always in principle, by putting them in Jesus' mouth in this combat with Satan. To be sure, the scholarly view just described does acknowledge Milton's preference for Scripture, but it does not consider how radical that preference is. Three instances of allusion in their contexts will demonstrate this radicalness before we consider the principle that transforms all Milton's allusions to ancient philosophy in *Paradise Regained*.

When Jesus rejects Satan's temptation to worldly glory, he echoes the ancient distinction between worldly fame and true glory: "For what is glory but the blaze of fame, / The people's praise, if always praise unmixt?" (III, 47–48). Merritt Y. Hughes notes that "Milton translates Seneca's question (*Epistles,* cii, 19): 'What distinguishes clear renown (*claritas*) from glory? Glory consists in the judgment of the many; renown in that of the good.' "[15] Yet Milton did not merely

14. Merritt Y. Hughes finds in Jesus a Christianized version of Aristotle's magnanimous man, in "The Christ of *Paradise Regained* and the Renaissance Poetic Tradition," *Studies in Philology,* XXXV (1938), 254–77. John M. Steadman finds the ladder of temptations of the second day Aristotelian in conception, moving from the voluptuous to the active to the contemplative life, in "*Paradise Regained:* Moral Dialectic and the Pattern of Rejection," *University of Toronto Quarterly,* XXXI (1962), 416–30. Lewalski finds components of several classical heroes in Milton's Jesus, in *Milton's Brief Epic,* 242–49. On the whole, she agrees with Irene Samuel, *Plato and Milton* (Ithaca, 1947), 69–95, that Jesus is most closely related to the Socratic-Platonic philosopher.

15. See Milton, *Complete Poems and Major Prose,* ed. Hughes, note to III, 47–48.

translate the question; he also transformed the answer. Jesus finds "true glory and renown, when God / Looking on th' Earth, with approbation marks / The just man" (III, 60–62). Milton has preserved the ancient contrast between the approval of the many, as "A miscellaneous rabble" (50), and the approval of the good, but the latter he locates only in God. The classical allusion is thus transfused with Christian meaning.

The same thing occurs in Jesus' assertion that he will "best reign, who first / Well hath obey'd" (III, 195–96). Walter MacKellar notes the antiquity of this principle, finding it in Solon, Plato, Aristotle, Cicero, and Seneca. Hughes quotes Plato (*Laws,* 715c) that "the administration of the laws must be given to that man who is most obedient to the laws."[16] This sound political principle is treated often in ancient philosophy.

In Jesus' mouth, however, it is not a political principle. He speaks it in response to the fourth temptation of the second day, the central one of the seven culminating in the vision of Athens. He is mentioning, for the first time in his temptation, the virtue for which he is celebrated in the poem, obedience. He affirms to Satan his willingness to be tried by sufferings—"By tribulations, injuries, insults, / Contempts, and scorns, and snares, and violence" (III, 190–91)—so that God may know the depth of his obedience. "Who best / Can suffer, best can do; best reign, who first / Well hath obey'd" (194–96) transforms the allusion to Plato. For in Plato, the prospective ruler must first obey the laws of the *polis.* Jesus, however, obeys the will of God, which not only will not protect him from insult and violence, as the laws of Plato's *polis* would protect its citizens, but will even expose him to these dangers, as he has already understood (I, 259–67). Jesus' obedience to God proves far more radical than obedience to the laws in Plato, just as Jesus' kingdom proves far different from an earthly *polis.* The classical allusion has an utterly unclassical meaning.

These two instances of allusion are transformed by their immediate contexts. The alteration in my final instance proves neither so immediate nor so radical, for it works in a different way. It occurs in Jesus' answer to Satan's offer of wealth as a means to gain his kingdom. Satan argues that the poor man can never come to power

16. See MacKellar, *Variorum Commentary, Paradise Regained,* note on III, 195–96, and Milton, *Complete Poems and Major Prose,* ed. Hughes, note on III, 194–97.

because he lacks "the gold" to get himself "puissant friends" (II, 425), so all his "Virtue, Valor, Wisdom sit in want" (431) while rich men rule. Jesus' answer, as MacKellar notes, contains a number of classical arguments. The state that lacks virtue is soon rent by the forces of its conflicting passions; external goods, like wealth, are merely a means to the acquisition of virtue; the person who governs himself is truly wise and truly a king.[17]

Near the beginning of his speech, Jesus gives several instances of virtuous men in Scripture who "have oft attain'd / In lowest poverty to highest deeds": Gideon, Jephtha, and David (II, 437–42). These men were raised up by God to do mighty works. As examples, then, they illustrate Jesus' faith in the Father, who will grant him his kingdom when the Father wills. This affirmation of faith and trust in God precedes and thus affects the classical arguments that follow it. After affirming that "he who reigns within himself, and rules / Passions, Desires, and Fears, is more a King" (466–67), Jesus affirms something kinglier still, his own mission:

> But to guide Nations in the way of truth
> By saving Doctrine, and from error lead
> To know, and knowing worship God aright,
> Is yet more Kingly; this attracts the Soul,
> Governs the inner man, the nobler part;
> That other o'er the body only reigns,
> And oft by force, which to a generous mind
> So reigning can be no sincere delight.
> (II, 473–80)

To be sure, these words reproduce a central distinction in ancient political thought, between rule by authority and rule by force. But Jesus employs the distinction in an unusual way, for he points to the true worship of God as the means for forming the soul and ordering one's life. Milton emphasized the point by placing these words almost at the end of Book II and by having Jesus reiterate them in the final lines of his rejection of Athens (IV, 347–64). If the ancient philosophers did not often treat divine worship and political life together,

17. See MacKellar, *Variorum Commentary, Paradise Regained,* notes on II, 433–86 and 466–67.

Plato explored them thoroughly in the *Laws,* where worship proves central to the moral formation (*paideia*) of the citizens and where, in the imagined *polis,* a religious festival takes place every day of the year.[18] From Milton's perspective, this laudable understanding of worship was vitiated by the gods worshipped. Plato did not know how to "worship God aright." In fact, his treatment of worship emphasizes civic participation in the rituals of sacrifice and celebration, as is common among the ancients. But Jesus' notion of worship looks to a quite different principle: religious faith, the worship of God "in spirit and in truth" (John 4:23).

Hence, in Jesus' rejecting Satan's temptation to wealth, the classical arguments are not transformed by their immediate context, as they were in the previous two instances. Nevertheless, Jesus surrounds these arguments with a subtle insistence on faith and trust in God as the principle of patient obedience. Jesus' faith and obedience animate his rejection of wealth, and these virtues stand beyond the scope of classical philosophy, though they are central to Scripture. Jesus frames the classical arguments with his insistence on these biblical virtues, thus coloring the philosophical arguments. They retain, as Jesus states them, their classical force, but they gain new force from Jesus' insistence on true faith and worship as the way to "[attract] the Soul" and "[govern] the inner man" (II, 476–77).

Jesus' use of Platonic arguments here does not so much transform as fulfill them. In one sense, it enacts the patristic notion that classical philosophy was a "preparation for the gospel," which completes and supersedes whatever is true in pagan thought. The Fathers also held that the ancient pagans had studied "the works of Moses" and had borrowed their insights from the Hebrews. This tradition remained vigorous in Milton's day, and Jesus asserts as much when he declares "That rather *Greece* from us these Arts deriv'd" (IV, 338).[19] In the light of this tradition, Milton's Jesus does not prove so much a Christian humanist as Plato was a Hellenic Judaist. Jesus is simply reclaiming what is rightly his own.

18. See Eric Voegelin, *Plato and Aristotle* (Baton Rouge, 1957), 228–39, 257–63, Vol. III of Voegelin, *Order and History,* 5 vols., and Zdravko Planinc, *Plato's Political Philosophy: Prudence in the "Republic" and the "Laws"* (Columbia, Mo., 1991), 215–60.

19. See McKellar, *Variorum Commentary, Paradise Regained,* note on IV, 338, for bibliography.

I do not contend that every classical argument in Jesus' speeches is biblically transformed or fulfilled by its context, but all of them are altered, in principle, by Jesus' uttering them in his combat with Satan. They do not have the same meaning spoken from Jesus' mouth, with his destiny, that they have on the pages of the ancient thinkers. All of the classical arguments Jesus makes have a radically unclassical meaning simply because he makes them, for they stand with Jesus under the shadow of the cross.

When the ancient thinkers argue against undue attachment to wealth, worldly glory, power, and so on, they are affirming, in contrast, the leisure (*schole* or *otium*) to pursue philosophy. This leisure was created by their refusal to spend time and energy on business and politics. They did not reject wealth per se, for most were independently wealthy, and Aristotle insists that wealth is needed in order to exercise certain virtues.[20] But philosophical inquiry requires free time and a free mind, and the pursuit of wealth and power allows for neither.

When Jesus rejects wealth, worldly glory, and power, however, he is affirming his complete obedience to God and trust in God's will. No comfortable leisure for philosophical contemplation lies in his future, as he knows, but only "Exaltation to Afflictions high" (II, 92). Hence, his use of classical arguments to reject these things not only possesses more than classical force but enjoys that force because it proceeds from the utterly unclassical principle of obedience in faith. Milton's Jesus seems not yet to know precisely how his ministry will end, but we know, and he has clearly accepted whatever is to come. Hence, his rejection of wealth, glory, and power is nothing less than his acceptance of the utter poverty, ignominy, and powerlessness of the cross. His obedient acceptance of the cross transforms the classical arguments he uses, for no ancient philosopher could have accepted such an ignominious "suffering for Truth's sake," not even the highly praised Socrates.

Miltonists have not recognized how fully this poem stands under the shadow of the cross. They have looked to Plato's tripartite soul and to the virtues of classical ethics in order to treat Jesus' heroic refusal of Satan's temptations. To be sure, these classical themes may be found in

20. See Aristotle, *Nicomachean Ethics,* trans. Martin Ostwald (New York, 1962), 1122b18–1123a20.

the structure and texture of the poem, and I do not deny their importance. *Paradise Regained* does hold up Jesus' temperance and courage as didactic models, and, admittedly, the poem does not dwell repeatedly on the "reproachful life and cursed death" (*PL,* XII, 406) that will form his redeeming ministry, though it recurs to his afflictions on more than one occasion. But then, the poem does not need to emphasize the cross. The end of *Paradise Lost* dwells on it, and all of Milton's audience knew that *Paradise* was *regained* through Christ's death on the cross. The poem does not so much affirm the classical virtues as point to the obedience in faith that transcends and fulfills them. Jesus' classical arguments are all infused by that biblical source. Moreover, the depth of his obedience is revealed in what it cost him on the cross. Jesus does not simply reject all the forms of kingship in this world offered by Satan. Rather, he accepts his mission as slave to humankind, "obedient unto death, even the death of the cross" (Philippians 2:8).

In sum, then, *Paradise Regained* was Milton's true Christian epic because it enacted his radical preference for Scripture in his choice of genre and in the heroism he depicted. He did not take the classical genres and put them together in an "original" way, and his biblical hero does not merely embody all the classical virtues. Rather, he took the supra-epic of the Book of Job with its biblical *controversia* as the model for his song "Above Heroic," because these genres treat properly of spiritual warfare. Furthermore, his hero embodies the classical virtues because Jesus' radical obedience to the Father utterly transcends them. His genre and his hero surpass the classical genres and their virtues because Milton's poem treated a spiritual depth and destiny beyond the vision of the ancients. That is to say, Milton based his genre and his hero centrally on Scripture. Even where Jesus uses classical arguments, they have an unclassical force and reach because they stand with him under the shadow of the cross.

In this way, *Paradise Regained* enacts Harold Bloom's revisionary trope of "transumption," though in a surprising fashion. Bloom finds in Milton his preternaturally "strong poet," and he calls Miltonic allusion "transumptive": "Milton's aim is to make his own belatedness into an earliness, and his tradition's priority over him into a lateness."[21] Bloom illustrates the point by analyzing the allusions in

21. Bloom, *Map of Misreading,* 125–43, esp. 129, 131.

Paradise Lost, I, 283–313, which describes Satan's size and shield as he walks to call the demons from the fiery lake. Bloom shows how the passage alludes to Homer, Vergil, Ovid, Tasso, Edmund Spenser, and the Bible. The poet, he argues, overgoes his predecessors by extravagantly describing a character who possesses the traits of previous literary characters yet who acts before even the beginning of time. In this way, Homer, Vergil, and the others are transumed, becoming later and defective imitations of "Milton."

In my view, Bloom is not writing about the historical Milton, but about the Bard in Book I of *Paradise Lost.* Moreover, though Bloom acutely describes what the Bard attempts to do, he mutes the fact that "transumptive allusion" necessarily fails. Insofar as it alludes, it affirms its "belatedness" and so cannot prove truly "transumptive." Bloom, and Milton's Bard, would have us believe that seizing primal events for one's subject constitutes an assertion of priority. But the assertion is silly on the face of it, and that, of course, is the burden of being a "late poet." The Bard's problem in Books I through VI of *Paradise Lost* is that he is a Bloomian. He does not yet understand true priority.

By the end of *Paradise Lost,* however, the Bard comes to Milton's understanding of true priority, and he enacts it in *Paradise Regained.* True priority consists simply in answerability to God's word in Scripture. Milton thought that Moses and the author of the Book of Job were historically prior to Homer. In turning to the Book of Job for his genre and to Scripture for his style, Milton was returning not only to the fount of truth, as he believed, but also to the historically earliest modes of its expression. Nevertheless, he had no interest in temporal priority for its own sake. It proved valuable only as an index to the divine truth, which is prior to all things, and this he found manifested in Jesus and the New Testament. In *Paradise Regained,* Milton allied himself with Jesus, his Savior and hero. As Jesus repeatedly affirms his faithful obedience to God, so did Milton faithfully submit himself to Scripture for his genre and for the virtues of his hero. If we measure them by the standards of classical literature, we cannot be adequate to Milton's genius in the poem. *Paradise Regained,* in its faithfulness to Scripture, presents itself as the standard whereby classical letters should be measured and found wanting, because it sings of "deeds / Above Heroic," of Jesus' acceptance of the cross as the way to regain Paradise for us.

Transumptive allusion does not appear in *Paradise Regained* because the poet does not care to be "strong." Rather, he transumes the ancient epic poets in a completely different way. The Bloomian strong poet, by his very efforts at self-assertion, merely affirms the priority of his predecessors and his own belatedness. Milton's Bard has done with all that foolishness. He simply looks to the truth of Scripture and seeks for an answerable style. Since the truths of Christianity surpass the achievements of the ancients, submission to Scripture and a style answerable to scriptural truth make the Christian poet superior. In this way, the humble poet, not the strong poet, surpasses the ancient epics, singing a song above heroic.

Similarly, in *Paradise Regained* the humble Bard surpasses the singer of *Paradise Lost,* especially of Books I through VI. Just as we are not to measure Scripture by classical standards but to measure classical achievements against the standard of Scripture, so we should not measure *Paradise Regained* by the standards of *Paradise Lost* but measure the Bard's earlier apprentice work against the achievement of his biblical epic. Hence, *Paradise Regained* is not a brief and relatively flat Christian epic compared to the splendors of *Paradise Lost.* Rather, *Paradise Lost* is a clumsily distended work, for it takes the Bard eight full books to reach the subject promised in its first line. *Paradise Regained* possesses greater artistic economy and integrity. Moreover, *Paradise Lost* achieved its splendors because its overgoing Bard often employs classical paradigms, so he often falters in his treatment of Christian truth, something he corrects within the poem and avoids in *Paradise Regained. Paradise Regained* never falters as a fully Christian poem, as *Paradise Lost* does so often in its first half. If we recognize the Bard's story in *Paradise Lost* and accept Milton's biblical standards for literary excellence, we will discern the reasons underlying the claim that *Paradise Regained* is his true Christian epic. These reasons may not suit our taste; we may reject, as a literary principle, "that Great / Or Bright infers not Excellence" whereas only "solid good" does; we may continue to prefer the sublimities and variety of *Paradise Lost* to all the virtues *Paradise Regained* may be said to possess. Milton's insistence on the superiority of *Paradise Regained* to *Paradise Lost,* declared in his opening lines, may be rejected by Miltonists. Nevertheless, his insistence was principled and consistent, and his reasons deserve our full recognition, if not our acceptance.

Jesus' rejecting the temptation of Greek learning has received considerable commentary as a crux in Milton studies. Tillyard claimed that

Milton was attacking "the dearest and oldest inhabitants of his mind." Douglas Bush found it painful "to watch Milton turn and rend some main roots of his being." Nonetheless, Bush understood Milton to be "asserting, with an earnestness born of ripened insight, his lifelong hierarchy of values," and Irene Samuel amplified the point in her oft-cited essay "Milton on Learning and Wisdom." Her position on the consistency in Milton's thought about the right relation of classical learning to true wisdom has been echoed by Howard Schulz and Arnold Stein, among others.[22] Scholars have also shown that Jesus' critique of classical learning was by no means extreme in Milton's day and proves more subtly careful than it may first appear.[23] Milton was qualifying the value of classical studies, not rejecting them. Jesus repudiates, not pagan learning *tout court,* but that learning as an end in itself.[24]

Milton and his Bard have the same understanding of these issues in *Paradise Regained* but not the same relation to them. Similarly, they have the same understanding of Christian epic in the poem and the same view of its superiority to *Paradise Lost,* yet they remain distinct with respect to the earlier work. As Harry Berger, Jr., observes, the Bard's spontaneous defects in *Paradise Lost* were Milton's deliberate and dramatic effects.[25] The Bard has reason to regret his use of classical paradigms for Christian subjects because his overgoing ambitions led him to falter as a Christian poet. But Milton knew exactly what he was doing: impersonating his ambitious Bard.

Similarly, while Jesus' rejecting the temptation to pagan learning represents Milton's consistently held view, for the Bard it proves an understanding realized only in the course of singing *Paradise Lost.* Although he always acknowledged the superiority of Christian truth to pagan learning, he did not always fully understand wherein that supe-

22. See Tillyard, *Milton,* 262; Douglas Bush, *The Renaissance and English Humanism* (Toronto, 1939), 125; Irene Samuel, "Milton on Learning and Wisdom," *PMLA,* LXIV (1949), 708–23; Howard Schulz, *Milton and Forbidden Knowledge* (New York, 1955), 89–92; and Stein, *Heroic Knowledge,* 97.

23. See Stein, *Heroic Knowledge,* 108–10.

24. Dayton Haskin admirably formulates the temptation as Satan's displacing the biblical understanding of spiritual reality for one philosophical and aesthetic. He argues that modern readers have been disturbed by Jesus' response because, as the heirs of the nineteenth century, we have accepted that displacement. See *Milton's Burden of Interpretation* (Philadelphia, 1994), 153.

25. See Berger, "Archaism, Vision, and Revision," 52.

riority lay. He did not understand how the humble style of the Gospels fits with its teaching that "God resisteth the proud" or with the Savior's redemptive self-emptying even unto the death of the cross. In short, the Bard has felt Satan's temptation to the splendor of classical eloquence. True, he never sought it for its own sake, apart from Christian truth. But he did seek it so as to exalt himself over his epic predecessors. He did prefer it to the style of Scripture in his singing—a preference he came to regret and correct.

The story of Milton's Bard does not end with *Paradise Lost,* even though the progress of his self-understanding is fully achieved there. *Paradise Regained* reflects critically on Books I through VI of *Paradise Lost,* albeit indirectly, much as do Books VII through XII. The Bard's self-critical reflections achieve their climax when they become explicit in Jesus' rejecting the temptation of Athens, but the poet has implied them from the beginning of his poem, largely by what he ascribes to Satan. For in *Paradise Regained* the Bard associates epic techniques and subjects wholly with Satan, even though in *Paradise Lost* he used them also for his divine characters. Moreover, though Jesus' speeches contain arguments from the ancient philosophers, and so are implicitly classical, the poem resoundingly links the explicitly classical with Satan. The Bard's associating classical references, techniques, and subjects with Satan in *Paradise Regained* marks his critical reflection on his earlier work.

The first explicit classical references in the poem pour forth from Satan. He is answering Belial's suggestion that he tempt Jesus with female beauty. Satan scorns the idea and portrays Belial as always lurking somewhere so as

> to waylay
> Some beauty rare, *Calisto, Clymene,*
> *Daphne,* or *Semele, Antiopa,*
> Or *Amymone, Syrinx,* many more
> Too long, then lay'st thy scapes on names ador'd,
> *Apollo, Neptune, Jupiter,* or *Pan,*
> Satyr, or Faun, or Sylvan.
>
> (II, 185–91)

Not only are these the first classical references in the poem, but they appear in a classical topos, the catalog. Classical references first appear in a classical technique, spoken by Satan.

Paradise Regained contains several catalogs, and all enter the poem through Satan's mouth or through his actions.[26] The Satanic banquet is presented in a series of brief catalogs (II, 340–65). Satan urges Jesus to seek glory with a short catalog of pagan conquerors (III, 31–42). He tempts Jesus to Parthian power with an extensive catalog of places (III, 269–302). The Bard places these in Satan's mouth, and when the poet presents the armies also shown to Jesus, a shorter catalog ensues (316–21). The poem contains only two other extensive catalogs and both are spoken by Satan: the places that send embassies to Rome (IV, 68–79) and the city of Athens (IV, 236–80), all of which are pagan.

Jesus speaks but one brief catalog in the poem, appropriately filled with classical names, but he speaks it with scorn, using the topos ironically. After Satan has set forth to him the splendors of Rome, Jesus is "unmov'd" by all "this grandeur and majestic show / Of luxury, though call'd magnificence" (IV, 109–11). He then says,

> . . . thou should'st add to tell
> Thir sumptuous gluttonies, and gorgeous feasts
> On *Citron* tables or *Atlantic* stone,
> (For I have also heard, perhaps have read)
> Their wines of *Setia, Cales,* and *Falerne,*
> *Chios* and *Crete,* and how they quaff in Gold,
> Crystal and Murrhine cups emboss'd with Gems
> And studs of Pearl, to me should'st tell who thirst
> And hunger still.
>
> (IV, 113–21)

The Bard gives Jesus this technique only as a retort to Satan's use of it.

Only at two points does Jesus refer to classical heroes with approval. The first comes in response to Satan's offer of wealth. Jesus lists four Romans in a single line (II, 446) as "Worthy of Memorial" (445) in their contempt of riches. He does so, however, only after mentioning the biblical examples of Gideon, Jephtha, and David (439–42). The second instance is Jesus' praise of "Poor *Socrates*" (III, 96), "For truth's sake suffering death unjust" (98). Yet he qualifies that high praise by naming Job first and calling Socrates the "next

26. For a brief study of the catalogs in *Paradise Lost,* see William B. Hunter, Jr., "Milton's Laundry Lists," *Milton Quarterly,* XVIII (1984), 58–61.

most memorable" (96). Compared to Satan's frequent references to pagan places and persons, all equally worthy of possession or emulation, Jesus' approval proves slight indeed. He rather features criticisms of pagan culture and values, for his censures are more frequent, extensive, and emphatic than these two brief notes of praise.

Since the catalog is an epic technique designed to lend magnificence to the action of a poem, Satan's catalogs in *Paradise Regained* emphasize the "greatness" of what he is offering to Jesus. Similarly, the Bard presented catalogs in *Paradise Lost* as part of his attempt to overgo the ancients. The overgoing topos, a related device, has the same magnifying aim as the catalog, to which it is often close in form. The two overgoing topoi in *Paradise Regained* (II, 358–61, and III, 337–43) are both presented by the Bard to set forth images created by Satan, and both are briefer than the overgoing topoi of *Paradise Lost*.

The second instance in the later poem has a parallel in the earlier, so they may be easily compared. The description of the Parthian army concludes with a comparison to one in Matteo Maria Boiardo, but it is nothing compared to the army of Hell of *Paradise Lost:*

> Such forces met not, nor so wide a camp,
> When *Agrican* with all his Northern powers
> Beseig'd *Albracca,* as Romances tell,
> The City of *Gallaphrone,* from thence to win
> The fairest of her Sex, *Angelica,*
> His daughter, sought by many Prowest Knights,
> Both *Paynim,* and the Peers of *Charlemagne.*
> (*PR,* III, 337–43)

> And now [Satan's] heart
> Distends with pride, and hard'ning in his strength
> Glories: For never since created man,
> Met such imbodied force, as nam'd with these
> Could merit more than that small infantry
> Warr'd on by Cranes: though all the Giant brood
> Of *Phlegra* with th' Heroic Race were join'd
> That fought at *Thebes* and *Ilium,* on each side
> Mixt with auxiliar Gods; and what resounds
> In Fable or *Romance* of *Uther's* Son
> Begirt with *British* and Armoric Knights;
> And all who since, Baptiz'd or Infidel

> Jousted in *Aspramont* or *Montalban,*
> *Damasco,* or *Marocco,* or *Trebisond,*
> Or whom *Biserta* sent from *Afric* shore
> When *Charlemain* with all his Peerage fell
> By *Fontarabbia.*
>
> (*PL,* I, 573–87)

If one knows that in Boiardo, Agrican of Tartary brings 2,200,000 troops to Albracca, the Parthian army shown to Jesus is impressive indeed.[27] If one does not know that, only the intention of the comparison denotes vast size, yet effectively enough. The Bard of *Paradise Lost,* in contrast, leaves no doubt about the size of the demonic army, even if one is unfamiliar with many of his references. It is larger than the combined armies of all classical and romance epics, with the giants and the gods thrown in. The Bard is displaying his learning and his ability to imagine, not simply the greatest army ever in poetry, but an army greater in size than all the poetic armies that ever existed in his tradition together, and with warriors of supernatural power and cunning. As I argued earlier, the Bard's heart here, like Satan's, distends with pride, as he, too, glories in the strength of his overgoing powers. Hence, his overgoing topos rather overdoes it. By the time he sings *Paradise Regained,* he uses the technique with greater restraint.

In *Paradise Regained,* then, Milton's Bard makes numerous classical references, composes several catalogs, and sings two overgoing topoi. All these techniques are linked with Satan, either placed in his mouth or describing his actions. All are associated with classical letters, either through explicit reference or because they are techniques from the epic tradition. All were practiced by the Bard in *Paradise Lost* in an effort to magnify his poem over classical and romance epics. The Bard of *Paradise Regained,* then, reflects critically on his earlier use of classical techniques and references by associating them so closely with Satan. At the very least, he implies limits on their use for Christian truth in poetry. Insofar as truth is illuminated by error, as virtue is by wickedness, a Christian poet might use these pagan references and techniques as the Bard has, to portray the darkness that sets off the light.

The Bard's position on the limits of the classical in true Christian poetry may also be seen in his use of the epic simile. Similes appear

27. See *Paradise Regained,* ed. Carey, note on III, 337–43.

rarely in the first three books of the poem. Not until Book IV do they appear with any frequency, and epic similes, not at all until then. On their first appearance, they describe how Satan is overmatched against Jesus (IV, 10–20).[28] This triple simile compares Satan to a man who continually tries to deceive another despite always being foiled, to a swarm of flies at a wine-press, and to waves dashing themselves against a rock. Granted, each of these implies Jesus, but only as a secondary figure. Primarily, they convey Satan's frustration and his vileness as their vehicles descend from man to flies to waves.

Although several similes ensue in Book IV, and some striking ones are spoken by Jesus (147–48, 149–50, 330, 343–44), none is longer than two lines. Epic similes do not occur until the final defeat of Satan and his fall:

> But Satan smitten with amazement fell
> As when Earth's Son *Antaeus* (to compare
> Small things with greatest) in *Irassa* strove
> With *Jove's Alcides,* and oft foil'd still rose,
> Receiving from his mother Earth new strength,
> Fresh from his fall, and fiercer grapple join'd,
> Throttl'd at length in th'Air, expir'd and fell;
> So after many a foil the Tempter proud,
> Renewing fresh assaults, amidst his pride
> Fell whence he stood to see his Victor fall.
> And as that *Theban* Monster that propos'd
> Her riddle, and him who solv'd it not, devour'd,
> That once found out and solv'd, for grief and spite
> Cast herself headlong from th' *Ismenian* steep,
> So struck with dread and anguish fell the Fiend. . . .
> (IV, 562–76)

Satan is compared to Antaeus vanquished by Hercules and to the Sphinx quelled by Oedipus. These are the longest similes in *Paradise Regained,* the only ones with vehicles drawn from classical literature, and they are used for Satan's fall. Again, they imply Jesus but just barely. He is given only a prepositional phrase in the first simile

28. The epic similes in Book IV are treated by Neil Forsyth, "Having Done All to Stand: Biblical and Classical Allusion in *Paradise Regained,*" *Milton Studies,* XXI (1985), 199–227, and by Rene E. Fortin, "The Climactic Similes of *Paradise Regained:* 'True Wisdom' or 'False Semblance'?," *Milton Quarterly,* VII (1973), 39–43.

("strove / With *Jove's Alcides*") and does not appear at all in the second. In the first half of *Paradise Lost,* in contrast, the Bard used epic similes for the loyal angels and the unfallen Eve, as well as for the demons. In the second half, he reserved the device largely, though not wholly, for Satan and his offspring. In *Paradise Regained,* he employs it only for Satan himself.

The Bard of *Paradise Regained,* thus, associates classical epic with Satan throughout his poem. Approving references to pagan places and persons pour forth from Satan yet are barely spoken by Jesus. Literary devices from the epic tradition are used unironically only by Satan and for his actions, never with regard to Jesus. This association marks the Bard's critical reflection on having used classical paradigms for divine characters in *Paradise Lost.*

His self-criticism also extends to certain subjects, most obviously to martial epic. As in Book XI of *Paradise Lost* (689–99), his critique of martial values argues his critique of the genre celebrating those values. Jesus reiterates its main points when he answers Satan's temptation to "glory" by military conquest. He insists that there is nothing glorious in conquest, which only destroys "all the flourishing works of peace" (III, 80). He also implies that there are no true virtues in it either: conquerors "swell with pride, and must be titl'd Gods" (81), but they are actually "Rolling in brutish vices, and deform'd" (86). Analogously, the poet who would celebrate the martial ethos while attempting to overgo the ancient epic poets runs the risk of swelling with pride as he seeks the divine titles awarded to Homer and Vergil. The Christian poet should not be possessed by ambition for that kind of glory but should seek something completely different—something unthinkable from a classical perspective: a hidden glory, invisible and inaudible. Jesus explains it this way:

> This is true glory and renown, when God
> Looking on th' Earth, with approbation marks
> The just man, and divulges him through Heaven
> To all his Angels, who with true applause
> Recount his praises; thus he did to *Job.* . . .
> (III, 60–64)

Clearly, the writer of the Book of Job relates a narrative of "true glory and renown," and so does the Bard of *Paradise Regained,* who imitates his supra-epic. Both writers, like their heroes, seek the approbation of an audience of One. The poet who glorifies warfare, perhaps especially angelic warfare, seeks the approval of the many and fails to understand true glory or virtue. He certainly fails to represent adequately "the better fortitude" of Christian heroism, which is won through spiritual, not physical, warfare. The Christian poet, according to the Bard of *Paradise Regained,* should not sing a martial epic.

This moral and artistic principle is underscored by the only time martial images are recounted in the poem: they are created by Satan. In the first of the three temptations from the mountaintop (III, 251 *ff.*), he shows Jesus the Parthian armies marching forth. Satan describes briefly their "martial equipage" (III, 304) and their "warlike muster" (308) before the Bard sets forth the sweeping movement in greater detail (310–46).[29] Warfare is not described for two reasons. The Bard will not represent warfare because he now believes it indecorous in a Christian poem. Also, Satan remembers Jesus' words against conquest. It therefore suits his purposes to present the splendor of military power to Jesus rather than its destruction. Milton's Bard clearly marks these images as Satanic. He thereby reflects critically on his war in Heaven and on his earlier ambitions to epic greatness.

Critical reflection does not amount to repudiation. On the issue of martial epic, *Paradise Regained* adds nothing of substance to Michael's critique of the heroic ethos in Book XI. It simply underscores the link between that ethos and Satan—a link that Michael already implied. Granted, the Bard began *Paradise Lost* by linking Satan and the demons with martial epic, and he employed the epic manner for them largely throughout the poem. But he did not reserve it wholly for them. In *Paradise Regained,* however, he uses the matter and manner of classical epic only for Satan. This represents an achievement in the Bard's self-understanding as a poet of Christian epic. He is now clear on the satanic implications of martial epic, at least within his oeuvre. His critical reflection on martial epic in *Paradise Regained* marks his corrective resinging of the war in Heaven. Yet the criticism does not constitute a rejection, for it remains implied and indirect.

29. See John Carey, Introduction, to *The Poems of John Milton,* ed. Carey and Fowler, 1075, for a fine discussion of how this passage "keeps itself just beyond the range of exact vision."

The Son's triumph in Book VI was the work of a pious, if ambitious, Bard, and it may well induce piety in a Christian reader. It cannot harm the well-intentioned. The Bard uses Michael's discourse to correct his misrepresentation of the Savior's heroism in Book VI, and in *Paradise Regained* he simply extends that corrective resinging: he sings a true Christian epic of spiritual, not military, warfare.

He correctively resings not only the matter but also the manner of epic. As many scholars have noted, the style of *Paradise Regained* continues the plainness and simplicity of Michael's discourse, and behind both lies the style of the Gospels.[30] Although this style has been criticized for bareness and lack of vigor, it has recently been ably described and defended. What C. S. Lewis attributed to Milton's fatigue in Books XI and XII proves more intelligible as the Bard's stylistic development, as a general movement away from the high, epic style of Books I through VI to one imitating the *sermo humilis* of biblical narrative. As Erich Auerbach observed, the Gospels transgress and transcend the hierarchy of genres in classical literature, narrating in a low style the most sublime events enacted among socially low persons. The church fathers understood this to be the literary effect of God's having become Man, in a humble station, to redeem humankind by the lowest possible death.[31] The Bard's singing Jesus' "deeds / Above Heroic" in a low style, compared to *Paradise Lost,* Books I through VI,

30. See Edward R. Weismiller, "Studies of Style and Verse Form in *Paradise Regained,*" in MacKellar, *Variorum Commentary, Paradise Regained,* 253–363: on the poem's gospel-like manner, see 305; on its similarity to *Paradise Lost,* Books XI–XII, see 316. See also Archie Burnett, *Milton's Style: The Shorter Poems, "Paradise Regained," and "Samson Agonistes"* (London, 1981), 112–38. Other discussions of style include Carey, Introduction, 1070–76; Philip McCaffrey, "*Paradise Regained:* The Style of Satan's Athens," *Milton Quarterly,* V (1971), 7–14; Emory Elliott, "Milton's Biblical Style in *Paradise Regained,*" *Milton Studies,* VI (1974), 227–41; Alan Fisher, "Why Is *Paradise Regained* So Cold?," *Milton Studies,* XIV (1980), 195–217; Henry J. Laskowsky, "A Pinnacle of the Sublime: Christ's Victory of Style in *Paradise Regained,*" *Milton Quarterly,* XV (1981), 10–13; and Mary Ann Radzinowicz, "How Milton Read the Bible: The Case of *Paradise Regained,*" in *The Cambridge Companion to Milton,* ed. Danielson, 207–23.

31. Erich Auerbach, *Mimesis: The Representation of Reality in Western Literature,* trans. Willard R. Trask (Princeton, 1953), 40–49, and *Literary Language and Its Public in Late Latin Antiquity and in the Middle Ages,* trans. Ralph Mannheim (New York, 1965), 38–42.

simply imitates the contravening of classical genres and styles found in the Gospels.

There are real differences between Jesus' style and Satan's in the poem. The flights of splendor in *Paradise Regained* belong to Satan, while Jesus' words and deeds are expressed more plainly and directly. Although Satan himself sometimes uses a plain style, he seems to be imitating Jesus, adapting his speech to the style of his opponent. Yet plainness is clearly not Satan's metier. He understands power and inclines to a style evincing splendor, profusion, strength.[32]

Furthermore, many Miltonists have treated these differences. Archie Burnett's study of adjectives in the poem exposes this contrast between Jesus and Satan statistically. He observes that "Milton's style in *Paradise Regained* accords in general with the hero's contempt for 'swelling epithets thick-laid' (IV, 343)." Only 9.4 percent of the words are adjectives, and only 13.0 percent of these convey sense impressions. If we contrast the incidence of adjectives in *Paradise Lost,* Books I through VI, it averages at 12.0 percent, almost one-third more than *Paradise Regained,* whereas Book XI has 10.3 percent, and Book XII, only 9.0 percent.[33] Moreover, Milton's 9.4 percent average in *Paradise Regained* is swelled by Satan's visions and storm, where adjectives occupy 13.5 percent of the words. In fact, the incidence of adjectives in these passages increases rather dramatically: from 11.7 percent for the Parthian armies, to 13.4 percent for Rome, to 17.0 percent for Athens and 16.7 percent for the storm. As one might expect from descriptions of visions and a storm, the incidence of adjectives conveying sense impressions proves much larger than that for the poem in general, close to 30 percent of the whole by my estimate, as opposed to 13 percent. In sum, *Paradise Regained* generally uses adjectives much less than *Paradise Lost,* Books I through VI, and it uses a great proportion of them for Satan's acts, where they convey sense impressions more predominantly than elsewhere in the poem. When Jesus rejects the "swelling epithets thick-laid" of classical epic, then, the Bard is reflecting critically on one of his earlier stylistic habits. He now associates that habit with Satan.

32. See Weismiller, "Studies of Style and Verse Form," 312–15.

33. See Burnett, *Milton's Style,* 113, 174–75.

The Bard's corrective resinging of his earlier style remains implicit in *Paradise Regained* until Jesus' critique of classical poetry. Yet that critique is foreshadowed in Jesus' rejection of Roman magnificence and its implied style of poetry. Magnificence is the central theme in Satan's offer of Rome to Jesus (IV, 25–108). Satan's temptation dwells on the variety and beauty of Rome's buildings (34–38, 45–60), on its political preeminence (68–80), on its "ample Territory, wealth and power, / Civility of Manners, Arts, and Arms, / And long Renown" (82–84). In substance, it proves yet another temptation to what Satan understands best because he cares for it most: glory through power. Jesus rejects it for many of the same reasons he earlier scorns Satan's temptation to glory through military conquest: Roman power destroys its provinces through "lust and rapine" (137; *cf.* III, 75–80), and the Roman people have grown arrogant through triumph and vicious from luxury (137–42; *cf.* III, 81–87). Jesus sees Satan's Roman greatness as only "grandeur and majestic show / Of luxury, though call'd magnificence" (110–11). True magnificence, that is, doing things truly great (*magna facere*), proves something else entirely.

Since epic poetry in Renaissance literary theory aims to treat of great deeds and weighty affairs in a lofty style, magnificence proves central to both its matter and its manner. The epic should evoke awe and wonder as much through its style as through its subjects. Renaissance poets often followed their Roman predecessors in representing poetic greatness through architectural metaphors. Horace's praise of his *Odes* in the final poem of Book III ("Exegi monumentum aere perennius") found many imitators, beginning with Ovid (*Metamorphoses*, XV, 871–79) and including William Shakespeare and Spenser. Milton's "build the lofty rhyme" in "Lycidas" (11) alludes to the Latin verb *condere,* which refers to the construction primarily of buildings but also of poems, as in the traditional *condere carmen.* In the Renaissance, the buildings of ancient Rome were the most signal examples of enduring magnificence. The great Renaissance poem usually aspired to be as enduring as Rome.

The Protestant Bard of *Paradise Regained* is profoundly critical of Roman magnificence in architecture and politics, and he implies a critique of the magnificent style in poetry—a style he practiced extensively in the first half of *Paradise Lost* to achieve epic greatness for his poem and himself. The style employs profusion and extravagance to suggest power. In the first six books, the Bard often aimed to display his poetic power in a profusion of images designed to overgo the ancients. The catalog and the overgoing topos, as we have seen, are two devices of profusion he employed in this attempt, though they are not the only means he used. Yet in *Paradise Regained* he reserves that style only for Satan's speeches and acts. Jesus never utters anything in that style of magnificence, except ironically. The Bard of *Paradise Regained* carefully distinguishes, throughout his poem, the Satanic style of magnificence from the plainer, biblical style he approves as proper to Christian truth in poetry. In so doing, he reflects critically on his earlier use of the magnificent style in *Paradise Lost.*

Throughout *Paradise Regained,* therefore, Milton's Bard associates the techniques and subjects of classical epic with Satan. Insofar as he employed these for his divine and unfallen characters in his earlier work, he reflects on it critically as improperly Christian. At the same time, the Bard takes up many elements from classical philosophy for Jesus' speeches, and he transfuses them with Christian meaning. In this way, he illustrates the proper use of pagan materials to convey Christian truth, not only Satanic temptation. Because the poem persistently associates the explicitly classical with Satan, because its style and its genre contravene the norms of classical epic to follow those of the Bible, we should not be surprised when Jesus rejects Greek wisdom and eloquence, proclaiming the superiority of "Sion's songs, to all true tastes excelling" (IV, 347).

For the Bard of *Paradise Regained* is not the same poet he was in the first six books of *Paradise Lost.* There he took his standards of literary achievement from classical epic, so he used classical paradigms for his Christian song to prove himself the greater poet. But he came to see the folly of this effort, abandoned his overgoing ambitions, submitted himself more fully to Scripture, and arrived at a clearer understanding of his vocation as a Christian epic poet. In *Paradise Regained,* he has had done with superiority contests, for they belong to Satan, the prince of this world, as the second day of temptations shows. The Bard has understood how and why Scripture proves superior to classical epic, not simply in its "inspired" truth but in the literary means fitted to render that truth. Hence, he takes Scripture as the model for his genre and style, subordinating his classical materials to it. The Bard has become Milton, the Protestant poet of a truly Christian epic. From his perspective, if we prefer the splendors of *Paradise Lost* in its first half to Jesus' austerity in *Paradise Regained,* we do not yet have the true taste that finds both literary and spiritual excellence in the Bible. Our poetic tastes are of the devil's party, and we ought to know it.

Bibliography

Addison, Joseph. *The Works of the Right Honourable Joseph Addison.* Edited by Richard Hurd. 6 vols. Vol. IV. London, 1811.

Alighieri, Dante. *La Divina Commedia.* Edited by C. H. Grandgent. Revised by Charles S. Singleton. Cambridge, Mass., 1972.

Allen, Don C. "Milton and the Descent to Light." *Journal of English and Germanic Philology,* LX (1961), 614–30.

Amorose, Thomas. "Milton the Apocalyptic Historian: Competing Genres in *Paradise Lost,* Books XI and XII." *Milton Studies,* XVII (1983), 141–62.

Aristotle. *Nichomachean Ethics.* Translated by Martin Ostwald. New York, 1962.

———. *Parts of Animals.* Translated by A. L. Peck. Cambridge, Mass., 1937.

Arnold, Marilyn. "Milton's Accessible God: The Role of the Son in *Paradise Lost.*" *Milton Quarterly,* VII (1973), 65–72.

Auden, W. H. *Collected Poems.* Edited by Edward Mendelson. New York, 1976.

Auerbach, Erich. *Literary Language and Its Public in Late Latin Antiquity and in the Middle Ages.* Translated by Ralph Mannheim. New York, 1965.

———. *Mimesis: The Representation of Reality in Western Literature.* Translated by Willard R. Trask. Princeton, 1953.

Augustine. *City of God.* Translated by Henry Bettenson. London, 1972.

———. *Le Confessioni.* Edited by M. Skutella. Revised by Michele Pellegrino. Rome, 1982. Vol. I of *Opere di Sant' Agostino.* 34 vols. projected.

———. *On Christian Doctrine.* Translated by D. W. Robertson, Jr. Indianapolis, 1958.

Berek, Peter. " 'Plain' and 'Ornate' Styles in the Structure of *Paradise Lost.*" *PMLA,* LXXXV (1970), 237–46.

Berger, Harry, Jr. "Archaism, Vision, and Revision: Studies in Virgil, Plato, and Milton." *Centennial Review,* XI (1967), 24–52.

———. "*Paradise Lost* Evolving: Books I–VI. Toward a New View of the Poem as the Speaker's Experience." *Centennial Review,* XI (1967), 483–531.

Berry, Boyd M. "Melodramatic Faking in the Narrator's Voice, *Paradise Lost.*" *Milton Quarterly,* X (1976), 1–5.

Blake, William. *The Poetry and Prose of William Blake.* Edited by David V. Erdman. Rev. ed. Garden City, N.Y., 1970.

Blakemore, Steven. "Pandemonium and Babel: Architectural Hierarchy in *Paradise Lost.*" *Milton Quarterly,* XX (1986), 142–45.

——. " 'With No Middle Flight': Poetic Pride and Satanic Hubris in *Paradise Lost.*" *Kentucky Review,* III (1985), 23–31.

Blessington, Francis C. "Autotheodicy: The Father as Orator in *Paradise Lost.*" *Cithara: Essays in the Judaeo-Christian Tradition,* XIV (1975), 49–60.

——. *Paradise Lost and the Classical Epic.* Boston, 1979.

Bloom, Harold. *A Map of Misreading.* New York, 1975.

Bonham, Sister Hilda. "The Anthropomorphic God of *Paradise Lost.*" *Papers of the Michigan Academy of Science, Arts, and Letters,* LIII (1968), 329–35.

Bowra, C. M. *From Virgil to Milton.* London, 1944.

Broadbent, John. *Some Graver Subject: An Essay on "Paradise Lost."* London, 1960.

Burden, Dennis. *The Logical Epic: A Study of the Argument of "Paradise Lost."* Cambridge, Mass., 1967.

Burnett, Archie. *Milton's Style: The Shorter Poems, "Paradise Regained," and "Samson Agonistes."* London, 1981.

Bush, Douglas. *English Literature in the Earlier Seventeenth Century, 1600–1660.* Oxford, 1945.

——. *The Renaissance and English Humanism.* Toronto, 1939.

Campbell, Lily B. *Divine Poetry and Drama in Sixteenth-Century England.* Berkeley, 1959.

Carpenter, Mary Wilson. "Milton's Secret Garden: Structural Correspondences Between Michael's Prophecy and *Paradise Regained.*" *Milton Studies,* XIV (1980), 153–82.

Carrithers, Gale H., Jr., and James D. Hardy, Jr. *Milton and the Hermeneutic Journey.* Baton Rouge, 1994.

Cavanagh, Michael. "A Meeting of Epic and History: Books XI and XII of *Paradise Lost.*" *English Literary History,* XXXVIII (1971), 206–22.

Christopher, Georgia B. *Milton and the Science of the Saints.* Princeton, 1982.

Cohen, Kitty. "Milton's God in Council and War." *Milton Studies,* III (1971), 159–84.

Comes, Natalis. *Mythologiae.* 1567; rpr. New York, 1976.

Condee, R. W. "The Formalized Openings of Milton's Epic Poems." *Journal of English and Germanic Philosophy,* L (1951), 502–508.

Cope, Jackson I. *The Metaphoric Structure of "Paradise Lost."* New York, 1979.

Crossman, Robert. *Reading "Paradise Lost."* Bloomington, Ind., 1980.

Crump, Galbraith Miller. *The Mystical Design of "Paradise Lost."* Lewisburg, Pa., 1975.

Curtius, Ernst Robert. *European Literature and the Latin Middle Ages.* Translated by Willard R. Trask. Princeton, 1973.

Danielson, Dennis Richard. *Milton's Good God: A Study in Literary Theodicy.* Cambridge, Eng., 1982.

——, ed. *The Cambridge Companion to Milton.* Cambridge, Eng., 1989.

Davenant, William. *Sir William Davenant's "Gondibert."* Edited by David F. Gladish. Oxford, 1971.

Davis, Walter R. "The Languages of Accommodation and the Styles of *Paradise Lost.*" *Milton Studies,* XVIII (1983), 103–28.

De Boer, C., ed. *Ovide Moralisé: Poème du commencement du quatorzième siècle.* Amsterdam, 1966.

Di Cesare, Mario A. "*Paradise Lost* and the Epic Tradition." *Milton Studies,* I (1969), 31–50.

Dobbins, Austin C. *Milton and the Book of Revelation.* University, Ala., 1975.

Drummond, C. Q. "An Anti-Miltonist Reprise: I. The Milton Controversy." *Compass,* II (December, 1977), 28–45.

——. "An Anti-Miltonist Reprise: II. Antagonistic Styles and Contradictory Demands." *Compass,* III (April, 1978), 39–59.

Dryden, John. "Dedication of the *Aeneis.*" In *Virgil's "Aeneid,"* translated by John Dryden. New York, 1909.

du Bartas, Guillaume de Salluste. *The Divine Weeks and Works of Guillaume de Salluste, Sieur du Bartas.* Edited by Susan Snyder. Translated by Joshua Sylvester. 2 vols. Oxford, 1979.

Durling, Robert M. "Deceit and Digestion in the Belly of Hell." In *Allegory and Representation: Selected Papers from the English Institute, 1979–80,* edited by Stephen J. Greenblatt. Baltimore, 1981.

——. *The Figure of the Poet in Renaissance Epic.* Cambridge, Mass., 1965.

DuRocher, David J. *Milton and Ovid.* Ithaca, 1985.

Elliott, Emory. "Milton's Biblical Style in *Paradise Regained.*" *Milton Studies,* VI (1974), 227–41.

Empson, William. *Milton's God.* London, 1961.

Ferry, Anne. *Milton's Epic Voice: The Narrator in "Paradise Lost."* Chicago, 1983.

Fichter, Andrew. *Poets Historical: Dynastic Epic in the Renaissance.* New Haven, 1982.

Fiore, Peter A. " 'Account Mee Man': The Incarnation in *Paradise Lost.*" *Huntington Library Quarterly,* XXXIX (1975), 51–56.

Fish, Stanley Eugene. *Surprised by Sin: The Reader in "Paradise Lost."* New York, 1967.

———. "Transmuting the Lump: *Paradise Lost,* 1942–1982." In *Literature and History: Theoretical Problems and Russian Case Studies,* edited by Gary Saul Morson. Palo Alto, Calif., 1986.

Fisher, Alan. "Why Is *Paradise Regained* So Cold?" *Milton Studies,* XIV (1980), 195–217.

Fixler, Michael. "Milton's Passionate Epic." *Milton Studies,* I (1969), 167–92.

———. "Plato's Four Furors and the Real Structure of *Paradise Lost.*" *PMLA,* XCII (1977), 952–62.

Forsyth, Neil. "Having Done All to Stand: Biblical and Classical Allusion in *Paradise Regained.*" *Milton Studies,* XXI (1985), 199–227.

Fortin, Rene E. "The Climactic Similes of *Paradise Regained:* 'True Wisdom' or 'False Semblance'?" *Milton Quarterly,* VII (1973), 39–43.

Freccero, John. *Dante: The Poetics of Conversion.* Edited by Rachel Jacoff. Cambridge, Mass., 1986.

Freeman, James A. *Milton and the Martial Muse: "Paradise Lost" and European Traditions of War.* Princeton, 1980.

Frye, Northrop. "The Typology of *Paradise Regained.*" *Modern Philology,* LIII (1956), 227–38.

Gagen, Jean. "Did Milton Nod?" *Milton Quarterly,* XX (1986), 17–22.

Gardner, Helen. *A Reading of "Paradise Lost."* Oxford, 1965.

Gilbert, Allan H. *On the Composition of "Paradise Lost": A Study of the Ordering and Insertion of Material.* Chapel Hill, 1947.

Golding, Arthur. *Shakespeare's Ovid: Being Arthur Golding's Translation of the "Metamorphoses."* Edited by W. H. D. Rouse. 1567; rpr. Carbondale, Ill., 1961.

Gransden, K. W. "*Paradise Lost* and the *Aeneid.*" *Essays in Criticism,* XVII (1967), 281–303.

Gregory, E. R. "Three Muses and a Poet: A Perspective on Milton's Epic Thought." *Milton Studies,* X (1977), 35–64.

Griffin, Dustin. "Milton's Hell: Perspectives on the Fallen." *Milton Studies,* XIII (1979), 237–54.

Grossman, Marshall. *"Authors to Themselves": Milton and the Revelation of History.* Cambridge, Eng., 1987.

Guillory, John. *Poetic Authority: Spenser, Milton, and Literary History.* New York, 1984.

Guss, Donald. "A Brief Epic: *Paradise Regained.*" *Studies in Philology,* LXVIII (1971), 223–43.

Hamilton, Gary D. "Milton's Defensive God: A Reappraisal." *Studies in Philology,* LXIX (1972), 87–100.

Hammond, Mason. "Concilia Deorum from Homer Through Virgil." *Studies in Philology,* XXX (1933), 1–16.

Hanford, James Holly. "Milton and the Art of War." *Studies in Philology,* XVIII (1921), 232–66.

Harding, Davis P. *The Club of Hercules: Studies in the Classical Background of "Paradise Lost."* Illinois Studies in Language and Literature, 50. Urbana, Ill., 1962.

Haskin, Dayton. *Milton's Burden of Interpretation.* Philadelphia, 1994.

Helms, Randel. " 'His Dearest Mediation': The Dialogue in Heaven in Book III of *Paradise Lost.*" *Milton Quarterly,* III (1971), 52–57.

Holloway, Julia Bolton. "Not *Babilon,* nor Great *Alcairo.*" *Milton Quarterly,* XV (1981), 92–94.

Horace. *Epistles, Book II; and, Epistle to the Pisones ("Ars Poetica").* Edited by Niall Rudd. Cambridge, Eng., 1989.

——. *Odes and Epodes.* Edited by Paul Shorey. Revised by Paul Shorey and Gordon J. Laing. 1919; rpr. Pittsburgh, 1960.

Hoyle, James. " 'If Sion Hill Delight Thee More': The Muse's Choice in *Paradise Lost.*" *English Language Notes,* XII (1974), 21–26.

Hughes, Merritt Y. "The Christ of *Paradise Regained* and the Renaissance Poetic Tradition." *Studies in Philology,* XXXV (1938), 254–77.

Hunter, G. K. *Paradise Lost.* London, 1980.

Hunter, William B., Jr. "The Double Set of Temptations in *Paradise Regained.*" *Milton Studies,* XIV (1980), 183–94.

——. "Milton on the Exaltation of the Son: The War in Heaven in *Paradise Lost.*" *English Literary History,* XXXVI (1969), 215–31.

——. "Milton's Laundry Lists." *Milton Quarterly,* XVIII (1984), 58–61.

Hunter, W. B., C. A. Patrides, and J. H. Adamson. *Bright Essence: Studies in Milton's Theology.* Salt Lake City, 1971.

Johnson, Samuel. *Selected Poetry and Prose.* Edited by Frank Brady and W. K. Wimsatt. Berkeley, 1977.

Johnson, W. R. *Darkness Visible: A Study in Virgil's "Aeneid."* Berkeley, 1976.

——. "The Problem of the Counter-Classical Sensibility and Its Critics." *California Studies in Classical Antiquity,* III (1970), 123–52.

Jordan, Richard Douglas. "*Paradise Regained* and the Second Adam." *Milton Studies,* IX (1976), 261–75.

Kates, J. A. "The Revaluation of the Classical Hero in Tasso and Milton." *Comparative Literature,* XXVI (1974), 299–317.

Kermode, Frank. "Milton's Hero." *Review of English Studies,* n.s., IV (1953), 317–30.

——, ed. *The Living Milton: Essays by Various Hands.* London, 1960.

Kerrigan, William. *The Prophetic Milton.* Charlottesville, Va. 1974.

——. *The Sacred Complex: On the Psychogenesis of "Paradise Lost."* Cambridge, Eng., 1983.

Knott, John. *Milton's Pastoral Vision.* Chicago, 1971.

Kranidas, Thomas, ed. *New Essays on "Paradise Lost."* Berkeley, 1969.

Labriola, Albert C. " 'Thy Humiliation Shall Exalt': The Christology of *Paradise Lost.*" *Milton Studies,* XV (1981), 29–42.

Laskowsky, Henry J. "A Pinnacle of the Sublime: Christ's Victory of Style in *Paradise Regained.*" *Milton Quarterly,* XV (1981), 10–13.

Law, Jules David. "Eruption and Containment: The Satanic Predicament in *Paradise Lost.*" *Milton Studies,* XVI (1982), 35–60.

Lawry, Jon S. *The Shadow of Heaven: Matter and Stance in Milton's Poetry.* Ithaca, 1968.

Le Comte, Edward. "Satan's Heresies in *Paradise Regained.*" *Milton Studies,* XII (1978), 253–66.

Lewalski, Barbara Kiefer. *Milton's Brief Epic: The Genre, Meaning, and Art of "Paradise Regained."* Providence, R.I., 1966.

——. *"Paradise Lost" and the Rhetoric of Literary Forms.* Princeton, 1985.

——. *Protestant Poetics and the Seventeenth Century Lyric.* Princeton, 1979.

——. "Structure and the Symbolism of Vision in Michael's Prophecy, *Paradise Lost,* Books XI and XII." *Philological Quarterly,* XLII (1963), 25–35.

Lewis, C. S. *The Discarded Image: An Introduction to Medieval and Renaissance Literature.* Cambridge, Eng., 1964.

——. *A Preface to "Paradise Lost."* London, 1942.

Lieb, Michael. *The Dialectics of Creation: Patterns of Birth and Regeneration in "Paradise Lost."* Amherst, Mass., 1970.

——. "Milton's 'Dramatick Constitution': The Celestial Dialogue in *Paradise Lost,* Book III." *Milton Studies,* XXIII (1987), 215–40.

——. *Poetics of the Holy: A Reading of "Paradise Lost."* Chapel Hill, N.C., 1981.

Lovejoy, Arthur O. *The Great Chain of Being: A Study in the History of Ideas.* Cambridge, Mass., 1936.

Low, Anthony. "Milton's God: Authority in *Paradise Lost.*" *Milton Studies,* IV (1972), 19–38.

——. " 'No Middle Flight': *Paradise Lost,* I.14." *Milton Newsletter,* III (1969), 1–4.

MacCaffrey, Isabel Gamble. *"Paradise Lost" as "Myth."* Cambridge, Mass., 1959.

MacKellar, Walter. *A Variorum Commentary on the Poems of John Milton.* Volume IV. *Paradise Regained.* New York, 1975.

Madsen, William. *From Shadowy Types to Truth: Studies in Milton's Symbolism.* New Haven, 1968.

Martindale, Charles. *John Milton and the Transformation of Ancient Epic.* London, 1986.

Martz, Louis L. *The Paradise Within: Studies in Vaughan, Traherne, and Milton*. New Haven, 1964.

———. *Poet of Exile: A Study of Milton's Poetry*. New Haven, 1980.

McCaffrey, Philip. "*Paradise Regained:* The Style of Satan's Athens." *Milton Quarterly,* V (1971), 7–14.

McCracken, David. *The Scandal of the Gospels: Jesus, Story, and Offence*. Oxford, 1994.

McQueen, William. "*Paradise Lost* V, VI: The War in Heaven." *Studies in Philology,* LXXI (1974), 89–104.

Mengert, James G. "Styling the Strife of Glory: The War in Heaven." *Milton Studies,* XIV (1980), 95–115.

Miller, George Eric. "Stylistic Rhetoric and the Language of God in *Paradise Lost,* Book III." *Language and Style,* VIII (1975), 111–26.

Milner, Andrew. *John Milton and the English Revolution*. London, 1983.

Milton, John. *Complete Poems and Major Prose.* Edited by Merritt Y. Hughes. New York, 1957.

———. *Paradise Lost.* Edited by Alastair Fowler. London, 1971.

———. *"Paradise Lost": A Poem in Twelve Books.* Edited by Thomas Newton. London, 1749.

———. *Paradise Regained.* Edited by John Carey. In *The Poems of John Milton,* edited by John Carey and Alastair Fowler. London, 1968.

Moore, O. H. "The Infernal Council." *Modern Philology,* XVI (1918), 169–93.

Murrin, Michael. "The Language of Milton's Heaven." *Modern Philology,* LXXIV (1977), 350–65.

Mustazza, Leonard. "Language as Weapon in Milton's *Paradise Regained.*" *Milton Studies,* XVIII (1983), 195–216.

Nardo, Anna K. "Academic Interludes in *Paradise Lost.*" *Milton Studies,* XXVII (1991), 209–41.

Norford, Don Parry. "The Sacred Head: Milton's Solar Mysticism." *Milton Studies,* IX (1976), 37–75.

Nussbaum, Martha C. *The Fragility of Goodness: Luck and Ethics in Greek Tragedy and Philosophy.* Cambridge, Eng., 1986.

Ovid. *Metamorphoses.* Edited and translated by Frank Justus Miller. Revised by G. P. Goold. 2 vols. Cambridge, Mass., 1977.

———. *Ovid's Metamorphoses: Books 6–10.* Edited by William S. Anderson. Norman, Okla., 1972.

Patrides, C. A., ed. *Approaches to "Paradise Lost": The York Centenary Lectures.* Toronto, 1968.

Pearce, James M. "The Theology of Representation: The Meta-Argument of *Paradise Regained.*" *Milton Studies,* XXIV (1988), 277–96.

Peter, John. *A Critique of "Paradise Lost."* New York, 1960.

Planinc, Zdravko. *Plato's Political Philosophy: Prudence in the "Republic" and the "Laws."* Columbia, Mo., 1991.

Pope, Elizabeth M. *"Paradise Regained": The Tradition and the Poem.* Baltimore, 1947.

Prince, F. T. "On the Last Two Books of *Paradise Lost.*" *Essays and Studies by Members of the English Association,* XI (1958), 36–52.

Quilligan, Maureen. *Milton's Spenser: The Politics of Reading.* Ithaca, 1983.

Quinn, Kenneth. *Virgil's "Aeneid": A Critical Description.* Ann Arbor, 1968.

Rajan, Balachandra. *"Paradise Lost" and the Seventeenth-Century Reader.* London, 1947.

——. "*Paradise Lost:* The Hill of History." *Huntington Library Quarterly,* XXXI (1967), 43–63.

Revard, Stella Purce. *The War in Heaven: "Paradise Lost" and the Tradition of Satan's Rebellion.* Ithaca, 1980.

Rewak, William J. "Book III of *Paradise Lost:* Milton's Satisfaction Theory of the Redemption." *Milton Quarterly,* XI (1977), 97–102.

Ricks, Christopher. *Milton's Grand Style.* Oxford, 1963.

Riggs, William G. *The Christian Poet in "Paradise Lost."* Berkeley, 1972.

Rollin, Roger B. "*Paradise Lost:* 'Tragical-Comical-Historical-Pastoral.' " *Milton Studies,* V (1973), 3–37.

Rosenblatt, Jason P. "Adam's Pisgah Vision: *Paradise Lost,* Books XI and XII." *English Literary History,* XXXIX (1972), 66–86.

——. "The Mosaic Voice in *Paradise Lost.*" *Milton Studies,* VII (1975), 207–32.

——. "Structural Unity and Temporal Concordance: The War in Heaven in *Paradise Lost.*" *PMLA,* LXXXVII (1972), 31–41.

Rudat, Wolfgang E. H. "Milton's Satan and Virgil's Juno: 'Perverseness' of Disobedience in *Paradise Lost.*" *Renaissance and Reformation,* n.s., III (1979), 77–82.

Ryken, Leland. *The Apocalyptic Vision in "Paradise Lost."* Ithaca, 1970.

Safer, Elaine B. "The Socratic Dialogue and 'Knowledge in the Making' in *Paradise Regained.*" *Milton Studies,* VI (1974), 215–26.

Samuel, Irene. "The Dialogue in Heaven: A Reconsideration of *Paradise Lost* III, 1–417." *PMLA,* LXXII (1957), 601–11.

——. "Milton on Learning and Wisdom." *PMLA,* LXIV (1949), 708–23.

——. *Plato and Milton.* Ithaca, 1947.

Sandys, George. *Ovid's "Metamorphoses": Englished, Mythologized, and Represented in Figures.* Edited by Karl K. Hulley and Stanley T. Vandersall. Lincoln, Nebr., 1970.

Sarkar, Malabika. " 'The Visible Diurnal Sphere': Astronomical Images of Space and Time in *Paradise Lost.*" *Milton Quarterly,* XVIII (1984), 1–5.

Sasek, Lawrence A. "The Drama of *Paradise Lost,* Books XI and XII." In *Studies in English Renaissance Literature,* edited by Waldo F. McNeir. Baton Rouge, 1962.

Schiffhorst, Gerald J. "Patience and the Humbly Exalted Heroism of Milton's Messiah: Typological and Iconographic Background." *Milton Studies,* XVI (1982), 97–113.

Schindler, Walter. *Voice and Crisis: Invocation in Milton's Poetry.* Hamden, Conn., 1984.

Schulz, Howard. *Milton and Forbidden Knowledge.* New York, 1955.

Sensabaugh, G. F. "Milton on Learning." *Studies in Philology,* XLIII (1946), 258–72.

Shaheen, Naseeb. "Milton's Muse and the *De Doctrina.*" *Milton Quarterly,* VIII (1974), 72–76.

Shakespeare, William. *The Merchant of Venice.* Edited by Brents Stirling. New York, 1970.

Shawcross, John T. *"Paradise Regained": Worthy T' Have Not Remain'd So Long Unsung.* Pittsburgh, 1988.

———. *With Mortal Voice: The Creation of "Paradise Lost."* Lexington, Ky., 1982.

Shoaf, R. A. *Milton: Poet of Duality: A Study of Semiosis in the Poetry and the Prose.* New Haven, 1985.

The Shorter Oxford English Dictionary: On Historical Principles. Third Edition. Oxford, 1980.

Shumaker, Wayne. *Unpremeditated Verse: Feeling and Perception in "Paradise Lost."* Princeton, 1967.

Sidney, Philip. *A Defence of Poetry.* Edited by Jan Van Dorsten. Oxford, 1966.

Sims, James H. *The Bible in Milton's Epics.* Gainesville, Fla., 1962.

Sims, James H., and Leland Ryken. *Milton and Scriptural Tradition: The Bible into Poetry.* Columbia, Mo., 1984.

Sloane, Thomas O. *Donne, Milton, and the End of Humanist Rhetoric.* Berkeley, 1985.

Stati, P. Papini. *Thebais et Achilleis.* Edited by H. W. Garrod. Oxford, 1954.

Steadman, John M. "The Idea of Satan as the Hero of *Paradise Lost.*" *Proceedings of the American Philosophical Society,* CXX (1976), 253–94.

———. *Milton and the Renaissance Hero.* Oxford, 1967.

———. *Milton's Epic Characters.* Chapel Hill, N.C., 1968.

———. "*Paradise Regained:* Moral Dialectic and the Pattern of Rejection." *University of Toronto Quarterly,* XXXI (1962), 416–30.

Stein, Arnold. *Answerable Style: Essays on "Paradise Lost."* Seattle, 1967.

——. *Heroic Knowledge: An Interpretation of "Paradise Regained" and "Samson Agonistes."* Minneapolis, 1957.

——. "Satan's Metamorphoses: The Internal Speech." *Milton Studies,* I (1969), 93–113.

Stocker, Margarita. *Paradise Lost.* London, 1988.

Summers, Joseph H. *The Muse's Method.* Cambridge, Mass., 1962.

Sundell, Roger H. "The Narrator as Interpreter in *Paradise Regained.*" *Milton Studies,* II (1970), 83–101.

Swaim, Kathleen M. *Before and After the Fall: Contrasting Modes in "Paradise Lost."* Amherst, Mass., 1986.

——. "The Mimesis of Accommodation in Book III of *Paradise Lost.*" *Philological Quarterly,* LXIII (1984), 461–75. Rpr. in Swaim, *Before and After the Fall.*

Tasso, Torquato. *Gierusalemme Liberata.* Edited by Lanfranco Caretti. Milan, 1979.

Taylor, Dick, Jr. "The Battle in Heaven in *Paradise Lost.*" *Tulane Studies in English,* III (1952), 69–92.

Tillyard, E. M. W. *Milton.* London, 1966.

Virgil. *The Aeneid of Virgil.* Edited by R. D. Williams. 2 vols. London, 1972–73.

Voegelin, Eric. *Plato and Aristotle.* Baton Rouge, 1957. Vol. III of *Order and History.* 5 vols.

Waddington, Raymond B. "The Death of Adam: Vision and Voice in Books XI and XII of *Paradise Lost.*" *Modern Philology,* LXX (1972), 9–21.

Waldock, A. J. A. *"Paradise Lost" and Its Critics.* Cambridge, Eng., 1947.

Walker, William. "Typology and *Paradise Lost,* Books XI and XII." *Milton Studies,* XXV (1989), 245–64.

Webber, Joan. *Milton and His Epic Tradition.* Seattle, 1979.

——. "Milton's God." *English Literary History,* XL (1973), 514–31.

Weber, Burton Jasper. *The Construction of "Paradise Lost."* Carbondale, Ill., 1970.

——. "The Non-Narrative Approaches to *Paradise Lost:* A Gentle Remonstrance." *Milton Studies* IX (1976), 77–103.

——. *Wedges and Wings: The Patterning of "Paradise Regained."* Carbondale, Ill., 1975.

Wickenheiser, Robert J. "Milton's 'Pattern of a Christian Hero': The Son in *Paradise Lost.*" *Milton Quarterly,* XII (1978), 1–9.

Wigler, Stephen. "The Poet and Satan Before the Light: A Suggestion About Book III and the Opening of Book IV of *Paradise Lost.*" *Milton Quarterly,* XII (1978), 59–64.

Williamson, George. "The Education of Adam." *Modern Philology,* LXI (1963), 96–109.

Winegarden, Karl Lewis. "No Hasty Conclusions: Milton's Ante-Nicene Pneumatology." *Milton Quarterly,* XI (1977), 102–107.

Wittreich, Joseph A. " 'All Angelic Natures Joined in One': Epic Convention and Prophetic Interiority in the Council Scenes of *Paradise Lost.*" *Milton Studies,* XVII (1983), 43–74.

———. *Visionary Poetics: Milton's Tradition and Its Legacy.* San Marino, Calif., 1979.

———. ed. *The Romantics on Milton: Formal Essays and Critical Asides.* Cleveland, Ohio, 1970.

Wood, Elizabeth Jane. " 'Improv'd by Tract of Time': Metaphysics and Measurement in *Paradise Lost.*" *Milton Studies,* XV (1981), 43–58.

Woodhouse, A. S. P. *The Heavenly Muse: A Preface to Milton.* Edited by Hugh MacCallum. Toronto, 1972.

Wooten, John. "The Metaphysics of Milton's Burlesque Humor." *Milton Studies,* XIII (1979), 255–73.

Wright, B. A. *Milton's "Paradise Lost."* New York, 1962.

INDEX